WOMAN:

HER RIGHTS, WRONGS, PRIVILEGES, AND RESPONSIBILITIES.

QUEEN OF THE FAMILY.

The most important office in the World.

WOMAN:

HER RIGHTS, WRONGS, PRIVILEGES, AND RESPONSIBILITIES.

CONTAINING A SKETCH OF HER CONDITION IN ALL AGES AND
COUNTRIES, FROM HER CREATION AND FALL IN EDEN TO
THE PRESENT TIME: HER PRESENT LEGAL STATUS IN

ENGLAND, FRANCE, AND THE UNITED STATES:

HER RELATIONS TO MAN, PHYSIOLOGICAL, SOCIAL, MORAL, AND
INTELLECTUAL: HER ABILITY TO FILL THE ENLARGED SPHERE
OF DUTIES AND PRIVILEGES CLAIMED FOR HER: HER TRUE
POSITION IN EDUCATION, PROFESSIONAL LIFE, EMPLOY-
MENTS, AND WAGES, CONSIDERED.

WOMAN SUFFRAGE,

ITS FOLLY AND INEXPEDIENCY, AND THE INJURY AND DETERIORA-
TION WHICH IT WOULD CAUSE IN HER CHARACTER, SHOWN,
AND THE BEST MEANS FOR HER REAL ADVANCEMENT
AND ELEVATION DEMONSTRATED.

By L. P. BROCKETT, M. D.,

ILLUSTRATED

BOOKS FOR LIBRARIES PRESS
PLAINVIEW, NEW YORK

First Published 1869
Reprinted 1976

301.412
B 864

STANDARD BOOK NUMBER:
8369-5274-X

LIBRARY OF CONGRESS CATALOG CARD NUMBER:
70-114869

PRINTED IN THE UNITED STATES OF AMERICA

ADVERTISEMENT.

(TO THE ORIGINAL EDITION)

It has been deemed desirable to illustrate this work somewhat largely, but with due reference to its high character as a book which should be in the hands of every family. The illustrations are some of them of historical incidents, relating to the condition of woman in foreign countries and former times; some refer to existing employments in other countries; some to the quiet beauty of a happy home; others to the various occupations in which woman has been, or is likely to be, engaged; while a few refer to that period, which we hope is far distant, when women will enter upon a political career, and forgetting the graces and delicacy which now cause them to be loved, honored, and reverenced, will become brawling politicians, greedy office-seekers, and bold, hard, unwomanly aspirants for place and power. We have sought, in these last illustrations, "to hold the mirror up to nature," not in an unkindly, but a dissuasive spirit, hoping that all sensible, thoughtful women, seeing what unseemly creatures they would become by plunging into a political career, might be led to avoid the danger, and give their powerful influence against it.

The Publisher.

PREFACE.

We are living in a period of moral, political, and social upheaval. The earthquakes and volcanic eruptions which within the past two or three years have desolated such wide tracts of the earth's surface are but the feeble physical analogues of those mightier revolutions which, within a half score of years, have overturned ancient abuses, unsettled institutions which had their roots deep in the foundations of society, have borne mankind onward in the path of progress with the swiftness of an avalanche, and are still threatening changes that may alter the entire character of our social organization.

We have seen, in the last decade, slavery and serfdom abolished, the greater part of Italy rescued from the temporal power of the Pope, the Concordat overthrown, the scepter wrested from the Bourbons of Sicily and Spain, the democratic power greatly increased in France, the franchise extended to a large body of the working class in Great Britain and to the African race in our own country, and are now face to face with two other great questions, the solution of which involves some of the profoundest topics of political economy and social organization—the entire severance of Church and State in Great Britain, and, as a corollary, the overthrow of the political ascendency of the British aristocracy—and the question of the reform in the legal status of woman, as involving her employments, her wages, and her claim to the exercise of the right of suffrage.

With the former of these questions, we, as Americans, have only the interest of our sympathy with universal liberty, and our common lineage. With the latter we are deeply concerned; for though the demand for these changes in the condition of woman is made in other countries as well as our own, it attains here its highest significance, and upon our action will depend in a great degree its success or failure elsewhere. Demands for enlarged freedom of action, assuming to be made in the interests of that spirit of universal liberty whose very name is so dear to us, are in danger of being yielded without sufficient scrutiny, and once yelded, no retrograde step, however desirable it may be, is possible.

It has seemed, therefore, to the writer, a matter of duty to examine this whole question of the political, social, and economical status of woman, in a spirit of thorough fairness and candor: to gather from past history and from present laws and customs, what are the actual wrongs, oppressions, and disabilities under which the sex suffer;

what are their present rights and privileges; what is their moral, intellectual, and social relation to man; what advances, either in economical, political, or social life, are within the limits of their capacities, and finally, what are the arguments for and against their exercise of the suffrage.

In this whole discussion, it has been the aim of the writer to avoid, alike from his high esteem for the sex, and his regard for that high-bred courtesy which is the surest mark of a gentleman, all resort to ridicule or sneers in the place of argument, and all levity of treatment of a subject which he regarded as too important, and involving too weighty interests, to be lightly esteemed.

It may be, that the conclusions to which he finds himself driven may not meet the views of all his fair readers, but he is confident that none of them will accuse him of doing them injustice, and he hopes, that in a careful second thought, they may be convinced that his arguments are such as their reason approves.

L. P. B.

BROOKLYN, *Sept.*, 1869.

LIST OF ILLUSTRATIONS.

CONTENTS.

who really lack it are in too feeble health to be able to work, or too indolent or weak-minded to desire it. Sad condition of the infirm poor. The inexorableness of the laws of trade on this subject. The unwillingness of a certain class of poor women to accept work, unless under precisely such circumstances as they desire. Instances in New York. Small classes who can not at all times find sufficient employment. The remedy for these, in improving their knowledge so as to be able to perform work of a higher grade. Ignorance, heedlessness, and unthrift, the causes of much of the wretchedness of unskilled workers, and of much of their ill-health. Difficulty of remedying their condition. Legislation impossible and useless. Charitable relief often ruinous both to the recipients and the tax-payers. Lodging-houses and model tenement houses do not reach them. Education and reformation, where possible, the best remedy. Why the wages of women are lower than those of men. Where supply exceeds demand, the lowest is the ruling price. A day's work of a woman, in manual labor, a little less than that of a man. In piece-work, when done as well, the price should be the same. Still, in view of prejudice, it might be a question whether it would not be expedient to submit at first to a slight reduction in order to secure the work. Remedies for low wages. Trades-unions, co-operation, better practical education. In higher grades of employment, wages of women nearly equal to those of men. No legislation can alter or improve this matter of wages. The possession of the ballot equally inefficacious. The only persons who could be benefited by making politics a profession, the educated class, who already command good pay for their work.

History of suffrage. Paternal, patriarchal, and kingly governments. Their natural outgrowth one from the other. Gradual development of an aristocracy. Rome. The progress and abuse of suffrage there. Greece. The *demos*. Popular suffrage. Abandonment of suffrage in the Middle Ages. Feudal barons. The middle class. Modern introduction of suffrage. Scandinavia. Switzerland. Hungary. The Saxon *Witenagemote.* The principle on which suffrage was based in all the countries of Europe. The property qualification always required. Formerly real property only represented. Of late years personal property of larger amount allowed a representation. The right of single women possessing property to vote on this ground contested in England. Petitions to Parliament. Reasons why their petition was not granted. The views of the author of "Woman's Rights and Duties" on this subject. The facts which give additional force to her reasoning. The history of suffrage in the American colonies. Variety of requirements. The Declaration of Independence. Fallacy of its doctrine of suffrage as now understood. Improbability that its authors ever really attached any such idea to their words. Dr. Bushnell's view. Another possible sense. This equally untrue. The action of the colonies on the subject of suffrage not affected by it. "Glittering generalities." Extension of suffrage for various causes. Probable effect of the fifteenth amendment of the Constitution.

What is suffrage, and in whom or what does the right of exercising it inhere? The savage theory of the French philosophers. Its influence upon our early statesmen. Its fallacies. The family the *unit* of society. What follows from this? All suffrage and official action, representation. Further limitations of suffrage within the just power of society. What restrictions it may not make. Another class of proper restrictions. Should property as property be represented? Justice of this. Methods of attaining it. Objections to most of these methods in the case of unmarried women and widows possessing property. Other views in regard to suffrage. The property qualification only. Manhood suffrage. Objections to it. An absolute government deemed preferable by some. Suffrage but a clumsy way of attaining a good government. The great opportunity of frauds which will affect the purity of the election. The Chinese method of selecting officers by competitive examination. Its advantages. Review of the argument.

The variety of grounds on which the suffrage was extended in the United States—performing military duty, fire duty, having served as a volunteer in either of our wars. Abrogation of the freehold qualification. The three-fifths rule in the South. Freedmen permitted to vote in Southern States. The injudiciousness of this as a general measure. The fifteenth amendment. Its possible evil effects. Only women and minors left. Why the suffrage should not be conferred on these,—or more particularly on women as women. This a different question from the English one, which relates to the bestowal of the suffrage on women as property-holders. Four classes of objections to woman-suffrage—political, social, intellectual, and moral. 1st. Political objections. 1. Woman has no need of the suffrage, since she is already represented in the municipality and the State. This representation much more full than can be otherwise attained. No reasonable request of women unheeded. Personal influence of woman on legislation. Examples: Vinnie Ream; Mrs. Husband; Mrs. Cobb. 2. The exercise of the suffrage by woman would be an attempt to make suffrage *individual* instead of *representative*, and so against the natural order of things. 3. By woman-suffrage women will gain nothing, while they will lose much. What they would lose. Women almost everywhere in a minority at the polls. Their votes would be often perverted to evil purposes. Their unfortunate position if elected to the Legislature, or to Congress. Their inability to control legislation as favorably as if they were not members. 4. No possible plea in justification of woman's intrusion into the realm of political action. Possible justification for the admission of some other classes—foreigners, colored men, the disfranchised. The case of woman different. There is no hostility to her. The only way to produce a feeling of antagonism would be to give her the suffrage. 5. It could not be in any case a remedy for any one of the wrongs under which women now suffer. Not low wages, want of employment, overcrowding in business, &c. What are the true remedies?

for pay, and without any intelligence or conscientiousness in the matter, for whichever side would pay best. The abandoned class would vote "early and often" for the candidates to whom their keepers had sold them. The pleasure of going to the polls in such company.

Objections to woman-suffrage from an intellectual point of view. Recurrence to first principles. In all free governments, the stability of the government dependent upon the intelligence of the voting population. If these are ignorant and venal, no government can long endure. From this cause, no Celtic nation has been able to maintain a republican government. To this cause is also due the constant anarchy and innumerable revolutions of Mexico, and the Central and South American republics. Chili, of late, an exception, owing to its greater intelligence. The efforts of Don Diego F. Sarmiento, President of the Argentine Republic, to educate his people, on this very ground. The application to the United States. Three classes who are already endangering our national existence by their ignorance and venality—viz.: the ignorant and low voters at the North, largely of foreign birth or parentage, and either vicious, or wholly under the influence of corrupt politicians ; the "poor white trash" of the South, always voting under influence and without knowledge, by whose votes the South was lately plunged into war; and the more ignorant and stupid of the negroes, who, however, are earnestly striving to improve. If we should add to these the very large classes of ignorant women of the dependent classes—servants, factory girls (of the lower grades), unskilled laborers, and the abandoned class, our peril would be almost infinitely increased; and if to these were to be added the Chinese, we should go down to swift destruction. If we must have universal suffrage, let us first have universal education, compulsory if need be. Woman-suffrage from the moral point of view. Our visions of the lost Eden. The sad sight of a pure and virtuous woman plunging into political strife. The fall of an ingenuous and pure-minded young man.

city missionaries. The exertion of influence for good, upon young men who are strangers in our large cities. Deaconesses. Their work. Kaiserswerth. Strasburg. Others. English Sisterhoods. Sisters of Charity. Deaconesses and Sisters in America. Summary.

Weakness of the arguments adduced by the popular advocates of woman-suffrage. Effect of this frothy declaration upon the community. The Working Women's Association in New York. The disgust of sensible people. The Chicago Sorosis. The organ of woman suffrage there. Miss Beecher's paper. "Gail Hamilton's" *exposé*. Women in general opposed to it. The argument that if any women want to vote, all women should be allowed to do so. Application to minors. Other forms of the proposition. Motives in the preparation of the work. Prevalence of these views. Progress. Not always in the right direction. The maiden of forty years ago. The wife of the same period. The life of the household at the present day. The educational errors of the present day in regard to women. Necessity of physical and moral training. Of what kind shall it be ? Good effects of the present agitation. Indications for good. Leave-taking.

Miss Beecher's Essay.

The marriage question. Reasons for not taking it up in the body of the work. Mr. Mill's avowals. What marriage is. No mere partnership. Views of some of the other leaders of the movement. Pernicious effect of these doctrines. "Gail Hamilton's" dangerous doctrines. The doctrine of the equality of the sexes at the basis of these. Its errors. The able argument on that subject by the author of "Woman's Rights and Duties."

INTRODUCTION.

In the investigation of any scientific question, there is no course so satisfactory as that of beginning with first principles; the foundation being well settled, the rearing of a suitable superstructure upon it is a work of comparative ease.

Let us, then, in the study of the difficult and intricate subject before us, revert to the Scriptural history of the creation of the first pair, and see what light it throws upon the true relations of the two sexes to each other.

In that wonderfully vivid, yet condensed, narrative of the creation and fall of man, contained in the first three chapters of Genesis, the following are the principal passages which refer to this subject: "And God said, Let us make man in our image, after our likeness: and let *them* have dominion over the fish of the sea, and over the fowl of the air, and over the cattle, and over all the earth, and over every creeping thing that creepeth upon the earth. So God created man in his own image, in the image of God created he him: *male and female* created he them.

2

And God blessed them, and God said unto them, Be fruitful and multiply, and replenish the earth and subdue it: and have dominion over the fish of the sea, and over the fowl of the air, and over every living thing that moveth upon the earth."—Genesis I. 26–28.

In the second chapter, the inspired writer enters somewhat more fully into the details of man's creation, and the circumstances which attended the predetermined creation of woman:

" And the LORD God formed man out of the dust of the ground, and breathed into his nostrils the breath of life; and man became a living soul. And the LORD planted a garden eastward in Eden; and there he put the man whom he had formed. And out of the ground made the LORD God to grow every tree that is pleasant to the sight, and good for food: the tree of life also in the midst of the garden, and the tree of knowledge of good and evil. . . . . And the LORD God took the man, and put him into the garden of Eden, to dress it and to keep it. And the LORD God commanded the man, saying, Of every tree of the garden thou mayest freely eat: but of the tree of knowledge of good and evil, thou shalt not eat of it: for in the day that thou eatest thereof, thou shalt surely die. And the LORD God said, It is not good that the man should be alone: I will make him an help meet for him. And out of the ground the LORD God formed every beast of the field, and every fowl of the air: and brought them unto Adam to see what he would call them: and whatsoever Adam called every living creature, that was the name thereof. And Adam gave names to all cattle, and to the fowl of the air, and to every beast of the field; but for Adam there was not found an help meet for him. And the LORD God caused a deep sleep to fall upon Adam, and he slept: and he took one of his ribs, and closed up the flesh instead thereof: and the rib, which the LORD God had taken from man, made he a woman, and brought her unto the man. And Adam said, This is now bone of my bones, and flesh of my flesh: she shall be called woman (Hebrew ISHA, feminine form of ISH, man) because she was taken out of man. Therefore shall a man leave his father and his mother, and shall cleave unto his wife: and they shall be one flesh."—Genesis II. 7–10, 15–24.

Again, after the sad history of the temptation and the fall, after sentencing the serpent, as the penalty of his crime, to become thenceforward a creeping thing, eating dust all the days of his life, Jehovah said to the woman: "I will greatly multiply thy sorrow and thy conception; in sorrow thou shalt bring forth children; and thy desire shall be to thy husband (*margin*, thou shalt be subject to thy husband), and he shall rule over thee. . . . . And Adam called his wife Eve (Heb. Chavah, Living :) because she was the mother of all living."—Genesis III. 16, 20

There are several points worthy of particular notice in this terse, condensed narrative; among these we may specify, first, the peculiarity of the creation of woman. In the creation of all the inferior orders of animals, both sexes were called into existence at the same time and from the same material; while in the human race, man was first created, and then, after a time, woman taken from his side to be a help meet, or fit, for him. This intimacy or oneness of structure indicated a more perfect unity of nature and purpose than was possible in the case of inferior animals, or than would be in any of the descendants of this first pair, not of different sexes. They were henceforth not twain, but one flesh; one body and one soul, though in differing forms. Sprung from a common source, inspired by common thoughts and emotions, there could be in their case no question of equality, any more than of the right hand and the left; they were parts of one whole, and neither was complete without the other.

It was a natural consequence of this unity of aim and purpose, that, though Adam was first created, and before the creation of the woman, gave the names to all the inferior orders of animals, *joint dominion* over these animals was given to the pair. Twice was the command repeated, "Let *them* have dominion," &c. Together they were to subdue the earth, together to dress and keep the garden of Eden. But one will, but one purpose, was to animate them both in the performance of their duties, and that a joint, a united will.

We may justly and fairly deduce from this narrative what was the Creator's purpose in this creation of the first human pair; they were to be united by the closest of all possible bonds, that of a common origin and nature; they were to be parts of each other, each the other's complement; the woman was to be a helper or aid, meet, fit, or adapted to the needs of the man; and these preliminaries observed, they were to be actuated by a common purpose and aim, and to possess a common dominion over the inferior animals, and the earth they were to subdue.

Has this purpose and plan of the Creator been thwarted and violated? It has, in the temptation and fall. Parting from Adam, and exercising her separate will and judgment, the woman fell a prey to the tempter's wiles, and, still by the separate exercise of her will and powers of persuasion, induced her husband to become a partaker with her in the transgression. What was the consequence of this assumption of separate and individual power? We have it in the sentence pronounced on her by Jehovah. "Thy desire shall be to thy husband (more correctly, as the margin has it, 'Thou shalt be in subjection to thy husband'), and he shall rule over thee."

It is as if he had said to the erring culprit, "Thou didst forget that thou wast to be one with thy husband,

in thought, in counsel, and in will; thou didst listen to
this inferior creature who is henceforth to crawl abjectly
upon the earth, in fear and terror of the race he has de-
ceived; henceforth, though the sway over the inferior creation is not taken wholly from thee, yet thou too shalt be
subject; the dominion shall no longer be a joint one, but
thy husband shall rule over thee, as well as over the brute
creation."

Does the sentence seem severe, as compared with that
inflicted on the man? It was because woman was the
greater transgressor; yet was it mingled with mercy. Not
only was there the dim promise of the coming Redeemer
to cheer her sorrows, and give hope of a better Eden, but
he to whom her desire was to be, and who was henceforth to rule over her, was bone of her bone, and flesh of
her flesh; and one bound to her by such tender ties could
hardly be a tyrant in his sway. Then, too, he whose labor
had hitherto been but a joyous pastime, was henceforth
condemned to hard, wearisome, unproductive toil, and, from
very weariness, could not become a severe task-master.
It is worthy of notice in this connection, that up to this
time Adam had only called his help meet *Isha*, woman—
henceforth she was *Chavah*, or *Eve*, the mother of all
living.

There are those who profess to regard this narrative of
the creation and fall of man, as only an allegory or myth;

but the fact stated by one of the ablest of living philolo-gists * before the Royal Geographical Society of London, that there is not, in all the East, a nation whose earliest traditions of the creation do not include a serpent, a fruit-tree and a woman, would seem to be conclusive that if an allegory, it must have originated in the infancy of the race, and have had a substratum of fact for its basis. For ourselves, we have no disposition to discard a record which bears upon its face such marked evidence of its truthful-ness and inspiration.

Having then shown what was the original relation of the sexes to each other, and how far it was modified by the fall, we have next to learn what has been the condition of woman in the ages which have since passed—what forms of oppression, cruelty, and wrong have illustrated the pre-diction, " he shall rule over thee." Unworthy and dishon-orable as this tyranny of brute force has been, and terrible as have been, in many lands, the cruelties inflicted on its innocent victims, a brief review of the condition of women in ancient times and different nations, may not prove unin-structive.

* Mr. Ferguson.

CONDITION OF WOMEN.

CHAPTER I.

THE knowledge we have of the condition of antediluvian woman is very meager, but some items of it are significant. In the Cainite branch, the women possessed extraordinary beauty, and powers of fascination equal to those which have since made such trouble in the world. That some of them were, also, endowed with high intellectual abilities, may be fairly inferred from the fact of their being the counselors of their husbands, and from the energy and inventive talent of their progeny. Polygamy was early practiced by these bold, bad men, but there is no evidence of any special depression or degradation of the sex in the period before the flood.

After the deluge, the condition of woman gradually grew worse, though in some nations it was much lower than in others. By slow degrees men sank into the savage state, and in that condition, selfishness being the governing law, woman was treated with greater or less consideration, according as she could accomplish more or less of the labor necessary for bread-winning. In the pastoral nations, she had the care of the tent, cooked the food, provided for the guests, and though required to occupy a separate tent, and in general to exhibit great reverence and respect for her husband, addressing him always by the title of Lord or Master, she possessed considerable power and authority in household matters, and in her marriage her consent was necessary to its validity. Polygamy as well as concubinage was common, but usually the first wife retained the substantial authority over the household.

In the agricultural nations, where the residence was fixed, the lot of woman was harder, and her authority and privileges more restricted. She was, except in the case of the highest classes, required to perform her full share, and generally more than her share, of the severe physical toil necessary in agricultural life. She plowed the soil, and among some nations, harnessed with the ox or the ass, drew the plow. She delved in the earth, gathered the crops, and in addition performed all the menial household duties, even to grinding the corn, slaughtering the animals for food, and preparing the repast. In many countries, she was not allowed to partake of the food thus prepared until the husband had eaten to satiety, and then humbly contented herself with what he left. Women were not permitted any

WOMAN DEGRADED TO A LEVEL WITH THE BEAST.

control over their male children, and these, at an early age, imitated their fathers, by treating them with cruelty and scorn.

Hard was the fate of woman in these nations. Her existence made wretched by excessive toil, continued throughout the entire life, with no kind words, no soothing attention, unloved and unloving, and devoid of hope in the future, with no knowledge of another life, it is not wonderful that she should destroy the lives of her female children, lest they should experience the same miseries, or that she should voluntarily terminate a life so utterly hopeless.

From this oppression, which thus made the woman a slave, the resort to physical violence was an easy step—and we find, accordingly, that among some of the nations of antiquity, as among the degraded Australian tribes, when the man would select a wife, he crept up behind her stealthily, and felled her to the earth by a heavy blow of his club, and flinging her upon his shoulder, strode away to his dwelling. If she recovered, she became his wife, and this first rude assault was but the prelude to other cruelties, which her lord and master inflicted at his will. If she died from the blow, there was no blame ; his wooing had been unsuccessful, and another maiden must undergo the same ordeal.

The Asiatic nations generally, in the early ages, treated their wives with cruelty, the higher classes making an occasional exception (more apparent than real) of some favorite, who, while her beauty and powers of fascination lasted, ruled her ruler, and had her every wish gratified; but when her beauty waned, or the capricious despot was won by another face, was cast aside, neglected, and often consigned to prison or death.

The power of the husband to put his wife to death, either with or without cause, was very generally recognized by the Oriental nations. Her condition was more lowly and abject than that of the slave, while it did not possess the slave's immunities.

It is no marvel that there should have been occasional revolts from this oppression, or, that, in rare instances, women should have availed themselves of the power of association, and have formed nations, in which no man was admitted except in a menial capacity. These protests against the cruelty of their oppressors were, however, in their nature, of but brief duration, and, though they maintained their position bravely for a time, they eventually again came under the yoke.

The Tartars, like other nomadic and pastoral nations, while still leading the nomadic life, treated their women with more respect, and made their slavery less galling than most of the Orientals; yet even among them the power of life and death was in the hands of the husband and father, and their oppression, though not physically degrading, was hardly less complete than that of other Asiatic tribes.

The doctrines of Confut-see (Confucius), in China, inculcated a more liberal and just treatment of women; but the actual condition of the sex in China has been, except, perhaps, in the very highest classes, in all ages, one of deplorable depression. The idea that they were to be regarded as slaves, and without rights, very early took possession of the Oriental mind; and their religious systems—Brahminism, Buddhism, and later, Mohammedanism, have all encouraged this view. In the Brahminic doctrine of transmigration of souls, one of the most fearful calamities which could befall the believer was to be born a female. To enter the body of an elephant, a horse, an ass, a dog, or even a pariah, might be endured, but to become a woman was to touch the lowest depth of wretchedness. More degraded than the outcast pariah, her touch more polluting to the high caste and devout Brahmin than that of an unclean dog, she was made to feel that her existence was something to be endured with difficulty, and that he was to be accounted happy, who, by any means, should dismiss her from this life, and give her the possibility of entering upon some other form of existence than that of woman.

The Buddhists treated woman with less cruelty, and recognized her ability to take a part in business affairs, but they denied her the boon of participation in the higher rites and privileges of their religion, and declared her utterly incapable of attaining to the bliss of *nirv-vana*, or the state of absorption of all earthly consciousness in the contemplation of the perfections of the divine nature. With them the woman was, in fact, a soulless drudge, of whose powers of usefulness the man was to avail himself, and whom, from motives of selfishness, he should treat with some kindness; but who was, nevertheless, in all the higher relations of life, an inferior being.

One other form of religion prevailed extensively in some portions of the East in the ages preceding the advent of Christianity, and is undoubtedly entitled to the claim of being a nearer approach to the religion of the early patriarchs than either of those we have named. It was the system of Zoroaster, or Zartusht, as developed in the Zend-Avesta.

The early Persians and Medes, and a part of the inhabitants of Arabia, as well as the colonies which went out from Persia, were the adherents of this faith, which has been incorrectly stigmatized as fire-worship. They were believers in a good and an evil spirit, the former omnipotent and omniscient; the latter inferior in power and knowledge, but possessing great and malign influence over the human race. They also recognized inferior spirits, subject to these two, active both

WOMAN WITH SEVERAL HUSBANDS.

for good and evil. The Parsees, or Guebres, as they were sometimes called, while assigning to their women a subordinate position, both in power and authority, treated them with great consideration, and made them participators in all their religious rites. Their position in the nation was, in many particulars, similar to that of the Jewish women, hereafter described.

Among the hill tribes of India there were some which did not give in their adhesion either to Brahminism or Buddhism, but retained some of the earlier Aryan forms of worship. In several of these tribes, owing, perhaps, partly to the excess of the number of men over the women, polyandry was, and still is, prevalent, many of the women having two, three, or more husbands, and the authority and control of the home being vested in the wife. As these hill tribes have been for ages low in the scale of civilization, and for the most part poor, the condition of neither the women nor the men was specially desirable.

In Egypt, where at one time civilization had attained a higher point than in any other country which practiced the worship of idols, we obtain occasional glimpses of the condition of woman from the Scriptures, as well as from the hieroglyphic records of the people.

In the higher classes, they possessed considerable liberty and influence, as is seen in the case of Potiphar's wife, Pharaoh's daughter, and later,

Solomon's wife. But as the entire population, except the priesthood, the royal family, and the chief nobles of the court, were slaves of the reigning king, the condition of the women of the middle and lower classes might naturally be supposed to be one of humiliation and toil. The pictorial records, discovered by Sir Gardiner Wilkinson and others, render it certain that this was the fact. Women are found engaged in all descriptions of menial labor, and the expression of fear and abjectness in their faces is universal. Under the Ptolemies, the nation had lapsed into a condition of gross licentiousness, which made the degradation of woman complete. In no nation on the globe was chastity so rare, or womanly virtue so impossible.

The influence of Mohammedanism on the condition of women belongs more properly to our consideration of the period subsequent to the Christian era; but as most of the Mohammedan countries are either Asiatic or African, it may, perhaps, as well come into the present chapter.

Mohammed was, by birth and education, an Arab, and his views of the character and condition of woman were neither better nor worse than those of his nation generally. In denying to them the possession of a soul, or the enjoyments of a future life, he demonstrated how low was the Oriental appreciation of women, and how little aid he expected from her in the propagation of his new doctrines. As, however, his religious system was to appeal to the passions of men for its sanction, and especially to the voluptuous tastes of the Oriental nature, he was compelled to provide his houris, as a substitute for women, in the companionship of man in Paradise.

The Mohammedans have ever regarded woman as a slave, and while, among the higher classes, she has, like other slaves, had her brief hour of favoritism, among the lower classes her condition has been abject and depressed. The life of the women of the harem is one of ignorance, indolence, petty jealousies, and intrigues, and often of almost unendurable *ennui*. Secluded from all society except that of their own sex, and the mutilated slaves to whose care they are assigned, their life is aimless and wretched.

The women of the lower classes, though less strictly guarded, lead a life of severe and constant toil, enlivened by no hope in the future; yet the women are, as a rule, more violent and fanatical in their adherence to Mohammedanism, and more zealous in its propagation, than the men. In those countries of Africa (in the Soudan and Senegambia, and the oases of the desert) in which an active propagandism of the Mohammedan faith is now in progress, the efforts of the missionaries of Islam are directed exclusively to the conversion of women, secure that they will prove the most active emissaries of the faith.

Mr. J. Stuart Mill speaks of it as a matter within his own official knowledge, that in the Mohammedan States of India, which are governed by native princes, where, as is not unfrequently the case, a princess is regent during the minority of her son, the State is always much better governed than when under the administration of a prince. This is certainly creditable to the executive ability of the princesses, but the best of these native governments has only the negative merit of doing less evil than its neighbors.

CHAPTER II.

The condition of women in European States and Palestine, before the Christian era, deserves some notice. In Greece there were two policies adopted, as diverse as the character of the commonwealths which resorted to them, yet both springing from the same general theory of the subject condition of women. In Athens, there were two classes of women : the one, composed of the wives and daughters of citizens, who were kept under the strictest surveillance, retained at home, or, if permitted to walk upon the street, required to be closely veiled. They were kept in ignorance of public affairs, and their life was but a long and close imprisonment, with nothing except their household duties to relieve its *ennui*. The other class, the so-called *hetairæ*, or companions, were educated and brilliant women, of fascinating manners, but abandoned life, who frequented the market places, the assemblies, and the public debates of the city, and were the associates of its statesmen, judges, and politicians. Their life was as free as that of the others was restricted, but it was a life of open and public vice.

In Sparta, the good of the State was paramount to that of the individual, and the position of woman was defined with reference to the benefit of the State. Political power was retained in male hands, and young women were disposed of in marriage by their parents, or, if orphans, by the king, but in every other respect they were placed very nearly on a footing of equality with the other sex. Their education was public, and included the athletic games and exercises elsewhere practiced by men only; they were encouraged to discuss the questions of public interest with the other sex; and as wives and mothers, to foster the patriotic spirit, to inculcate prudence, fortitude, courage, patience, and the manly virtues generally. Their virtue was unimpeached, and the influence they exerted over their nation, in its best days, was, perhaps, more beneficial than that of any women of ancient times.

In all the Dorian States there was greater freedom allowed to the women, and they took a more active part in public affairs, than in any other part of Europe. In Corinth and in most of the other large cities of the peninsula, there was, on the other hand, a most deplorable state of morals, and, almost without exception, the women were the degraded slaves of lust.

In the early periods of the Roman republic, the Roman matrons were distinguished for their virtue and dignity. With them the interest of the nation often prevailed over their private claims, and they gloried in making patriotic sacrifices. They were never secluded, either before or after marriage, and they became, in many instances, possessed of great wealth, and were able to dispose of it as they pleased. They took an active part in public affairs, and often exerted great influence over the Senate by their petitions and pleas for favorable legislation. Yet the early laws gave the husband the same absolute right to the services and even the life of his wife, as he had to those of his slave. He could punish her in any manner he pleased, short of death, for any offense; and if the offense was great, he could summon a tribunal of her relatives, try her before them, and if she was convicted, put her to death. He could divorce her for infidelity, for poisoning, and for having false keys. By the laws of the Twelve Tables, the women were granted the power of divorcing themselves from the men. In the later republic and the empire, this unlimited facility of divorce led to the most deplorable results upon the public morals. Chastity, honor, and virtue became the rare exceptions, and the prevalence of lust in its grossest and most degrading forms, the almost universal rule. The women of highest rank, the wives and daughters of the emperors and triumvirs, were the leaders in the most horrible and degrading crimes, and yet, vile as their character were known to be, they exerted a controlling influence over their fathers, husbands, and sons.

The fall of pagan Rome was due quite as much to the terrible degradation of its women, and their reckless thirst for scenes of excitement and bloodshed, the natural fruit of their profligate lives, as to the luxury and demoralization of its men.

The Jewish nation had attempted to preserve, as nearly as possible, in their purity, the institutions of their great lawgiver, but he, in compassion to their Oriental origin and training, had permitted polygamy and divorce, and had given to the parents and husbands very stringent authority over their daughters and wives. Whoever revolts against the idea of the subordination of woman, must find the authority for his course elsewhere than in the laws of Moses. So far as these can be regarded as an exposition of the sentence of Jehovah on woman after the fall, they only add to its severity. Yet the Jewish lawgiver was too wise and too just not to make laws which should protect woman from the brutal instincts of the semi-barbarous Israelites, which should confirm her in the possession of property, and render her condition more tolerable, under the liberty of divorce.

We can not, however, regard the Mosaic law as intended to be in this or its other legal aspects, an authoritative development of the will of Jehovah for all phases or conditions of society. It

was intended to influence, control, and improve
a semi-barbarous people, just emerging from slavery, of Oriental origin and ideas, and gradually
to lift them to a higher plane. Of course, rapid
progress was out of the question, and their prejudices and ancient practices must be conciliated to
some extent. What would be adapted to such a
people, would in many particulars be wholly out
of place in a more enlightened and cultivated
commonwealth, in other times and under other
circumstances.

Either from these laws, or from the peculiar
condition of the Hebrew people, we find that
during the existence of the Hebrew common-
wealth, women enjoyed a very considerable degree of liberty, and in exceptional instances great
authority and influence. Unlike other Oriental
nations, there was no attempt at seclusion either
of married or unmarried women; they took a considerable and almost uniformly patriotic interest
in public affairs; in one notable instance, a woman,
and she a wife, Deborah, the wife of Lepidoth,
judged Israel for many years, and, in association
with Barak, led the national forces against the
Canaanites. In the later history of the nation we
find women taking a prominent part in the national
rejoicings, and the wives and mothers of the Is-
raelitish kings influencing and controlling their
action. Two of these queens, Jezebel and Atha-
liah, stand out in a bad pre-eminence, which indi-

cates alike their despotic power and their evil disposition. Still later, in the Maccabean wars, Judith, the slayer of Holofernes, and deliverer of her people, is a commanding figure in Jewish history.

The hope of being privileged to become the mother of the long promised Messiah gave a dignity and glory to the character of the Judean woman, which manifested itself as well in her moral as her physical beauty—and through the ages this blessed expectation had its share in keeping her pure, chaste, and holy.

Yet, with all this measure of freedom, the Jewish woman was, in many respects, subordinate; and, especially among the lower classes, her lot was hard, her toil constant and severe, and her task-master, who was also her husband, was exacting and stern.

Both Cæsar and Tacitus portray the social condition of the Germans as remarkably attractive, and describe the position of their women as one of more freedom and equality than was found elsewhere; but while there has been, from the earliest times, among the Teutonic tribes, a stronger attachment for home and family than in the Celtic nations, these descriptions are to be taken with some allowance, both from their necessarily superficial character, and from the proneness of both writers to make history the vehicle for the inculcation of their own views and theories. The

WOMEN AS HOD CARRIERS. SCENE IN VIENNA, AUSTRIA.

Germans were barbarians, and though of a noble and generous nature, and free from many of the vices of barbarism, there is no reason to believe that they abdicated their authority over the women of their nation, or exempted them from the hardships which they suffered in most barbarous nations. This is the less probable since, even to-day, when they have become a highly intellectual and cultivated nation, and all the ameliorating influences of Christianity and mental culture have for ages exerted their influence in improving the condition of woman, the German women of the lower, and, to some extent, of the middle classes, are subjected to greater hardships than the women of any other nation of Europe. The farm-laborer, the mechanic, and even the small farmer, makes his wife or mother his drudge, and compels her to perform the most menial and severe labors, while he sits or walks by her side unemployed, smoking his pipe. Within a few years, American citizens have witnessed, in Vienna, women acting as masons' tenders, carrying bricks and mortar up to the walls of lofty brick buildings in course of erection. There, as well as here, German women, often the mothers of families, are chiffonnières and scavengers.

3

CHAPTER III.

THE advent of Christianity exerted a favorable influence on the condition of women throughout all the countries in which it was propagated. In the mission, the sufferings, and death of the Messiah, a part of the sentence pronounced on the serpent, and the serpent's prompter, had been fulfilled; the seed of the woman did bruise the serpent's head. And in the whole life and teachings of the Redeemer, there was a compassionate thoughtfulness for woman, an evident desire to raise her from her lowly condition, and to confer upon her some relief from the severity of the sentence pronounced in Eden, which was without any precedent in the world's previous history. It seemed as if, in his view, woman, in bringing into the world the second Adam, had measurably atoned for her transgression in leading the first Adam into temptation, and henceforth her lot was to be less wretched, her sorrows to be diminished, and her joys increased. Women rendered conspicuous services to the Saviour himself, and to the early Church; though never admitted to the exercise of authority, their zeal, their labors, in public and private, in the diffusion of Christianity, and their abundant charity, were commended both by Christ and his apostles, nor were they ever censured for their Christian activity, even though it at times must have encroached on the household duties, which, then as now, were considered by many as paramount.

At an early period in the history of the Church, Christian women, aside from the instruction of their households in the doctrines of the Christian faith, taught the catechumens, prepared the love-feasts, and made provision for the eucharist; exercised, in large measure, the duties of a hospitality more exacting than that of the present day, visited the sick and the prisoners, encouraged those who were destined to martyrdom, and often, with heroic courage, refused to deny their Lord, and suffered death in the most terrific forms which the cruelty of tyrants could devise. For the first six hundred years of the Christian era, or, at least, as soon as the number of the disciples of Christianity had increased sufficiently to warrant the organization of Christian communities, the Christian woman was practically free from the subjection under which she had formerly been bound. Her new ties, aside from those of the family, were to the Church, to the care of the sick, to religious instruction, and to the cloister; for the life of voluntary seclusion for religious meditation and improvement had many charms for the unmarried and widowed. The wealthy and high-born women of the Roman empire gave their money and influence for the ransoming of slaves, for the establishment of hospitals, asylums for the sick, and monasteries, which, at first, included also schools for the instruction of the poor and ignorant.

To say that there were no instances of the oppression of women in these early centuries, would be to falsify history. The Roman laws, and later, the Justinian code, were in force, and neither recognized, so fully as they ought, the rights and immunities of woman; but then, as before and since, the practice of the community was materially better than the laws, and in her social position, woman enjoyed more of freedom than at a later period.

We may not urge it as any fault of the sex that as the ages drew on, ignorance, darkness, and moral degradation constantly increased. They would have done so inevitably under existing circumstances. There were, in Southern Europe, the dregs of the old Roman empire, which had perished from its own rottenness; a conglomeration of nationalities, having as yet no bond of union, not even the nominal Christianity which but a part of them had professed; a bitter strife between the middle classes, the nobles, and the peasants; and a Church which was fast declining from its high estate of purity and self-sacrifice into a condition of hypocrisy, selfish greed, and gross licentiousness. The monasteries and nun-

EMPRESS HELLENA AND HER MAIDENS ATTENDING THE WOUNDED SOLDIERS.

neries were no longer places of devout meditation and Christian instruction; but in them, gluttony, drunkenness, lust, and murder, ran riot. The priests, under the new *régime* of celibacy, were no longer the ministers of Christ, but wolves which debauched and destroyed the flock, and all things seemed tending toward utter ruin and desolation.

It is to the honor of the sex, that we have to record, that in every century of these dark ages, there were found women who sought to raise their sex from the degradation which seemed so inevitable; daughters of nobles and princes, who, by the establishment of schools and institutions of learning, and by public instruction, attempted to turn the attention of their sisters from frivolity and dissipation; and daughters of toil as well, who established manufactories, asylums for the poor and infirm, and sisterhoods for the relief of the suffering.

The development of knight-errantry and the age of chivalry, during this period, was a protest against the lawless outrages of the time, from which women were the greatest sufferers, and an effort to establish the domination of a great reform of morals and manners, on an inadequate basis, and in an age which was not ripe for it. It accomplished some good as well as some evil; the high-born dames whom the knights recognized as their ladyes, were pledged to lives of purity and good works, and their approval infused new courage, and incited to greater efforts, their knights; but the excessive flatteries addressed to them by the troubadours, and the almost religious adoration bestowed upon them, tended to excite the vanity and to raise the self-esteem of these women, whose education was but meager, and whose judgment was hardly more developed than their intellect.

It should be remembered, too, that in the days of chivalry, it was only the noble and high-born to whom the knight pledged his sword, and from whom he received his "favors;" the wives and daughters of the peasants, and, indeed, of the tradesmen, had no rights which these knights were bound to respect; and often was the lowly home made desolate, and the peasant-woman dishonored, by a knight who had vowed perpetual fealty to some proud beauty in castle or chateau.

But these dark ages could not always last. The Reformation came, and brought an improvement both in morals and manners. The revival of letters, which partly preceded and was partly contemporaneous with it, had opened the way for the intellectual culture of the sex, and in the century which followed, we find a considerable number of female names illustrious for scholarship; the new faith had its eloquent advocates among women as well as among men, though the Reformers themselves discouraged any public ministration of women. Luther, however, pressed women into service, as instructors of the young, and recognized them as able assistants in many departments of Christian activity.

The power of woman, if not her freedom from subjection, was recognized, especially in the higher classes. In the century which followed the Reformation, more than half the principal thrones of Europe were occupied by queens, some of them illustrious for their virtues and abilities, others equally conspicuous for their vices.

Isabella, of Spain; Catherine de Medicis, of France; Mary and Elizabeth, of England; Elizabeth, of Hungary; Mary, Queen of Scots, were the most remarkable of these female rulers, and whether their success was due, as has been alleged, to the able men they selected as counselors, or not, it must be admitted that their reigns do not generally compare unfavorably with those of the kings, who preceded or succeeded them.

In the following century women played a prominent part in the government of France, Spain, and England, but it was oftenest as favorites, who ruled the kings through their passions, and disposed of offices, places and treasure, for the gratification of their own caprices rather than for the good of the people.

The eighteenth century was also remarkable for its intellectual women, some of whom have never been surpassed in the vigor and purity of their style, while others exhibited a grasp of intellect and a power of grappling with important questions of finance and political economy, which had hitherto been supposed beyond the abilities of the sex.

The religious reformation in England, and the organization of Wesleyan Methodism, developed another element of womanly power. Wesley's distinguished patroness, Selina, Countess of Huntingdon, was herself active as a writer in defense of his doctrines, and the women of the middle and lower classes, who made up somewhat the larger portion of the converts under the preaching of both Wesley and Whitfield, found liberty of utterance in their meetings, and often discoursed with great power, and sometimes with considerable vehemence, in behalf of the new doctrines.

It was, however, reserved for the nineteenth century to witness the higher and much more general intellectual development of woman, and her advance in the attainment of those legal rights, which, under English common and statute law, had hitherto been unjustly withheld from her. In literature she has achieved a high, though hardly the highest position; her fictions have shown considerable creative power, and are hardly more deficient in originality than those of the most eminent male novelists; in poetry she has attained a high rank, and though still falling below the great masterpieces of English verse, she is entitled to rank with the best poets of our own time. In science a few great names have appeared, to demonstrate the capacity of the sex for high attainments in astronomy, mathematics, natural history, political economy, psychology, and moral philosophy.

In the mechanic arts, though seldom inventing any important machines, they have exhibited a tact and skill in manipulation, in many departments, which have secured for them high positions and great responsibilities.

In trade and commercial pursuits, women, who have been trained to them, often exhibit decided abilities both in financial management and in sales.

But it was left for the Crimean war, the late war in the United States, and the still more recent war in Germany, to exhibit most fully the remarkable executive ability of woman, in the labors of the hospital, in the management of depots of supplies, in the purchase of goods, the disbursement of hospital stores, the conducting of extensive correspondence, the erection of hospitals, asylums, and homes for the wounded, the organization and successful management of monster fairs, and the control, in general, of an expenditure of nearly eighty millions of dollars.

In this great work, of the thousands who took part in it, many fell victims to over-work and over-anxiety; some, as delicate as the others, but with better powers of endurance, survived the

3*

great struggle, but, thoroughly disabled, sank a year or two later into untimely graves; and others, recovering from the terrible strain of brain and nerve, still live to bless the world.

It is the testimony, not grudgingly given, of the men who were associated with them in this work, that it was well, admirably done; that much of it could not have been done so well by men, since it required womanly tact and tenderness; and that none of it could have been accomplished with more skill, system, and promptness, by men trained all their lives to business, than it was by women who had previously been the ornaments and pets of society.

To these noble and generous-hearted women, however, the " pace was killing;" the effort was too great for their delicate and frail constitutions; and though there was no faltering, no shrinking from toil, till the last invoice was made out, the last consignment shipped, or the last patient cared for, they went to their homes, many of them, when all was done, only to lie down and die. To men, under similar circumstances, there would have come for a time intense weariness, and a craving for rest; but the bow, long bent, would have recovered its elasticity, and the power of work have returned.

The brief review of the condition of woman in all ages being thus concluded, let us proceed to define what is woman's present position before the law.

CHAPTER IV.

THE greater part of the provisions of our statute books in relation to woman have been based on the common law of England, modified of late years by special statutes, granting particular privileges or immunities to women in certain relations or conditions in life. In Canada, to some extent, and in Louisiana and Florida almost entirely, the French laws either of the code Napoleon, or the old communal law, prevail. What the English common law on this subject is, has been briefly but justly expressed in an old Black-letter volume published in 1632, and attributed to Sir John Doderidge, Solicitor-General, and subsequently Judge of Common Pleas and of the King's Bench. The book is entitled the "Lawe's Resolution of Woman's Rights." The following passage, quoted by Mrs. C. H. Dall in her "The College, the Market, and the Court," contains the pith of many a long page of Black-letter :—

"The next thing that I will show you is *this* particularity of law. In this consolidation which we call wedlock is a locking together. It is true that man and wife are one person; but under-stand in what manner. When a small brooke or

little river incorporateth with Rhodanus, Humber,
or the Thames, the poore rivulet loseth her name:
it is carried and recarried with the new associate;
it beareth no sway; it possesseth nothing during
coverture. A woman, as soon as she is married,
is called *covert*; in Latine, *nupta*—that is, 'veiled;'
as it were, clouded and overshadowed; she hath
lost her streame. I may more truly, farre away,
say to a married woman, Her new self is her
superior, her companion, her master." . . .

"Eve, because she had helped to seduce her
husband, had inflicted upon her a special bane.
See here the reason of that which I touched before—that women have no voice in Parliament.
They make no laws, they consent to none, they
abrogate none. All of them are understood either
married or to bee married, and their desires are to
their husbands. I know no remedy, though some
women can shift it well enough. The common
lawe here shaketh hand with divinitye."

Mr. John Stuart Mill, in his "Subjection of
Women," published in the summer of 1869, thus
states the present provisions of the common law
of England, in relation to the condition of married
women, after all the recent statutory modifications:

"The wife is the actual bond-servant of her
husband; no less so, as far as legal obligation goes,
than slaves, commonly so called. She vows a life-
long obedience to him at the altar, and is held to
it all through her life by law. Casuists may say

that the obligation of obedience stops short of participation in crime, but it certainly extends to every thing else. She can do no act whatever but by his permission, at least tacit. She can acquire no property but for him; the instant it becomes hers, even if by inheritance, it becomes *ipso facto* his. In this respect the wife's position, under the common law of England, is worse than that of slaves in the laws of many countries. By the Roman law, for example, a slave might have his *peculium*, which, to a certain extent, the law guaranteed to him for his exclusive use. The higher classes (in England) have given an analogous advantage to their women, through special contracts setting aside the law, by conditions of pin-money, &c.: since, parental feeling being stronger with fathers than the class feeling of their own sex, a father generally prefers his own daughter to a son-in-law who is a stranger to him. By means of settlements, the rich usually contrive to withdraw the whole or part of the inherited property of the wife from the absolute control of the husband : but they do not succeed in keeping it under her own control; the utmost they can do only prevents the husband from squandering it, at the same time debarring the rightful owner from its use. The property itself is out of the reach of both ; and as to the income derived from it, the form of settlement most favorable to the wife (that called ' to her separate use ') only precludes the husband from receiving it instead of her; it must pass through her hands; but if he takes it from her, by personal violence, as soon as she receives it, he can neither be punished nor compelled to restitution. In the immense majority of cases there is no settlement; and the absorption of all rights, all property, as well as all freedom of action, is complete. The two are called 'one person in law,' for the purpose of inferring that whatever is hers is his, but the parallel inference is never drawn, that whatever is his is hers; the maxim is not applied against the man, except to make him responsible to third parties for her acts, as a master is for the acts of his slaves or his cattle. I am far from pretending that wives are, in general, no better treated than slaves; but no slave is a slave to the same lengths, and in so full a sense of the word, as a wife is. Hardly any slave, except one immediately attached to the master's person, is a slave at all hours and all minutes; in general, he has, like a soldier, his fixed task, and when it is done, or when he is off duty, he disposes, within certain limits, of his own time, and has a family life, into which the master rarely intrudes. But it can not be so with the wife.*

* Mrs. Dall illustrates this practical servitude of the wife, under the English common law, by the following incident, which occurred in one of the London courts in 1858 —

"A delicate, much-abused woman unmarried, but who had been, in her own phrase, 'living for some time' with a man, brought an action

"While she is held in this worst description of slavery as to her own person, what is her position in regard to the children in whom she and her master have a joint interest? They are by law *his* children. He alone has any legal rights over them. Not one act can she do toward, or in relation to them, except by delegation from him Even after he is dead, she is not their legal guardian, unless he by will has made her so. He could even send them away from her, and deprive her of the means of seeing or corresponding with them, until this power was in some degree restricted by Sergeant Talfourd's act.

"This is her legal state. And from this state

against him for assault. Erysipelas had inflamed her wounds, and endangered her life.

"'Had she died, sirrah,' said the magistrate, addressing the criminal, 'you must have taken your trial for murder. What have you to say in your defense?'

"'I was in liquor, sir,' pleaded the man. 'I gave her some money to go to market. I told her to look sharp; but she was gone more than an hour, your worship; so, when she came back, I—I was in liquor, your honor.'

"The magistrate leaned over his desk, and speaking in the most impressive manner, thus endeavored to cut short the defense:—

"'This woman is not your slave, man. She is not accountable to you for every moment of her time. She is not,' he continued with increasing fervor, but a growing embarrassment, 'she is not—she is not—'

"A suppressed titter ran through the court: for every married man knew that the words, 'She is not your wife,' were those which had sprung naturally to the worthy magistrate's lips; and must have passed them, had not honest shame prevented. The man then attempted to defend himself on the ground of jealousy, but this was instantly set aside; the unmistakable impression left on the mind of the assembly being, that the illegality of the relation was wholly in the woman's favor."

she has no means of withdrawing herself.   If she
leaves her husband, she can take nothing with her,
neither her children, nor any thing which is rightfully her own.   If he chooses, he can compel her
to return, by law, or by physical force; or he
may content himself with seizing for his own use
any thing which she may earn, or which may be
given her by her relations.*   It is only legal separation by a decree of a court of justice, which
entitles her to live apart, without being forced
back into the custody of an exasperated jailer—
or which empowers her to apply any earnings to
her own use, without fear that a man, whom she
has not seen for twenty years, will pounce upon
her some day and carry all off.   This legal separation, until lately, the courts of justice would only
give at an expense ($4,000 or more) which made
it inaccessible to any one out of the higher ranks.
Even now it is only given in cases of desertion or
the extreme of cruelty; and yet complaints are
made every day, that it is granted too easily.   No
amount of ill-usage, without adultery superadded,
will in England free a wife from her tormentor,
that is, by a full divorce."

Well may Mr. Mill remark of such laws as
these, that the laws of most countries are far

* The husband of the Hon. Mrs. Norton actually enforced this outrageous provision of the law against his wife; seizing the income from her
settlement, all her personal effects, her literary earnings, and the gifts
of her friends.

worse than the people who execute them, and many of them are only able to remain laws by being seldom or never carried into effect.

The English common law is somewhat more just to single women, though still oppressive in some particulars.

A single woman has the same rights of property as a man; she is entitled to the protection of the law, and has to pay the same taxes to the State. If her parents die without a will, she shares equally with her brothers in the division of the personal property; but her eldest brother and his issue, even if female, will take the real estate as heirs at law. If she be an only child, she inherits both the personal and real property of her parents.

Being "duly qualified," that is, possessing a certain amount of property, she may vote on parish questions and for parish officers.

As the English law of suffrage is based on a property qualification, it was contended that single women possessing the required amount of freehold property (this was before the recent suffrage reform) might cast a vote for members of Parliament; and it is a matter of record that in one or two instances they have done so. The attempt by any considerable number of women to cast a vote under these conditions would, however, have imme diately caused a legal prohibition. In June, 1866, fifteen hundred single women, property-holders, petitioned Parliament to provide for the representation of householders without distinction of sex, alleging that the possession of property justly carried with it the right to vote for representatives in Parliament, and that their exclusion was an anomaly in the British constitution. Though their construction of the British constitution was unquestionably logical, and the number of voters to be added by such a change was not large, yet the prayer of the petitioners was, without hesitation, rejected, though defended with ability by Mr. J. Stuart Mill, who had presented it.

The Church and all State offices are closed to women. In rare instances they have been appointed to rural post-offices, or made parish clerks, overseers of the poor, or governors of small local prisons. They are not excluded from the highest of all positions in the realm, that of sovereign; but there, the power, under the constitution, is much more nominal than real, since the real sovereignty is lodged in the cabinet. In almost all periods of English history, women have, through court favor or particular circumstances, held some one of the great offices of the kingdom, sinecures, of which there are so many in Great Britain; but these were only exceptional cases, and the recurrence of any one of them is highly improbable.

No single woman, having been seduced, has any remedy at common law, neither has her mother or next friend. If her father can prove *service* rendered, he may sue for loss of service.

The conservative principle is so strong in the English people, that they suffer these laws, and others equally odious, to remain on the statute book, when the enforcement of some of them has not been attempted for generations, and they could not, probably, in any given case, be enforced. Still, it must be acknowledged that women have a right to claim more liberal legislation, and the abrogation of the old principle of force from the statute book, in its application to their condition.

In England there is no provision for the protection of a married woman who goes into business in her own name. Be her husband ever so profligate or worthless, he has the right to seize all her earnings and her goods, convert them to his own use, and turn her penniless into the street, and she has no redress.

In France the provisions on this subject are better. The code Napoleon, it is true, resembles the English common law in this respect; but all parties, at their marriage, are allowed to choose whether they will be governed by this law, which, in its relations to the property of married women, is called the *dotal*, or by another called the *communal* law, and the choice once made can not be revoked. The communal law makes the woman a citizen, equally liable with her husband for the State and other taxes, and gives her the authority to make her own bargains and control her own property, which is not responsible for her husband's debts. She has no suffrage; but on the other hand, she is not liable for military service.

In France, women sometimes hold office; they may be post-mistresses, inspectors of schools and public asylums, may take charge of bureaus of wood and tobacco—government monopolies—and in relation to these subordinate offices they enjoy all the rights of the men, except the right of promotion.

The French law, in other particulars, gives the husband much the same personal rights over the wife as the English common law, with the added disadvantage, that, as a Catholic country, there is no legal separation, and no divorce but for adultery. The dread of this perpetual bondage has been in the lower classes, among the working people (*ouvriers*), students, &c., the cause of a form of illicit connection—the grisette system—which is more prevalent there than in any other country of Europe, and which has proved subversive of public morals to a frightful extent. The single woman has no redress against her seducer, even under the promise of marriage; and in general her position, except in the protection of her property, is worse than in England. The French law, in all its provisions in regard to women, seems not so much desirous of protecting her as of hedging her about, by laws, to protect society against her: yet there has been progress even in France; the position of woman in that country is bet ter now than it was fifty years ago, and would be better than it is, were it not that the low state of public morals begets a contempt for women which is but thinly veiled in the habitual politeness of the French people. We turn to the United States, and ask, What is the legal *status* of woman here?

Thirty years since, the English common law was, with but slight modifications, the paramount law in regard to the legal condition of woman; but changes were incorporated into the statutes of the new States, and these were speedily introduced in the older commonwealths, till now the greater part of the disabilities under which they formerly suffered are abolished. There is, however, a great want of uniformity in the legislation of the different States on this subject; some going much further than others in their enactments for the benefit of the sex. In most of the States, the wife is allowed to hold property separate from her husband. In New York, Massachusetts, Connecticut, and most of the Western States, she can conduct business in her own name, or have a partner other than her husband, and her separate property is not subject to seizure by him, nor is it liable for his debts. She can receive property by inheritance or gift after her marriage, and dispose of it independently of her husband. In several of the States the married woman can make a will, and bequeath absolutely her separate property to whomsoever she pleases. In most, she receives as her dower, at her husband's death, one-third of his real and one-half of his personal estate.   If they are childless, she receives, in some States, the whole of his personal and half of his real estate, if he dies intestate.   She is by statute of most of the States, a guardian of her minor children, on their father's death, except in cases of mental incompetency. Divorce is granted for several causes in all the States, and equally to either party; in some of the States it is granted for any cause, or without cause, a facility which is productive of the worst results.

The courts punish with greater or less severity the brutality of the husband who treats his wife with violence; and wife-murder is more frequently punished with death by hanging than the murder of any other person.   This is as it should be.

The condition of the single woman who possesses property, is the same as that of any other citizen. She does not vote at any public election, State or national; but, on the other hand, she is not subject, either to military or jury duty; she is taxed both by the State and national governments, and receives the benefit of the taxation in the protection accorded to her person and property.

A single woman who has been seduced, can, in several of the States, bring a civil, and, in two or three, a criminal action against her seducer, and in a civil suit usually obtains exemplary damages; or in most or all of the States her father, mother, or next friend can bring a suit for her.

A few offices or places under the national and State governments are allotted to women. A considerable number are postmistresses, some of them in important cities. From five hundred to one thousand women are clerks in the various departments at Washington. In the offices of the State governments there are a considerable number employed as clerks. An attempt has been made but we believe as yet unsuccessfully, to secure for them, in one or two instances, the position of assessor or collector of internal revenue. A few are employed in the Custom-house at New York, and perhaps in some of the custom-houses in other cities. They do not yet, as clerks, receive equal compensation with male clerks of the same grade; and partly for the reason, that with some honorable exceptions, their work is not equal, either in quality or quantity, to that of the male clerks. That some of them do as much, and do it as well as the men, is undoubtedly true, and that most of them could do so, is equally true; but the system of appointing these women clerks has been very corrupt. They were generally appointed on the urgent requests of members of Congress, and were usually relatives or favorites of those who solicited their appointment. They were often incompetent for the duties of their positions, as, indeed, competency had little or nothing to do with the matter;

they were often gay, frivolous girls, who cared more for flirtations than work. If the Civil Service bill were passed, and those only appointed who could sustain a competitive examination, there would be no difficulty in regard to salaries ; the same work would command the same pay, whether the clerk were man or woman.

The only approach to the grant of the suffrage to women which has been made by any of our Legislatures (except Minnesota), is a law passed by the State of New York, authorizing all persons who contributed regularly to the support of public worship in any religious society incorporated under a general law of the State, to vote at the regular meetings of such society. In Minnesota, the Legislature passed an amendment to the State constitution in 1868, admitting the participation of women in the suffrage, and it was ratified by the people by a small majority early in 1869, but no election has yet been held under it. It is, as we have said, desirable that there should be a greater uniformity in the legislation of the different States in regard to the rights and conditions of women. On some points, as for instance in the facility of divorce, and in the case of Minnesota, the conferring the right of suffrage, a few of them have gone too far ; but on matters of much greater moment, some are far behind their true position, and in some particulars none have fully come up to their duty. The true standard for legislation in relation to woman, can be ascertained by regarding her as the help-meet, the associate, the complement of man, and, as thus, entitled to equal justice with him in regard to her person, her property, her moral, intellectual, and social condition. In the marriage relation, though her duties and her sphere of activities may be different from that of the man, yet, if she performs honorably and truly her duties, she should be entitled to an equal share of the property, and of the responsibility with the husband; no restrictions should be placed on her inheritance as his widow, which would not be placed on his as her widower; she should be placed in the same relation as guardian of their children, that he would be, in the event of her death; and in the disposition of the property accumulated by their joint labors, she should not be hampered any more than her husband would have been.

In regard to education and intellectual culture, it is rather the practice than the law which needs reformation, and on this subject we shall have more to say by-and-by. Meantime we may remark, that there seems to be no good reason why, in this country, as well as in France, women should not, very frequently, and wherever competent women can be found, be appointed inspectors of schools, not to the exclusion of male inspectors, but in connection with them. We believe that the public interest in the schools, and

4

their consequent improvement, would be greatly promoted thereby. There are medical schools for women in several of our large cities, and the course of instruction is, we believe, as thorough in some of them, as in the medical colleges for men. The States have authorized them to grant medical degrees, and the prejudice which at first existed in regard to them has greatly abated.

The legislation on moral questions involving the rights of women has not as yet come up to its true standard, and will not until the principle is fully recognized that the guilt of the man should receive the same measure of punishment and of social reprobation as that of the woman. If the one is to be reckoned an outcast for her offenses against the purity of society, let the other be banished from society also; if society receives the one on evidence of his penitence (too often is he now received without that evidence), then let the erring one of the other sex, who seeks pardon from God and man, be permitted to make an effort for a better life, and encouraged to succeed. Seduction should be severely punished, and the libertine driven from society as infamous.

The progress which has been made in the last few years in the legislation in regard to women, indicates, that, in an enlightened Christian community, the legislators have no intention of oppressing women; that they are willing to do them justice, when they understand fully their claims and their rights; and though the progress of legislation may be slow, it will be sure in the end to give to the sex all they can rightfully claim. We could de sire, indeed, that woman should not have occasion to claim as a right, what should be freely and promptly bestowed as a boon; but the wheels of legislation always move tardily. Still we are satisfied, that women will sooner be invested with all their rights by an appeal to the justice of men, than they would by an attempt to obtain them through personal legislation for themselves. We do not despair of the millennium, because its coming is delayed, when we see with each year new triumphs of right over might, of justice and right-eousness over ages of hoary wrong, of gentleness and peace over outrage and bloodshed. So, too, we may not yield to discouragement in regard to the prevalence of that fairness and chivalric honor, which is ready to yield somewhat more than absolute justice, in its desire not to wrong those who have placed their interests in its keeping—when we see such progress as the past twenty years have witnessed, toward giving woman her rightful place in society, and in the common-wealth.

CHAPTER V.

HAVING thus defined the present legal status of woman, we proceed to consider what are her true relations to man, what the specific characteristics of her mental organization, and wherein she differs from man in her physical, mental, and moral structure.

These inquiries we deem necessary to the determination of her capacity for, and adaptation to, the various pursuits and employments in which of late it is deemed, by some, desirable that she should engage.

And here, at the very threshold of our investigation, we are met by the positive assertion of Mr. J. Stuart Mill, that it is impossible, in the present state of society, to know any thing correctly on the subject of woman's nature or capacities. Mr. Mill is a philosopher and political economist of distinguished ability, and his declarations are to be received with respect, even where we are compelled to differ from them. From his stand-point it *may be* impossible to come at any correct conclusion on these subjects, just as it is impossible for an observer who stands at the water-level of the great cañon of the Colorado

River, to discern the character of the landscape at the top and beyond the perpendicular wall, which rises more than a mile above him.

But looking at the subject from a different point, and regarding woman as created by the Almighty for a definite purpose and end, we beg leave to affirm, with all due respect to Mr. Mill, that *it is possible* to know something of her nature, her relations to man, and her capacities. That, under other circumstances, she might develop abilities which have hitherto remained latent, is very probable, and should be taken into the account in any estimate of what she may accomplish; but we are more concerned at present with the powers she has developed in the past six thousand years, than with those which are yet in abeyance.

To any one who has read carefully and thoughtfully those portions of the first three chapters of Genesis which we have quoted in our introduction, it will, we think, be evident, that the All-wise Creator, in the formation of woman, intended to put her in certain peculiar relations to man which had no parallel in the rest of his creation.

With the inferior animals, their creation in pairs had, for its primary object, the propagation of their several species, and any other distinction was wholly subordinate to this; but in the creation of the human pair, other purposes and designs mingled with this, in the mind of the Creator. This is evident from the period which elapsed between the creation of the man and the woman; from the duties which he performed in that period; from the sense of want of a companion—a help meet or fit for him—which he had experienced, and his Maker had observed; from the circumstances of her creation; from the apparently divinely inspired declaration of Adam : " This is now bone of my bones, and flesh of my flesh : she shall be called woman, because she was taken out of man ;" and from the conferring of a joint dominion upon the pair over the animal tribes.

We can infer that it was not the intention of the Almighty to create as a help-meet for Adam, one who should be in all respects his peer or equal, else would he have created another man to be his associate, or a woman from material entirely distinct from his body, and of stature and physical power equal to his. To have done this, would have almost inevitably led to strife in regard to authority and precedence, and perhaps eventually to the division of the earth between equal and opposing chiefs.

But the woman is taken from his own flesh and bones. She is a part of himself, and her sympathies, her affections, and her nature, are so identical, that while she is to be his associate and helper, she is but a part of himself. Yet this very language of both Adam and the Creator implies, in some degree, a subordination to the man, whose helper she is to be. With the Divine approval, Adam assumes the right to assign to her a name, as he had previously done to the animal creation ; and while that name of itself implies the nearness and dearness of the relation, it also implies that he is the head, the ruler, while yet also the associate.

We have already noticed how this authority of the man, and subordination of the woman, is still more distinctly stated in the sentence pronounced upon the woman, after her temptation and fall, and in part, we must believe, because she had undertaken to act independently of her associate and head : "Thy desire shall be to thy husband, and he shall rule over thee," or, more literally, "Thou shalt be subject to thy husband, and he shall rule over thee."

We have shown, in our historical sketch, how cruelly and harshly this sentence had been enforced by the selfishness of barbarous and half-civilized nations ; and how even the cultivated Greeks and Romans had made woman either a drudge in domestic life, or the slave of their lusts. We have seen how, in the dawn of Christianity, its Almighty Founder compassionated the condition of woman, and though not removing the yoke of subordination, yet lightened its weight, and sought to infuse into the hearts of men that gentleness which should substitute the law of love for the law of force. In the ages since, men have too often recurred to the sentence in Eden, and interpreted it in its harsh and oppressive sense, rather than in the spirit of Christ.

That the Creator, who understood thoroughly, if his creatures do not, the relations which the pair he had created bore to each other, intended that the woman should be in some sense subordinated to the man, seems evident, not only from the circumstances of her creation, and the penal sentence, but from the nature of things. While there are instances in which the woman possesses the sounder judgment and the clearer intellect of the two, the presumption is in favor of the possession in greater degree by the man, of those faculties which go to make up the governing power. In a family, as in the State, the control must be exercised by a single mind, so that the design of the Creator seems to have been that the man should be the head, as he is so often called, and the woman his vicegerent. To this view accords the physical differences in the two sexes; the man —of larger, sturdier frame, of commanding port and presence, with a voice heavy, thunderous, and fitted to command—able to take the lead in all enterprises requiring strength and power of executing the purposes he has conceived; the woman smaller in stature, and more delicately and finely built, her form and features attractive, with a beauty which we are accustomed to designate as *feminine ;* her voice sweeter, softer, and more melodious, except in the high notes, her whole figure slighter, and giving the impression of litheness and grace, rather than of great strength.

Keeping in mind that woman was to be a help-*meet* (or fit) for man, that is, the complement of his nature, supplying those faculties and qualities which were most deficient in his more rugged nature, we turn next to her intellectual characteristics, and find, as we might expect, that she is strongest where he is weakest, and weakest where he is strongest. Her intuitive faculties surpass those of man. She leaps to a conclusion, and usually a correct one, which he reaches only by a long and painful process. In the elementary studies of our schools, she easily outruns her male competitor, committing her lessons to memory with wonderful facility, and generally forgetting them as readily; unraveling with ready skill the intricacies of the lower mathematics; having a special fondness for the acquisition of a long list of geographical, historical, or scientific names, which she repeats with parrot-like readiness, and a fortnight later can not remember them; acquires a moderate but superficial knowledge of languages easily, but very rarely has any thorough mastery of their structure, or any acquaintance with their literature; is fond of rhetoric, and generally of composition; but has a great horror of logic, or analytical science. She is strongest in the studies depending upon the exercise of the perceptive faculties, and weakest in those which

4*   F

require the use of the reasoning or analyzing faculty.

Woman has but little genius for invention; she may apply or adapt an invention to some purpose for which it was not at first intended, though she does this but rarely; but of the hundreds of thousands of inventions which have received letters patent, very few, and those mostly not of great importance, are the inventions of women.

This lack of creative power manifests itself also in her writings. Many women write well; some eloquently. Most women describe any person or thing they have seen, well; many narrate incidents brilliantly; but even in the best novels written by women, how seldom do we find a real creation, a character at the same time life-like and original. Grant that not all, or perhaps the greater part, of the male novelists are successful in the creation of men and women who are not automatons, the fact remains, that, in our own times, there are at least a half-score of them who can fairly lay claim to this credit; but while there are at least ten novels written by women to one written by a man, it would be difficult to find three among them all who have manifested any creative genius. We are aware that one name will rise to the lips of many of our readers, as that of a novelist possessing great creative power; but, while we honor highly Mrs. Stowe's genius and ability as a writer, we are forced to the con-

WOMEN ENGAGED IN THE FINE ARTS.

clusion by her later works, that she only describes what she has seen, drawing her pictures with great truthfulness and beauty, but that she has never created a character, in all her numerous fictions.

In the fine arts, painting and sculpture, the same defect has characterized their compositions. They have described on canvas, and in the more enduring marble, what they have seen, what they have read, what they have heard or dreamed, but so far as we can learn, they have never been successful in putting an original conception, or creation, on canvas or in marble. We have no disposition to say that they can not : we have a very high opinion of the genius and talent of women, and would deny no possibility of their future ; but as to the sex in general, we do not believe that their abilities are greatest in that direction.

In their moral and social nature we find a similar distinction between men and women as in the intellectual faculties, so far as such distinction is possible. In woman the emotional nature is most developed; in man, the judgment and will. Woman is naturally more religious than man; her tendencies to worship and reverence are stronger, and her religious experience is usually deeper and more abiding; the exaltation of her mental faculties, under the influence of intense religious emotion, is greater than that of man, and hence there have been many more instances of triumphant deaths among women under circumstances of great physical suffering, or even under the terrors of martyrdom, than among men.

Women are usually more patient and tolerant of suffering than men; a larger measure of it usually falls to their lot, and they endure it with less complaint.

On the other hand, they are seldom as persevering as men; and if the result desired is not reached within a moderate time, they more readily weary of the pursuit. Still temperament has much to do with this; there have been instances of feminine perseverance which would do the highest credit to either sex.

The imagination being more active in women than men, the temptation to that form of untruthfulness, known as "white lying," is somewhat stronger with them than with the other sex. This tendency is particularly observable in that condition of the health known as hysteria, though it would not be just to regard a morbid manifestation as an inherent fault of woman's nature.

The sympathetic nature of woman is one of the chief glories of her moral character. Men are, in general, harder and more cruel than women. Herself often a sufferer, woman has learned to enter into the heart of the suffering, and can comfort and console them under the deepest sorrows. In all the Christian ages, woman has ministered, with tender hand, to the suffering and sorrowing, to the sick and the wounded, the prisoners and those appointed to die. In our own time, Florence Nightingale, and her noble companions in the Crimean war, the thousands in our own four years' struggle, and Miss Safford, Madame Mario, and their associates in the recent German war, have demonstrated the remarkable executive ability of woman in the organization and develop ment of great philanthropic enterprises.

This organizing and executive faculty is a more general endowment of woman than has been usually acknowledged. It differs materially from the governing faculty, which Rev. Dr. Bushnell, in his very able essay on "Women's Suffrage," contends, on somewhat insufficient grounds, that they do not possess. The faculty of organizing and managing affairs successfully depends rather upon tact and the intuitive perception of human character, and of the fitness of things (all womanly traits), than upon any demonstrative power of governing. The executive officer of a ship of war is not the commander, but one who, in subordination to his chief, arranges the details of the ship's service, and sees that every man performs his duty. For positions somewhat analogous to this, our great merchants and manufacturers say that women, properly trained, are superior to men.

There have not been wanting instances, notable ones, in which, though the governing faculty is regarded as properly and appropriately the heritage of man, women have acquitted themselves admirably in its exercise. We will not speak of queens, since some part of their apparent skill in governing is doubtless due to the able male counselors who constitute their cabinets; but how can we deny the ability to govern and control to such women as Joan of Arc, or to the Countess Teleki of Hungary, who, in the Hungarian war of 1848, led a division of cavâlry in three several assaults upon a body of Austrian troops, and, twice repulsed, rallied her troops the third time, and with her helmet doffed and her beautiful golden hair streaming in the winds, shouted the war-cry, "Eljen Kossuth," and hurled them upon the enemy; and, in the words of the Austrian commander, "Neither men nor devils could have resisted that onset; we were swept down like grass before the mower's scythe." The beautiful countess fell in the assault, but she had proved her ability to command. Who could question the faculty for command of that noble Michigan woman, Mrs. Anna Etheridge, who, at the battle of Chancellorsville, seeing the regiment to which she was attached flying from the field, seized their flag, and with a "For shame, boys! go back to the field! I will lead you," checked their retreat, and led them back into the thickest of the fight?

Nay, do we not often find in our public schools and academies, female teachers whose skill and tact in the government of their schools enables them to bring into willing subjection grown boys who have proved an overmatch for male teachers?

In this analysis of the differences, physical, mental, social, and moral, between the two sexes, it must be remembered that we have only dealt in general characteristics of the sexes. There are numerous exceptions under each, but none, we believe, which will invalidate our general estimate.

We conclude, then, that there is evidence in the Scriptures, and in the physical, mental, moral, and social constitution of the sex, that her Creator intended woman to be the ally, the helpmeet, the associate, and co-worker with man, but so far in subordination to him, that he is to be recognized as the head, and possess the chief authority in the family, but always with due regard to the wife, as his vicegerent, and next in authority and power.

CHAPTER VI.

BEFORE proceeding to consider the employments of women, it may be well to give some account of the present system of education of the sex, and to show its faults and disadvantages.

In England, aside from the dame schools and the national schools, in which, for the most part, only the children of the poor, of both sexes, are taught, the only schools for the education of girls are the endowed female schools, which are few in number, and the female seminaries or finishing schools, which are generally very expensive. There is a provision for girls in some of the great charity schools, such as Christ Church and Westminster, but very few girls ever enter. The middle and higher classes very generally employ governesses for their daughters, giving them a year or two at the finishing schools before they "come out," as the phrase is.

While the education of the women of the poorer classes in England is greatly inferior to that of a corresponding class here, a large proportion being unable to read or write, the girls of the middle and higher classes receive generally a more thorough training than the daughters of families possessing a competency here. The system of education is defective, being directed largely to what may be called "accomplishments," rather than to true mental culture. The English girl who has received the diploma of a fashionable finishing school, if she has a taste for music, usually plays well—artistically—on the piano and harp, and if she has a good voice, sings correctly and with expression; she generally draws with accuracy, and if she possesses artistic taste, sketches from nature very effectively; she is usually quite perfect in her French grammar and pronunciation, and often writes and speaks the language correctly, though she has no considerable knowledge of its literature. In many cases she has a fair knowledge of Italian and German also, and an elementary one of Latin. In English studies, the range is not as extensive, as in American schools for girls, but they are more thoroughly mastered. Generally, physical science is ignored in the English schools for girls, though a few teach the elements of chemistry, philosophy, and botany. The range of studies taught to the English girl is not great, and, as we have said, is altogether too much in the way of "accomplishments;" but what is taught, is, for the most part, very thoroughly acquired, and not readily forgotten. One reason of the peculiarities and the thoroughness of this system probably is, that among the middle class, and even the lower ranks of the nobility and gentry, owing to the law of primogeni ture and the loss of position, office, or property, as in the case of the families of clergymen, army officers, civil officers, &c., so large a proportion of the daughters are obliged to teach for a livelihood, either as governesses, or in the finishing schools.

Yet the course of instruction for girls is much narrower, and less productive of mental development than that of the boys; and we all know how defective in every thing, except classical and mathematical training, is the higher education of young men in England.

In France, the education of women is conducted on a plan which is calculated to dissipate and enfeeble the intellect; and can never develop, successfully, the mental powers. It makes showy women, brilliant in their early youth, but superficial, and with no desire for higher or more thorough culture. Much of the education of girls is conducted in convents, and is intensely superficial. Dissatisfied with this, Louis Napoleon has caused the establishment of numerous schools for girls, corresponding to the colleges or lyceums for boys in Paris. But his Minister of Instruction, M. Duruy, regarding, as most Frenchmen do, the female intellect as greatly weaker, and less capable of grappling with abstruse studies than that of man, has caused a series of text-books to be prepared especially for female schools throughout the empire (some of them were prepared by M. Duruy himself), which are avowedly simpler and more superficial than those in use in the colleges and lyceums. They are, really, mere surface books, containing not quite so much information in regard to their respective topics as would be communicated in an average popular lecture on the subject; and the knowledge thus imparted is so diluted and overlaid with verbiage, that there is hardly an idea to a lesson. A Frenchwoman, who acquires a thorough education, must do so in the face of great disadvantages, and deserves great credit for her energy and perseverance.

In Germany, the education of women is conducted on a more sensible and practical plan. The training of the public schools in most of the German States is compulsory, and the girls pursue the same studies, and from the same text-books, as the boys. In the schools of higher education, the course of instruction, though giving more attention to accomplishments than that of the gymnasia or universities, still requires thorough and exact scholarship.

Indeed, under existing circumstances, we should regard some of the German schools for girls as better adapted to impart a thorough education to a young woman, than, with a very few exceptions, any in England, France, or the United States.

Female education in the United States needs a thorough and radical reform. In our public schools, where, except in the large cities, the two sexes receive their elementary education together, the instruction is tolerable; though, partly from defective text-books, and partly from the lack of competent teachers, it is less thorough than it should be. In a considerable number of the large towns of New England and New York, and in some of the larger cities of the South and West, graded, high, or union schools, are established, into which a considerable number of girls from the public grammar schools are admitted, and have the opportunity of acquiring, usually in connection with the other sex, a fair English education, and, in some of them, a moderate amount of Latin, Greek, French, German, and vocal, but not often instrumental, music. The training, in the branches taught in these schools, is generally thorough, and those who have been educated in them, though deficient in some of the "accomplishments," have really a far more practical education than the graduates of the most popular female seminaries.

In the West, there are now about twenty-five "colleges," some of them hardly more than ordinary high schools, which receive students of both sexes, and conduct their education in the same classes, and in all respects precisely alike. The professors and instructors in these colleges are of both sexes, and the classes are generally very full. In some, as at Oberlin, Ohio; Antioch College, Yellow Springs, Ohio; Adrian College,

A USEFUL AND APPROPRIATE EMPLOYMENT.

Adrian, Mich., &c., the course of instruction is full and tolerably thorough, and they have graduated many distinguished men and women. The plan of admitting both sexes works well where there is a capable and efficient faculty. Dr. Bushnell, whose qualifications for giving an opinion on this subject, all will admit, says in his recent work: "The joining, for example, of the two sexes in common studies and a common college life—what could be more un-university-like, and morally speaking, more absurd? And as far as the young women are concerned, what could be more unwomanly and really more improper? I confess, with some mortification, that when the thing was first done, I was not a little shocked even by the rumor of it; but when, by and by, some fifteen years ago, I drifted into Oberlin, and spent a Sunday there, I had a new chapter opened that has cost me the loss of a considerable cargo of wise opinions, all scattered in loose wreck, never again to be gathered. . . . . . I learned, for the first time, what it means that the sexes, not merely as by two-and-two, but as a large open scale of society, have a complementary relation, existing as helps to each other, and that humanity is a disjointed creature, running only to waste and disorder, where they are put so far asunder as to leave either one or the other in a properly monastic and separate state. Here were gathered for instruction large numbers of pupils, male and female, pursuing their studies together, in the same classes and lessons, under the same teachers; the young women deriving a more pronounced and more positive character in their mental training from association with young men in their studies, and the young men, a closer and more receptive refinement, and a more delicate habitual respect to what is in personal life, from their associations with young women. The discipline of the institution, watchful as it properly should be, was yet a kind of silence, and was practically null—being carried on virtually by the mutually qualifying and restraining powers of the sexes over each other. There was scarcely a single case of discipline, or almost never more than one, occurring in a year. In particular, there was no such thing known as an *esprit de corps* in deeds of mischief, no conspiracies against order and the faculty, no bold prominence in evil aspired to, no lying proudly for the safety of the clan, no barbarities of hazing perpetrated : and so the ancient traditional hell-state of college life, and all the immense ruin of character propagated by the club-law of a stringently male or monastic institution, was totally escaped and put away. What we see recurring always, where males are gathered in a society by themselves, whether in the prison, or the shop, or the school, or the army—every beginning of the *esprit de corps* in evil is kept under, shamed away, made impossible by the association of the gentler sex, who can not co-operate in it, and can not think of it with respect.

"And what so long ago was proved by this earliest experiment, has since been proved, a dozen or twenty times over, by other experiments under other forms of religion, as well as under all varieties of literary culture and social atmosphere. Thus, if any one should imagine that the success of this first trial at Oberlin (which has now been in existence thirty-five years) was due to the particular, very strongly pronounced, type of religious influence there established, he may hear (the late) President Mann, of the Unitarian College at Antioch (Ohio), where also the two sexes were combined in the same studies, uniting in the testimony: 'We have the most diligent, exemplary institution in the country. We passed through the last term, and are more than half through the present; and I have not had occasion to make a single entry of any misdemeanor in our record book—not a case for any serious discipline. There is no rowdyism in the village, no nocturnal rampages making night hideous. All is quiet, peaceful; and the women of the village feel the presence of our students, when met in the streets in the evening, to be a protection rather than an exposure. It is almost five years since I came here, and as yet I have had no practical joke or college prank, as they are called, played upon me, not in a single instance.' A very intelligent writer in the *Westminster Review*,* acquainted with this and many other colleges, testifies to the decisive superiority here in moral behavior, and puts double honor on the name before so transcendently honored, by saying, in a touch of pleasantry, that 'male students were first called gentlemen at Antioch.'"

Mrs. Dall, who visited both Oberlin and Antioch colleges in 1867, gives later testimony to the success of what she calls the double system, *i. e.*, having pupils and teachers of both sexes. After a vivid description of the success of a young woman of color, born a slave, but a graduate of Oberlin, in teaching the classics, winning, as she did, the affection and confidence of all her pupils, Mrs. Dall continues : " Everybody at Oberlin was loud in praise of the double system ; no one would teach now in any other sort of college. The presence of women secured discipline. There was no chance for hazing or any other antiquated folly. Pupils and teachers, who had gone from Oberlin to Vassar, both missed the pleasant excitement of the old life."

Dr. Bushnell's remarks on this subject of the higher education of the two sexes together, are so just and admirable, that we can not refrain from quoting them :—

" The two sexes brought together in this man-

* Believed to be Rev. Moncure D. Conway.

ner, it is hardly necessary to say, will be rapidly discovering their true scale of merit. It matters little whether they are found to be equal or unequal in their talent of scholarship, for it does not follow that the greatest facility of acquirement will be issued in the greatest power, or will even be felt as having now the greatest practical breadth and volume. Enough that both sexes will better understand, and more respect each other, and will learn to take their relative places more exactly and gracefully. That they have, in fact, a complementary nature one to the other, will be distinctly felt, and all but visibly seen; and the college itself, in its double combination of male and female impulse, will be only a more complete man or humanity than it otherwise could be. The male talent, and the female, will be a great deal more exactly apprehended than they have been. It will even be seen that sex is predicable of talent as of organization, and both sexes of mind will be receiving qualities and contributions from each other in their cross relations, such as answer with general exactness to the husbanding and meet-helping of the marriage bond itself.

" Educated on this footing of equality, women will very soon escape their unrighteous disabilities, and obtain a place in the scale of estimation that exactly corresponds with their personal weight and capacity, and more than that they have no right to ask. Employment will be open to them,

5   G

just according to what they are best qualified to do, and their wages, like the wages also of men, will be in the exact compound ratio of what they can do and what they persönally are. And as what they personally are, includes a great deal of favor to their woman's look and voice, they will scarcely miss the full reward of their industry. As they have been educated with men, they will also become educators with men, and if they can fill the highest, most responsible places of management and presiding trust, they must and will obtain such places, and the rewards that men have in the same. They will have professorships allowed them such as they can more appropriately fill—not of mechanical philosophy, perhaps, or chemistry, or metallurgy, or fortification, but of the languages, of botany, of moral science, and not improperly, of the exact mathematics."

In regard to this last, we doubt. The mastery of the higher branches of the exact mathematics, so thoroughly as to be qualified to teach them, requires an analytical power, and a close, persevering application, which do not seem to be conspicuous qualities of the female intellect. We should be more ready to assign her the chair of chemistry, geology, or natural history, or astronomy, in all of which studies, women (exceptional cases, certainly) have distinguished themselves.

But to return to our consideration of the condition of female education in the United States.

Aside from these colleges on the double system, many of the normal schools, or training schools for the education of teachers, admit pupils of both sexes; and their course of instruction being intended to qualify the pupil-teachers to give instruction in the various grades of the public schools, the course of study is eminently practical, and the teaching generally very thorough. In this course very few of the so-called " accomplishments " are included. Drawing, in its elementary forms, and vocal music, to enable the teacher to lead the music of the school, are among the studies, but both are prosecuted only so far as to enable the future teacher to give instruction in their rudiments.

It is certainly desirable, and we hope may at no distant day be found practicable, to have most or all our colleges and universities receive young women as students, to pursue the same studies with the young men. It would, we believe, result in great benefits to both sexes, and would in a few years settle the vexed question of the comparative intellectual abilities of the two.

At present, the education of those girls who are able to acquire a so-called " higher education," aside from those who are or have been connected with the public high schools, the colleges on the double system, and the normal or training schools, is only obtained in the female academies, female seminaries, colleges for women, and boarding-schools, which abound in every part of the country. Nearly four-fifths of the girls who receive any thing more than a common school education, are taught in these schools. There are, perhaps, half a dozen, and we should include in that number, Vassar College, Packer Collegiate Institute, Elmira Female College, the Troy Female Seminary, Mt. Holyoke Female Seminary, and a seminary in Central Illinois founded years ago by Miss C. E. Beecher, which are honestly striving to give. their pupils a thorough education; but they all, as well as all the rest, are engaged in an impossible task.

The years which girls devote to school life are fewer than those which boys spend in getting their education. The boy, after spending his boyhood in a public school, or academy, at about the age of fourteen begins to fit for college; and, about two years later, enters. His four years' college course completed, he is ready to study a profession, which usually requires three years more.

The girl, after a course of elementary instruction, more or less full, and regularly attended up to her twelfth or thirteenth year, but which is generally only sufficient to make her tolerably familiar with the mere rudiments of common school studies, enters one of these boarding-schools, or seminaries, from which, at the longest, she is expected to graduate in four years. In this short space of time, she

WHAT IS TAUGHT IN FASHIONABLE FEMALE BOARDING-SCHOOLS.

is to acquire a competent knowledge of instrumental music, drawing, and painting in water-colors, Latin, French, and perhaps German and Italian, higher arithmetic, algebra, geometry, natural philosophy, chemistry, geology, botany, natural history, physiology, Butler's analogy of religion, intellectual and moral philosophy, political economy, &c., &c. She must also keep up her familiarity, or acquire it if she had it not already, with geography, grammar, history, penmanship, &c.; and must write, usually weekly, exercises or compositions of some kind. Her musical practice must be constant, and usually from one to two hours per day; and amid all her mental labor, she must find time for gymnastics, or, as it is the fashion to call them, calisthenics. Even Sunday shines no Sabbath day to her. What with Bible classes, and analyses of sermons, her poor brain is nearly as much overtasked on that day as any other.

The boy who should attempt to master all these studies in four years, with no more previous preparation than the girl has, would, if he survived the second year, be a candidate for an insane hospital or an idiot asylum before he had completed the third; and so would the girl, if she really acquired any thorough knowledge of the greater part of these studies; but she does, in fact, merely skim over most of them, half learning some, and omitting others, but attaining no clear or accurate

knowledge of more than one or two. At seven-
teen or eighteen, the girl has completed her
school course, and in most instances gladly aban-
dons her books, never desiring to open them again.
Of all the studies with which she has been cram-
med, during the previous four years, she has no
interest in, and hardly any valuable remembrance
of any one; even her music, which has occupied so
many weary hours of her school life, is abandoned,
or seldom practiced. She "comes out," is soon
married, and all thought of further mental culture
is abandoned.

That we have not overdrawn the picture, the
following *naïve* confession of a graduate of one
of these "Female Colleges," communicated to
the New York *Tribune* in July, 1869, amply
demonstrates :—

" SIR :—A thorough education in four years !
Yes, that is the tutorial cry of the country : met-
aphysics, languages, history, philosophy, mathematics, zoology, &c., &c., not to mention the
modern accomplishments, so modernly indispensable, of playing the piano and singing. But after
all their studying, resolving, reciting, thrumming,
and 'unparalleled advantages,' what do they
know ? That is the question, and one, too, that
may be speedily answered : They know remarkably little. 'But,' says some one, 'our girls
are surely bright, quick, and do study ; while with-

out doubt our professors, preceptors, and lecturers are all that they are represented to be!' Certainly our girls are bright, are quick—but, shall I say it, that is about all. I was a pupil at one of the first female colleges in the country, and being observant, I had tolerably good opportunities of judging of the training received there. In the first place, the girls rarely studied, they generally 'knew' their lessons, just by means of that same brightness and quickness, fond father and mother, which Julia, and Kate, and Melisse are so overflowing with. The lessons were practically 'learned' and said off; but an hour after the recitation, I know that nine-tenths of those girls could not have told what their lesson was about— and why? Because the American girl is terribly deficient in brain. There is no mistake about it, although it is very hard to say it, they care no more for knowledge than a man would care to wear a new-fashioned bonnet. In proof of this, find me the girl, who, on leaving college, school, or seminary, thinks her education incomplete, or dreams of studying at home by herself. There are none, or almost none. 'Study, indeed! Have I not just graduated at —— College? Study! oh, no, I am going to enjoy myself, and it's about time, I should think!' How many times I have listened to words like these. Poor things, little do they know (or, I may add, care) that the foundation of their education only is laid. But, it is said, 'they must know some-thing, to pass such examinations before such learned committees!' Let me initiate you, Mr. Editor, into the mysteries of an examination. Six years ago I was a pupil at the college I mentioned before, and a member of the second French class. I did not know how to read French understand-ingly, I could not compose a single sentence grammatically, but I had a correct pronunciation. Examination day grew nigh, and I was almost frightened out of my wits by being informed that I was to speak a long selection in French before the august committee. I studied the allotted piece, however, and recited it womanfully, on the appointed day, amid the applause of delighted spectators. I received the first honor of my class, and was spoken of as wonderfully proficient in the Gallic tongue. Thus were the audience duped, the judges duped, and, I may add, that I was almost duped myself. This is the way in which most of our examinations were prepared for; even the com positions read and lauded on these interesting occasions were not unfrequently *verbatim* copies of essays clipped from unfamiliar works recom-mended by one of our teachers as containing 'useful ideas on the subject you are about to undertake, my dear.' Oh! it disgusts me com-pletely when I remember the paltry tricks we were encouraged in, and that were suggested to us there. If, as children, we went to school to

be instructed in the art of deceiving, what wonder
that we are adepts in it now ?   M. F. A."

How poorly qualified is a young woman who has
had only such a training as this, to enter upon the
duties of married life. Her knowledge on any
subject is the merest smattering; she has no
definite or clear ideas of the structure and functions of the body which she tries to adorn with
gay and fashionable clothing; the sacred mysteries of motherhood, and the life and welfare of
the little one she may be called to cherish, are
things of which she is profoundly ignorant;
intellectually she is entirely unfit to be a help-
meet for her husband; she knows nothing of business matters, nothing of the public affairs in which
he, as a citizen, is interested. She can not read
any thing except the most sensational and vapid
of modern novels, or a periodical literature
equally trashy, "all sober reading is so horrid
dull," and "sober reading" includes every thing,
except fiction and fashions. Her moral culture
is equally imperfect. She may go to church, may
possibly have a class in the Sunday school, but
if so, the class is to be pitied ; for, having no religious ideas, no comprehension of religious truth,
she can, of course, communicate no knowledge to
her pupils. of the great moral principles which
underlie our earthly life, of her duty to her husband, to her neighbor, to community, to God, she
5*

has no definite idea; if she acts rightly and generously, it is from the instincts of her early training; if she errs in any or all her duties, she is really as much to be pitied as blamed.

But suppose that she fails to marry, and that some change in the circumstances of her family render it desirable that she should do something for her own support. What shall she do? She can not teach; she has no definite or thorough knowledge on any subject which is ordinarily taught; she has not even learned how to study, much less to impart knowledge to others; even the music, on which so large a portion of her school years has been spent, is utterly distasteful to her, and she has never acquired that knowledge of its principles, which would enable her to teach others. A wealthy New York merchant, with three grown daughters, and who had recently married a second wife, young and fashionably educated, said to the writer: "I don't know how it is; I am passionately fond of music; I have a superb Chickering grand piano in my house, and my wife and daughters have had, for years, the best musical instruction in New York; and yet I can never hear a single tune at home; my piano is locked from one month's end to another, and not one of them will touch it; they all say they had enough of that at school." This was perhaps an extreme case—one where the parties had no natural fondness for music; where the natural

taste exists, it would be strange if years of practice did not enable a young woman to play a few
tunes passably well; but it is very seldom the
case that one of these graduates of a fashionable
school knows enough of music to become, whatever the necessity, a successful teacher.

Shall this unwedded girl attempt to acquire
the knowledge of medicine requisite to become a
physician. She must go back then to the first
elements of education, and learn how to study; for
the study of medicine requires thought, memory,
comparison, analysis, synthetic power, mathematical skill, logical reasoning, and a capacity for
sound deduction. In all these her training has
been worse than useless; it must all be unlearned.
Shall she seek a position as a government clerk, a
book-keeper, an accountant, a cashier in a store,
or manufactory? Could she be more incompetent
than she is for either? If her penmanship is not
utterly ruined by that abomination, the "fashionable handwriting for ladies," she might pass muster
on the chirography; but the spelling—how seldom
is the fashionably-educated woman accomplished
in that! And the accounts—how is she who can
scarcely reckon correctly the change she receives in
a shopping excursion, to be expected to possess any
ability for the intricacies of book-keeping? She
is driven, *perforce*, to take a place as saleswoman,
or to wear out her life in the drudgery of the
needle. There is hardly any evil of our national

life which so imperatively demands reform as this.

This so-called fashionable education is ruining the health and the intellects, and greatly impairing the moral character of thousands of our young women, and it should be abolished forthwith. Something might be accomplished by making the course one of six years instead of four, requiring a rigid examination and a considerable range of attainments for admission, and then diminishing the number of studies by at least one-half. With these changes, and careful thorough teaching, it might be possible for a young girl to go through a course of study, and graduate with some knowledge of the subjects of her study, some fondness for intellectual pursuits, and some capacity to teach others.

But the best and most effective system of female education is that which trains the two sexes together, and while inspiring a moderate emulation, develops the intellectual and moral faculties more perfectly and harmoniously than it can be otherwise accomplished. Still, the vested interests in boarding-schools, female seminaries, and female colleges are so vast, that we despair of seeing them relinquished, or so thoroughly reformed as they should be, in our generation. Much could be done, indeed, by women in this matter, if they would give their attention to it; for a large proportion of the principals and proprietors of these finishing schools are women. Not until this reform is completed, can woman ever hope to take the positions to which she aspires; for not until then will she be so educated as to fill them successfully.*

* See APPENDIX A.

CHAPTER VII.

In treating of the employments of women, we necessarily give the first place to that which is her normal position—the charge of the household, and especially her calling as wife and mother. By far the larger part of the women of any generation hold one or both these relations to man.

We are not disposed to say, as some have done, that this is the only fitting occupation for woman ; or, in the words of the old monkish catechism of the Middle Ages, in answer to the question, "What is the dutie of woman ?" "Woman's whole dutie is to spinne, to sew, to say her *aves* and *paters*, and to love her husband." Nor, on the other hand, would we scoff at this, as menial labor, unfit for women of culture.

We have said, in a former chapter, that in the woman the affections predominate. Woman needs something to love and cherish, something which shall stir the fountains of her heart, and waken those emotions which elevate her above common humanity. When a pure-minded, intelligent, loving woman is united, not only by the marriage tie, but by the bonds of a true affection, to a man every way worthy of her, one who can sympathize fully with her, and whose mental and moral traits form the just complement of hers, she enters upon a relation which is higher and nobler than any other in this life; and when such a woman presses her first-born to her bosom, the life of her life, the young immortal given to her, to educate and rear for usefulness and activity here, and for glory hereafter, she has tasted of as much joy as often falls to the lot of mortals.

The vocation of the wife and mother—the mistress of a household—is one which, for the proper performance of its duties, requires the highest culture and the best development of the body, mind, and soul. Of the body, since activity, strength, skill, and elasticity of constitution are required; no tight-laced, fashion-distorted, pale, puny daughter of Eve can perform the duties of a good wife, much less those of a mother, successfully; pain, weariness, and nervous disorder will make her duties burdens, her very existence a prolonged agony. Development of the mind, for she is to be the companion, the associate, the help-meet of her husband; wise to aid and counsel him; skillful to help him when needful in his duties; intelligent to manage affairs, when his absence may render it necessary. Mental development is requisite also, in the early training of the child; the knowledge of what is best for its health and growth; knowledge of the best method of unfolding its dawning capacities ; knowledge of the way of restraining its too ardent thirst for learning, and of the best means for the symmetrical expansion of its intellect.

The highest degree of moral culture is also desirable, to insure the observance of those relations between the wedded pair which shall make their union fruitful in all good works and noble deeds ; for the cultivation of those Christian graces and amenities, which will make *home* most like *heaven* in its serenity, unselfishness, and attractiveness ; and desirable, also, that the mother may implant in the mind of her child those seeds of purity, truthfulness, conscientiousness, justice, and liberality, which shall make it a blessing to its parents and to the world.

Such homes there are, such wives, and such mothers ; women who find in this home-life and its duties ample employment for all their time, and the rich intellectual gifts with which God has endowed them ; and who take more delight in making their homes happy, in aiding their companions in the performance of their duties, and in rearing their children for lives of virtue, intelligence, and usefulness, than they would in swaying listening senates by their eloquence, winning the applause of the world by their wit and wisdom, or wielding the scepter of power in the empire of the Cæsars.

And if there comes, as in God's providence

there sometimes does, the angel of death to these happy homes, and takes from them a husband beloved, or removes a cherished and idolized child, the stroke, bitter as it is, does not shut out all sunlight from that dwelling, does not consign that wife and mother to hopeless despair, and the helplessness of an unavailing and indolent grief. Bereaved and afflicted, she yet finds solace in the household activities, and the opportunities for a more active and extended benevolence.

To the married woman, then, who understands her duties, and has the will and ability to perform them, there is no occasion, and indeed, no opportunity, for other employments; she can only engage in other pursuits by neglecting some of her home duties, or by delegating them to others less competent to perform them well; for, if she is so situated as to have and require servants, the superintendence of her household, the care and nurture of her children, if she is a mother, the necessary time occupied in planning for her own wardrobe and that of her family, and the claims of society, occupy all of her time not devoted to moral and religious duties.

Even Mr. J. Stuart Mill, the ablest and most radical of the defenders of what are sometimes called "women's rights," admits, that "when the support of the family depends not on property, but on earnings, the common arrangement by which the man earns the income, and the wife superintends the domestic expenditure, seems to him in general the most suitable division of labor between the two persons. If," he argues, " in addition to the physical suffering of bearing children, and the whole responsibility of their care and education in early years, the wife undertakes the careful and economical application of the husband's earnings to the general comfort of the family, she takes not only her fair share, but usually the larger share of the bodily and mental exertion required by their joint existence. If she undertakes any additional portion, it seldom relieves her from this, but only prevents her from performing it properly. The care which she is herself disabled (by other employments) from taking of the children and of the household, nobody else takes; those of the children who do not die, grow up as they best can, and the management of the household is likely to be so bad, as, even in point of economy, to be a great drawback from the value of the wife's earnings. In an otherwise just state of things, it is not, therefore, I think, a desirable custom, that the wife should contribute by her labor to the income of the family." Further on, he says: " Like a man, when he chooses a profession, so, when a woman marries, it may in general be understood that she makes choice of the management of a household and the bringing up of a family, as the first call upon her exertions, during as many years of her life as may be required for the purpose; and that she renounces not all other objects and occupations, but all which are not consistent with the requirements of this. The actual exercise, in a habitual or systematic manner, of outdoor occupations, or such as can not be carried on at home, would by this principle be practically interdicted to the greater number of married women."

There are cases, as we all know, where, from the indolence, intemperance, or inefficiency of the husband, and the straitened circumstances of the family, the wife and mother feels compelled to resort to some employment, which will give her the means of supporting her family. She is thus placed in worse circumstances than the widow, for she has usually the worthless husband also to feed and support.

It is obvious that under these circumstances, and they are such as should call forth our pity and sympathy, the labor of the woman must usually be fragmentary, for she can seldom leave her family for many hours at a time. This seriously complicates the question of employment, reducing it to those classes of occupations which can be carried on at home, with frequent interruptions, or in brief and irregular absences from home. If only capable of physical labor, she may take in washing, may go out at times as a charwoman, may cultivate or gather small fruits, or may sew, knit, or drive a sewing-machine; if she is educated,

she may teach a small school at home, or perhaps
take a place as assistant teacher in some public
school, or she may teach music, or drawing, or
French, or German, if she can obtain pupils, or
manage a small store. This comprises about the
entire list of occupations which are within her
reach, and all are precarious and often inadequate
for her purpose, while many of them involve so
great a neglect of her children, if she has any, as
to be perilous to their future. I do not include in
this catalogue literary labor, because, although a
few married women with families do succeed in it,
the number is very small; the payments usually
so precarious and so long delayed, that it can not
be considered as in any respect a dependence.
Yet, bad as this state of affairs is, it is not very
much worse than that of the man, who is from
any cause, such as the care of a helpless family,
illness, or lack of continuous employment, compelled to devote only a fragmentary part of his time
to bread-winning labor. In either case, the probability of obtaining an adequate livelihood is not
very great, and both are just objects of the assistance of those who are blessed with a larger share of
this world's goods, though that assistance should
be rendered in such a way as not to impair their
self-respect or independence. Additional compensation for labor, an increase of patronage,
obtained by personal effort, supplementary wages,
an addition to supplies of fuel or winter stores,

an unexpected credit of a given amount at a store, or other ways skillfully managed, of doing good by stealth, will often save such a wife and mother from giving up in despair, and infuse new life and energy into her desperate and unequal struggle for the support for her family. No form of charity is more productive of good than this.

CHAPTER VIII.

In a perfectly normal condition of human society, the number of adult men and women should be just about equal, and every woman in ordinary health, and of ordinary physical and mental capacity, should have the offer of marriage, being, of course, perfectly free to accept or reject it, as she pleased. In such a state of things the number who did not choose to marry would be comparatively small, and the question of occupations for them of no great-importance.

But, human society is never in a perfectly normal state; it is always vibrating from a condition like that of England, where there are nearly five hundred thousand more adult women than men, to one like that of California a dozen years ago, or Montana and Idaho now, where there are five or ten men to one woman, where it was said, that in 1850, miners came from the mountains two or three hundred miles to the Bay of San Francisco, to get a glimpse of a woman's face.

In the majority of old and long settled countries and states, military service, the vicissitudes of travel and outdoor occupations, and above all, emigration, have a constant tendency to aggravate the disproportion between the two sexes. In Great Britain and Ireland, this disproportion has reached a point which is startling; and in most of the Eastern or Atlantic States of our own Union, it is large enough to occasion some anxiety. In Massachusetts, it is stated that there are seventy thousand more women than men, and in most of the New England States the proportion is nearly as great. In the Middle States it is somewhat less, though the absolute excess is large. In the Southern States, owing to the great loss of men in the recent war, the disproportion is more marked than at the North.

But the equality or inequality in the numbers of the two sexes is no gauge or standard of the number of adult married women. A very considerable proportion of the men in any community, from one cause or another, do not seek to marry; and in the existing and constantly increasing extravagance of young women in dress, especially in our cities and large towns, and their entire ignorance of household duties, may be found a very cogent reason why this class is multiplying rapidly.

"I would be very glad to marry and have a home of my own," is a very common remark with young men who have the making of good hus bands in them, "but I could not keep house and support Grace (or Jennie, or Minnie, as the case may be) as she is in the habit of living at home, for less than four or five thousand dollars a year, and as my salary (or income) is but fifteen hundred or two thousand dollars, I must give up all thought of it."

With a very large proportion of the young women of our cities and larger towns, the idea of marriage is one of romance merely. They expect their home, if they keep house, or their suite of rooms, if they board, to be of palatial elegance; like the lilies, they toil not neither do they spin, and yet in the costliness and gorgeousness of their apparel, Solomon in all his glory was not arrayed like one of them. The idea which dominates the mind of a fashionable young married woman of the present day, is not how she shall be a help-meet to her husband, managing prudently, and spending judiciously what he has earned by severe toil; it is not how she may accomplish the most good with moderate means, or so order her household as that there shall be no waste, and thus the more to be left for benevolence or thrift; it is not how her home can be made most happy, and her husband, as he comes to it, worn with the fatigues of the day's duties, find solace and joy in her society and the attractiveness of the home circle; it is how she may surpass this acquaintance, equal that one, or excite the envy of a third, by the number, the splendor, and the costliness of her dresses, and her reckless display of them, in all weathers, and under all circumstances. Abroad she is the bird of paradise, glorious in her beauty, and the observed of all observers; at home, the gay plumage is laid aside, and it is much if she does not greet her husband in soiled and disordered apparel.

The sums expended on fashionable dress are beyond the belief of those who have not investigated the matter, or had painful personal experience of them. Even among a class not wealthy, the clerks, tellers, and cashiers of our banks, clerks in wholesale warehouses, men just fairly started in business, or having a moderately prosperous trade, master mechanics, &c., the expenditure of the women of the family, for dress, frequently ranges from one thousand to ten thousand dollars each, per annum. Among the wealthy still higher sums are expended. "My girls tell me that they are so economical that they feel as if they were almost mean in their dress," said a wealthy merchant, "and yet here are bills for over twelve thousand dollars, for the outfit of two of them for Newport, this summer. I wonder what they would spend, if they were extravagant."

This reckless expenditure, in many instances, ruin young men who marry, and who find that they can not, by any honest means, pay such enormous bills. How many of the defalcations, bank robberies, stock speculations, gambling losses, false entries in books, and abstractions of money,

6

within the past five years in all our large cities, have been prompted by the desire on the part of the offenders to indulge their wives in dress, which seemed to be the great subject and end of all their thoughts.

But the evil does not end here. This fashionable extravagance having become the rule, the young woman, whose father's purse is strained to the utmost to provide her with the luxuries which she insists are essential, and who looks forward to marriage as her probable destiny, has already fixed it in her own mind that she must have all, and much more than all, the luxuries she now has, in her married life. If she is cool and calculating, she resolves to marry no man whose income is not large enough to admit of her extravagance, and she becomes a fortune-hunter; if she is impulsive and romantic, she rushes on her fate without misgivings, encourages her somewhat timid admirer to propose, and they marry, only to find that ruin is before them. Where, as is the case in instances unfortunately too rare, real affection and an undercurrent of good sense co-exist, the wife may try to adapt herself to her husband's humble circumstances; but even in these cases, she knows so little of real economy and good management, that an effort at the most rigid retrenchment is almost sure to be followed by some reckless piece of extravagance, which more than swallows up the previous savings.

SENSIBLE.

ABSURD AND EXTRAVAGANT.

It is no matter for wonder that young men of moderate means are afraid to marry under such circumstances, and as it is almost impossible for the young to exist without social enjoyment, they become attached to their clubs, their drinking saloons, and not unseldom to association with the impure, and the acquisition of habits which drown the soul in perdition.

If women would but be wise in these matters! If they would remember that not all the adorning which the *modiste* can bestow, will impart beauty to those who do not possess it, and that to the beautiful and attractive, a plain and simple dress is infinitely more becoming than the most magnificent silks and laces, the shawls of India and Cashmere, and the most brilliant diamonds and gems which ever flashed from crown or coronet —then might there be hundreds of happy homes and hearts, where now there is sorrow, disgrace, and ruin, either present or impending.

We have thus accounted for a portion of the yearly increasing class of the unmarried; of the great mass yet remaining, some (we are speaking now of women), from one cause or another, do not desire to marry; some do not fancy the offers they receive, and prefer a single life to one of possible unhappiness; some, from their health, from hereditary tendency to disease, from their attachment to infirm parents, or, (rarely, we think) from lack of personal attractions, or infirmities of temper, are not sought in marriage. Another very considerable class of single women are those who are widowed.

There are no statistics available to show, with any approach to accuracy, what portions of these are dependent upon their own exertions for a support, and hence require an occupation or employment.

Two large classes of working women first demand our attention; domestic servants, and the female employés in the great manufacturing establishments, cotton and woolen factories, hoop-skirt factories, shirt and collar factories, laundries, ready-made clothing establishments, book-binderies, power presses, &c., &c.

In both classes, there are more or less married women, but generally those living apart from their husbands, and so, for practical purposes, to be reckoned as single women. Domestic service has come, of late years, to be almost exclusively occupied by women of foreign birth or foreign parentage. It is very rare in our cities, and is getting to be so in the country, to find a female domestic (excepting the large class of colored servants of whom we shall speak by and by) who is not either of Irish, German, English, Scotch, French, Swedish, Norwegian, Italian, or Spanish birth or parentage, and generally in about the order, as to numbers, which we have stated. There has been in this respect a gradual but very complete change within the past thirty years. While we would give all due credit to the enterprise of these women of foreign birth, in thus monopolizing one of the most important departments of feminine labor, we can not but regret that they have been able to do so. Our families are not so well served, a very large proportion of those seeking situations being new comers, unfamiliar with our language, habits, and customs, and having but limited and very imperfect notions of cleanliness and good order, and generally unskilled in even the rudiments of cooking, or the laundress' art. With a pride, which however we may lament it, we can not regard as wholly unjustifiable, the class of American girls, daughters of parents in humble circumstances, whose mothers and aunts, thirty years ago, would have willingly accepted situations in good families, shrink from this service, now that these ignorant foreign women have crowded the intelligence offices, because they feel that it would be a disgrace and dishonor to be associated with them. We can hardly wonder at this; for the foreigners are, with some exceptions certainly, ignorant, rude, bigoted, and fanatical, not always cleanly, and often dishonest; and to be classed with them would be, to some extent, unfortunate. Yet, in relinquishing this calling wholly to them, our girls of American birth have shut themselves out of an employment which, with all that there is disagreeable about it, is greatly preferable, in its compensation, its healthfulness, and its social consideration, to the drudgery of the needle, or the confinement and often injurious associations of the manufactories.

If women of good sense and practical skill in household matters, women of good character and intelligence, would oftener undertake these positions, they might secure to themselves kind friends in their employers, a higher and more confidential relation between mistress and servant, and a compensation which would be much higher than that which the majority of teachers, needlewomen, saleswomen, &c., receive.

The labor in this employment is not, on the average, so severe as that in the manufactories; it is much less, and less injurious to health, than needlework, or the driving of a sewing-machine. It is service, and implies obedience to a mistress; but who among those, men or women, who are compelled to work for a livelihood (we should rather say, perhaps, are privileged to work), has not his or her employer? Who is not in the service of some one? And whether this master or mistress be the head of a household, an officer of the State or nation, the proprietor of a great manufactory, a merchant, a judge, or a bishop, a congregation, or the great public, the service is as often wearing and irksome in the higher, as in the lower realms of service. Another objection urged by American girls occasionally, has, we are inclined to believe, more weight with them than all the rest. It is that they do not like to be subject to other women, and, above all, to their own country-women. We can easily see the force of this objection. Women are, as a rule, more exacting with their servants than men, and amid this prevalence of foreign help, the fashionably educated American woman, while herself ignorant of household duties, not unfrequently puts on a haughty and domineering air, which none will submit to, except those who have been all their lives menials, and even they only accept the situation with a view to revenging themselves for the insults they receive, by defrauding or robbing their employers.

A more thoughtful, just, and liberal course of conduct toward their employes would secure to mistresses better servants, and might open the way for the return of some of those invaluable women to service, who formerly were the humble and attached friends of the families with whom they lived. Colored servants are much more numerous at the South than in the Northern States. In the latter, indeed, they are comparatively rare. In some instances they are very faithful, trusty, and skillful, but many of them have the vices bred of a slave life—heedlessness, recklessness, a lack of neatness, untruthfulness, and petty dishonesty. In other vices, still more disreputable, there is very little difference between the colored and the foreign servants. The standard of morality is lower than it should be in both.

The reign of European female servants is destined, however, to be short. Already, in California, Chinese men have taken their place almost entirely, and the same change is destined to occur in our Eastern cities and towns. What may be the result of this revolution remains to be seen

But if the foreign element has driven our American women from domestic service, it has also, to a considerable extent, done the same thing in relation to their employment in manufactories. Thirty, or even twenty-five years ago, in the great cotton and woolen mills and print-works of New England, it was a very rare thing to find a factory girl of foreign birth or parentage. Now, the majority are Irish and Germans. In the great manufactories of New York, Philadelphia, Cincinnati, and other cities, a large (we believe the larger) proportion are of foreign birth or parentage. In the large book-binderies, as yet, American girls are in the ascendency.

CHAPTER IX.

TEACHING is an employment for which woman possesses some eminent qualifications. It is the duty and privilege of the mother to give her child its first and most indelible mental and moral training; and so important is this early maternal culture, that it is a rule, almost without exception, that a man's character, intellectually and morally, is molded by his mother's influence. For the instruction and management of young children, women are more successful, as teachers, than men; they have more tact, more skill in interesting and amusing them, and more ability to lead them on, by the slow and short steps by which alone most children can advance in their knowledge of science. The exercises of the *kinder-garten*, or child's garden-school, were, indeed, first invented by a man, but they have been practiced with greater success by women than by men. The system of object-teaching now so popular in England and the United States, has had its greatest triumphs in the hands of female teachers.

If, as the most eminent educators of our day assert, the crucial test of the ability to teach is found in the capacity for imparting instruction to the youngest, the weakest, and the least intelligent, then must the honor of being the most successful of teachers be given to women.

In our public schools women are largely in excess of men, as teachers, having charge in the graded schools, of the primary, and a part of the intermediate departments, and being assistants and sometimes principals in the grammar and high schools. Formerly, when young men taught school in winter, to eke out the year's wages, or furnish the means for the prosecution of academical, collegiate, or professional study; and young girls undertook the summer district school to earn some extra finery, or to procure the means of adding to the outfit for the housekeeping that was to come ere long, there was very little of the professional zeal of the teacher in either, and the vocation of teaching was at a low ebb. The standard of qualifications required of the teacher was low, and not very rigidly enforced. If the young man was not conversant with arithmetic beyond the "rule of three," or was at fault in grammar, geography, or history, yet if the school was small, and he would come for a low price, the examining committee generally thought it was best to give him a certificate. And if the young applicant for the honors of schoolmistress was slightly faulty in her spelling, had very indefinite ideas about the boundaries of the States, and could not (perhaps from timidity) explain why *one* should be carried for every *ten* in addition, yet it was only a summer school, and she would doubtless do well enough with the few little children she would have, and so she, too, got the certificate. These matters are all changed now. What with normal schools, and teachers' institutes, associations, drills, and periodicals, that must be a *very* rural district which has not a normal teacher, either male or female, or at least one who is making teaching a profession, and who has taken pains to qualify him or herself for the now honored calling.

As a consequence, the candidates for positions as teachers are generally qualified to undergo the somewhat searching examinations they are called to pass, and are seldom deficient in their technical knowledge of the topics they are to teach, at least so far as they are pursued in the popular textbooks. Whether they possess an aptness to teach, and the knowledge how to impart instruction on the subjects which they are expected to understand, is another question. The ability of female teachers to enforce discipline successfully, is also somewhat in doubt.

From an opportunity of observation extended over many years, we are inclined to the belief that, on both points, women on the average succeed quite as well as men, and in maintaining order and discipline, usually better than men. The course pursued in our normal schools is very

well calculated to impart skill in teaching, where
the natural faculty of teaching exists. As to
government, a young woman of tact and spirit
controls her pupils quite as much by her womanly
dignity and her personal magnetism, as by any
direct exercise of authority. She rules the tur-
bulent boys in her school very much as the
wisest and shrewdest of her sex rule men outside,
by seeming not to do it. Even the clownish,
overgrown boy feels ashamed to do any thing to
vex the schoolmistress. She is such a nice little
lady, and he who would be constantly plotting
mischief against a schoolmaster, because he was
" a man of his size," becomes mild and gentle,
considerate and well-behaved, toward a little woman, whom he could take up with one hand and
carry out of the schoolroom, simply because she
is a little woman, whose gentle and lady-like manners have fascinated him. It is the old story of
Una and the lion over again.

In the female seminaries, French colleges, and
finishing schools, the quality of female teaching
is, we are inclined to believe, considerably lower
than in the higher grades of public schools. Generally, music and French are taught by men,
though sometimes a French lady is employed for
modern languages; but very much of the teaching
in other studies is of that careless, superficial,
slipshod sort, which does no real credit either to
instructor or pupil. The petty deceptions and

subterfuges practiced in many of these institutions, to give the parents and guardians of the pupils the impression that the course of study is very extensive and thorough, and that their children are paragons of learning, would disgust any really honest teacher.

It is too late in the day to raise the question of the capacity of woman for becoming a teacher in the higher studies of the college or university. In all the Christian ages, there have been a few women, eminent alike for the soundness of their judgment, the clearness of their perceptions, and the extent of their erudition, who have, either voluntarily or involuntarily, become the teachers of their time. In the earlier centuries of the Christian era, they taught in public, and their lectures or expositions were largely attended. In the Middle Ages, we find them professors in the universities of Italy and France, and attracting great numbers of students to their teachings. In more modern times, they have kept up the reputation of their sex, if not in direct instruction, at least by their books, which were in many cases models both in their style and in the thoroughness with which they handled abstruse topics. In our own day, there have been a small number of women whose attainments in the highest walks of science have been fully equal to those of the ablest male scholars on the same topics. Mrs. Somerville, though now, we believe, in her ninetieth year, has demonstrated the vigor of her intellect even at that great age, by the careful revision of her great work on physical geography, and has called forth from Sir R. I. Murchison, himself, perhaps, the ablest physicist of our time, the encomium, as truthful as it is remarkable, that she was the peer, in her extensive and profound knowledge of physical science, of any living philosopher. In the difficult and abstruse science of political economy, in which so many of the finest male intellects have failed, two women, Miss Harriet Martineau and Mrs. J. S. Mill, have manifested an ability second to no writers on the subject in our time. In astronomy, Miss Maria Mitchell has proved as successful an observer and as sagacious a discoverer as any of her male *confrères*. In profound knowledge of the great principles of law, Miss Hannah Bonvier was in no way inferior to her father, one of the great jurists of our age. The late Mrs. Hill, wife of Rev. Thomas Hill, D. D., late President of Harvard University, died at the age of thirty-one, the victim of her earnest zeal to acquire such a knowledge of the highest mathematics as is attained by hardly one man in a generation. We might multiply, almost indefinitely, the number of names of women in various departments of science and literature, whose attainments justified them in becoming public instructors. And these attainments have been made, it must be remembered, under a generally faulty and superficial system of education. Were the opportunities for a thorough and complete education of women as ample as those of men, there can be no question that the number of highly educated women would be vastly greater than it now is. At present the number qualified to fill college professorships is small, though increasing. The education required to fill such positions can not be obtained before the age of eighteen, especially with those who have marriage in immediate prospect. Neither science nor literature allow those of their votaries, who wish to attain the highest honors, to give them a divided homage. Long and close application is necessary to qualify the accomplished teacher for her work. Yet this is a field where prizes await those who are qualified to receive them. In the present zeal for the founding of new colleges, there is a demand considerably beyond the supply for highly educated and skillful teachers, and many of the chairs might be filled advantageously by women.

In all the branches which constitute a liberal education, women have demonstrated their ability to teach successfully, but in a college admitting pupils of both sexes, it would be desirable that the female professors should occupy those chairs which did not require the exercise of great physical power. Surveying, the practical branches of geometry, fortification, mining, metallurgy, chemistry, and especially chemical technology, would not, on these grounds, be professorships which women would desire to fill. For another reason, viz., the general impatience of women with the slow processes of logical deduction, logic, and moral and intellectual philosophy in their highest development, would seldom be topics which women would teach with success. Usually, a woman may be trusted (in the higher walks of education) to teach any science, for which, from special training, she feels herself competent.

From teaching, as an employment, the transition is easy and natural to the practice of what are usually called the learned professions. There are not wanting examples of women having filled with considerable success the clerical office. One denomination of Christians, the Friends, have had for two hundred years and more their women preachers, some of them of great eloquence. These fair preachers, it must be acknowledged, have not generally lost, to any appreciable extent, their womanly modesty and delicacy by their public exercises. The extreme plainness, simplicity, and freedom from formality in the religious exercises of the Friends, have prevented any injurious results from these utterances. The Moravians, too, have had for a long period their women preachers, and, we believe, in one or two instances, women bishops. Of other religious denominations, the Universalists, in this country, have several ordained women preachers and pastors; the Unitarians have five or six; and the Methodists, two or more. There are also some among the minor denominations. That a well educated and deeply religious woman may be able to write a sermon as systematic, earnest, pungent, and practical, as most clergymen, and could perform many of the pastoral duties which fall to the lot of clergymen, successfully, can not be denied, yet we must confess that we greatly prefer that they should not occupy the pulpit. There is something contrary to our ideas of propriety and womanly delicacy in a woman's standing up before a great congregation as their spiritual leader and guide. She may be competent for the position, intellectually and morally, but the office of the preacher and pastor implies the power of government—bearing rule—a thing for which we look in vain in the history of the early Church.

We do not lay so much stress as some do, upon the prohibitions of Paul: "I suffer not a woman to teach;" "Let the woman learn in silence with all subjection;" "Let your women keep silence in the churches, for it is not permitted unto them to speak; but they are commanded to be under obedience, as also saith the law;" "For it is a shame for women to speak in the church," &c., &c. These prohibitions were to some extent partial, intended only for particular churches, especially for that in the corrupt city of Corinth,

where the general gross and infamous demoralization of the entire community, rendered special
restraints necessary, to create a sense of modesty
and refinement which had not hitherto existed.
They are also partly modified by other declarations of the apostle in the same and other epistles,
which show conclusively that it was a public
teaching, and not an· exhortation or testimony to
the truth to which he objected. We have our
doubts whether, as some suppose, allowance should
also be made for the apostle's natural sternness
and decision of character, and the influence which
his single life and homelessness may be supposed
to have exerted upon him, as modifying in a degree the tone of the revelation, so far as he de-
clares it, inspired by God. Still, viewing the
work of the ministry, as it unquestionably
is, as one form of exercise of the governing
power, we can not but regard the entering
upon it by woman as a thing to be deplored. If,
as sometimes occurred in the Jewish common-
wealth, God calls a woman to be a spiritual
leader of his people, we believe that he will make
her call manifest by such visible signs that she
will be readily and heartily received by the
Church, and her divine mission recognized. Exceptional cases of this sort may possibly arise—
but till they do, we can not help believing that
the public religious exercises of woman should be
confined to exhortation, or bearing her testimony

to the truth and vital power of the religion which she professes.

Of public speaking of a secular character by women, now becoming very prevalent, we have only to say, that while we have in some instances been instructed, and in others amused, by these feminine orations, we can not desire any considerable increase in the number of these speakers. That some of them have done service to the causes they have advocated, that some both write and speak eloquently, is true; but that in thus attempting to edify or amuse the public, they almost inevitably divest themselves of something of that maidenly modesty and delicacy which are such essential charms in the character of woman, is also true. There may be those who are called to this work; if so, let them perform it, but let every woman who thinks of undertaking it, be sure that it is her vocation.

CHAPTER X.

As to the medical profession, there seems to be no serious objection against its being undertaken by women who are properly qualified for it. For some departments of medical study and practice, such as, for instance, diseases of her own sex, and of children, and the practice of obstetrics, woman possesses some peculiar qualifications and advantages. If she has the natural abilities, and has acquired the previous systematic and thorough mental training which will enable her to become thoroughly familiar with the science of medicine in all its relations, there is no reason why she should not be eminently successful as a medical practitioner. The practice of medicine requires, however, qualities of so high an order—tact, quick perception, readiness of resource, sound judgment, comparison, the power of discrimination, both of the symptoms of disease and the nature and application of remedies, and in some of its departments, such complete self-possession, firmness, control of the emotions and sympathies, patience and thorough knowledge of the human structure, and of the modifications in its physiological action affected by disease—that even its most eminent professors often feel their incompetency for its practice.

The greatest difficulty which women have to contend with, in the study and practice of this profession, is, that their early training has been so superficial and desultory that they are unfitted for the severe study and close application requisite for its mastery, and are hence strongly disposed to take up with some of the forms of quackery, which promise them results which can really be attained only by careful and protracted study and adequate knowledge of the subject.

There are, however, a considerable number of women, now, as there have been some in past generations, who have distinguished themselves by their high attainments in medical knowledge and skill; such women as the Blackwell sisters, and others whom we might name, who have demonstrated that a woman can attain, in some walks of the profession, an eminence equal to that of the most distinguished physicians of our time.

Great physicians, those who rank very high in their profession, are never to be found in great numbers, and necessarily their number must be smaller among women than men, since fewer enter on a course of medical study, and many of them have not had the preliminary training which would qualify them to take high rank in it; and the facilities for the prosecution of medical study in the way of dissections, museums,

&c., for women, are not yet equal to those for men.

Yet there is a very considerable sphere of usefulness opened here for brave, studious, clear-headed women. They are especially adapted to be the physicians of children; the tact and skill, the knowledge how to manage and interest a child, which seems almost intuitive in many women, is a great advantage, as every physician knows, in their treatment of the little ones.

If women trusted each other more than they do, and were more willing to believe and confide in the superior knowledge of any of their sex, we should hope to see the day when the entire medical treatment of women and young children was in the hands of highly educated, capable female physicians, as those best qualified for it; but so long as very many women openly avow their preference for male medical attendants, irrespective of the question of their qualifications, it seems to us that a long time must elapse before women will become very generally the physicians of their sex.

It is very seldom the case, we think, that women, however highly qualified they may be, desire to go into general practice, and the fact is creditable to their good sense and sound judgment. There might be circumstances, though we can hardly conceive of them, in which a woman would be justified in undertaking the cases of a

FEMALE PHYSICIAN MAKING A MIDNIGHT VISIT.

general practice; but there would be so much that was distasteful and unpleasant about such a practice, that we should apprehend that the principal danger would be that of her abandoning the profession altogether, in utter disgust. There is just now a very considerable demand for women physicians as missionaries, who could treat their own sex, especially in Mohammedan countries, where no male physician is admitted into the harem under any circumstances. It is urged, and with great truth, that in addition to their medical services, they might become propagandists of Christianity to these secluded women, and thus benefit both soul and body.

A knowledge of medicine also qualifies them the better for the position of a skillful and highly trained nurse and attendant upon the sick, which so many filled with such signal advantage to their patients, during the late war. There is a wide opening in this direction for profitable and useful employment for women.

We have alluded already to the prevalent reluctance of women to enter upon general practice, and the indication which it furnished that they understood well what was their true position in the matter. For the same as well as other reasons, women are not well adapted to the practice of surgery, and should never undertake it. Their more delicate nervous organization, their more ready sympathy, and their instinctive aversion to the use of the operating knife, even where it was indispensable, would affect alike their diagnostic power, and their ability to operate; and the woman who could subdue all these emotions, and hold herself ready to pass the trying ordeal of performing a great surgical operation, might be brave, heroic, skillful, if you will, but before reaching this point, she must have crucified her woman's heart, and have become that undesirable thing—a manlike woman.

For the reasons given in another chapter, it would be unwise for a married woman, the mother of a family, to engage in the practice of medicine, unless in the rare case where she is the wife of a physician, and as thoroughly trained in her profession as her husband. Even in such a case, there would be much to annoy her and impair her efficiency; her household duties would necessarily distract her thoughts, and her children, if she has any, would very surely be neglected; but in any other case, though the development of the maternal instincts would not be without its advantages in many instances, yet, with the exception already made, the practice of medicine should be strictly confined, so far as women are concerned, to single women or widows.

There will be, as any female physician in full practice can avouch, full as many annoyances and disabilities for these, as they will care to meet. The night's rest so constantly and thoughtlessly disturbed, the midnight rides in dark nights and over rough roads, the querulousness and peevishness of hypochondriacs, the mad antics of hysterical patients, the deep feeling of responsibility when a wife and mother, the cherished idol of her husband's heart, is passing through her great agony, or lies insensible and in imminent peril of sudden death; the sense of the powerlessness of medicine, when the beloved child, the pet of the household, is passing on, by slow but sure steps, to the grave; the uncertainty whether, in a given case which has proved fatal, there may not have been some medicine, or some method of treatment, unknown to the physician herself, yet within the bounds of human knowledge, which, if resorted to, would have saved this precious life.

I speak not of any financial difficulties, of the unwillingness which every physician finds among a certain portion of his patrons to pay for services rendered; of that class, unhappily too numerous, by whom, on the recovery of the patient, "death and the doctor are alike forgotten," or of the want of conscientiousness so prevalent, which, unmindful of the benefits rendered, considers the physician's bill the last one to be paid, if paid at all. Of all these troubles the woman physician will have her full share, and owing to the prevalence of the idea in the loutish minds of the unintelligent, that women's work should not receive the same pay as men's, she may have a few extra worries peculiar to herself.

But there is a place and a need for well-educated female physicians, and they shall have from us nothing but a " God speed them in their profession, and give them abundant success in it."

The question whether woman should enter the legal profession has given rise to much animated discussion. Some of the most advanced defenders of woman's rights contend that she ought to take those places at the bar and on the bench, which are now occupied solely by men. There are several serious objections to this. The advocate who addresses a jury, or a bench of judges on an important case, not only requires thorough preparation of all the law points, and a complete mastery of the great principles on which his argument is to be based, but he must be an adept in the difficult and often unpleasant art of cross-examination, and he must be prepared with a retort—not always courteous—for the sophistries and subterfuges of a, perhaps, not over-scrupulous adversary. If he is addressing a jury, he must make a favorable impression on them, either by his real dignity, his apparent candor and conscientiousness, his clear and transparent logic, or his tact, humor, and wit. If his plea is made before the full bench of judges, he must present, in the strongest light, the great legal principles which underlie his case, must fortify it with authorities, decisions, and precedents, must hedge it about with logical arguments, and in the whole, there

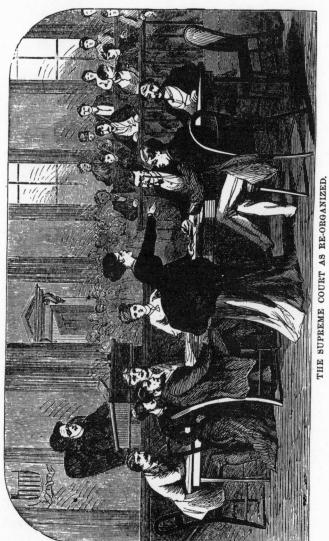

THE SUPREME COURT AS RE-ORGANIZED.

must be no extraneous ornament, no diffuseness of oratory, no *ad captandum* appeals, or he loses his case inevitably.

To a true woman, there would be much in both of these branches of the profession which would be distasteful and unpleasant. Granting the ability, which may exist in rare instances (though women are seldom close and skillful logicians, or disposed to terse and condensed argument), there would yet be many of the necessary incidents of a trial scene which would be exceedingly painful to a woman of sensitive and delicate temperament, and through which she could not pass, without detriment to that refinement and delicacy which should ever characterize woman.

To her presiding on the bench there would be objections of a different class. Women seldom make good presiding officers, partly from the fact that they do not often possess that thorough self-possession, that calmness and dignity of manner, and that thorough knowledge of parliamentary rules and usage, which alone prevent confusion and discord in the assembly, and mortification and embarrassment on the part of the presiding officer. The parliamentary rules they might acquire, but seldom or never do, and even with the knowledge of them, the other difficulties would be serious. The judge requires, in addition to these qualities, that judicial faculty, that power of discriminating between the true and the true-seeming, of sifting evidence, discovering perjury, weighing precedents and authorities, and divesting himself of preferences, leanings, and prejudices, and that profound knowledge of legal principles, all of which go to the making of the character of the just, upright, and learned judge, and render his position the grandest and most responsible in the community.

In some of these qualities, woman is, we may believe, deficient from the structure of her mental constitution ; in others, her deficiency is one which might possibly be remedied by long and patient culture ; but, with the rarest of exceptions, the function of the judge is not one to which she would do well to aspire.

There are, however, other departments of the legal profession which woman can fill as well as man, and some of them among the most lucrative. Conveyancing and its kindred branches of business appertaining to the disposal of real property, the searching of titles, the preparation of pension and bounty papers, the drawing of deeds, wills, contracts, agreements and affidavits, and generally the consulting business of an attorney's office, can be done as well by a woman as a man, if the woman will but give her whole thought and mind to it. So, too, the preparation of a case for trial, the preparing the brief, the hunting up and arranging the authorities under each point, are matters within the scope of woman's powers. Our great lawyers usually have partners or confidential clerks on whom these duties now devolve, and these partners or clerks never open their mouths in court.

There are also the places of clerks and reporters of courts, which might well be filled by women.

We conclude, then, that in some departments of the legal profession there is room for women, while there are others which would not be appropriate for them, and which they could only undertake, by first relinquishing that modest and womanly demeanor which is their highest charm.

Of the other professions introduced in connection with our military, naval, scientific, polytechnic, mining, and agricultural and technological schools, which are multiplying so rapidly, there are but few which are adapted to the physical capacities of woman. The peasant woman of France, Italy, Germany, and Switzerland may indeed vie with man in her ability for coarse, hard, severe out-door labor; she may plow, reap, mow, and dig as well and stoutly as her husband; she may bear as heavy burdens, and compete with him in all rough and muscular employments; but in so doing, she soon loses her beauty, her grace, and her refinement of manners, and becomes a clod. We have no desire ever to see an American woman undertake any of these employments, even if they had the strength for them. In the case of the educated classes, there is, moreover, a physical inability for the greater part of these new professions. The West Point course, for instance; granting that a young woman, by dint of extraordinary physical ability and vigor, succeeded in passing through it, what could she do with the education there obtained?

We are sure that no one, with the possible exception of the editors of the *Revolution*, would contend that a military career was desirable for a woman. Under peculiar and exceptional circumstances, in times of great national danger, women (one or two in a century) have, it is true, taken the lead of military enterprises, and with success in some cases; but, would it be worth while, for such a possible contingency, to educate women for a military life? Is the army career calculated to develop the graces or amenities of life? No! when the great emergency comes, if it ever does come, when a woman is needed to lead our forces to battle, we may be sure that a better leader can be found among the volunteers than we could train for the work, if we graduated a hundred from the military academy every year.

Of the special sciences taught there, such as fortification, military and topographical engineering, &c., there are few or none which a woman could practice successfully. The construction of

WOMEN IN THE ARMY—THE DRESS PARADE

RAILWAY TRAIN OFFICERED ON THE NEW SYSTEM OF ENLARGED SPHERE OF LABOR FOR WOMEN.

forts and batteries, the laying out and building of railroads, military roads, canals, breakwaters, &c., are not avocations in which women are likely to distinguish themselves. The duties of the surveyor, superintendent, or engineer of mines, of the locomotive engineer, the technological chemist, the navigator, the captain or engineer of a steamship, the constructor of a sewer, the foreman of a fire-engine, the superintendent of a great manufactory, or manager of a machine-shop, are all of a class which women would very seldom have the physical strength to perform well, and which, except in those rare cases which bid defiance to all rules, it would be undesirable that they should undertake.

Some departments of agriculture and horticulture do furnish appropriate employment for women. In the late civil war, when the draft weighed heavily upon the farming population of the newer Western States, great numbers of the patriotic women of Illinois, Minnesota, Wisconsin, Iowa, Missouri, and Kansas, the wives, sisters, and daughters of the men who had gone to fight the nation's battles, undertook most of the heavy farm-work—a few held the plow, and many more "cultivated" the corn, drove the mowers and reapers, gathered, bound and stacked the grain, or raked, loaded, and housed the hay, gathered, husked, shelled, and sent to market the corn, thrashed the wheat, oats, and barley, and sacked and shipped them, and cared for the live-stock, doing nearly as well as if the men had been at home to attend to their duties themselves. We trust the time will never come when they will be called to such severe labor again; though we doubt not that it would be undertaken cheerfully from similar motives. But there is much work on a farm which women may perform with success and honor to themselves. The mother of a farmer's family, or, in case of her absence or inability, some other woman of the household, will always, on a large farm, have abundant labor and care in the management of the household affairs. The providing meals for so large a family, the care of the clothing and the training of the children, and their education, which to a considerable extent must come upon the mother; the care of the fowls and small animals of the live-stock, will keep her time very fully occupied; if the farm is partly or wholly devoted to dairy products, her cares will be increased, though not so much, in these days of cheese and butter factories, as formerly. But it is often the case that a young, spirited, and enterprising woman undertakes the management of a farm herself, and if she is intelligent in regard to farm work, and possessed of fair executive ability, she usually succeeds well.

But it is especially in market-gardening, and garden truck and small fruit farming, that women have been most successful. For many miles around our large cities there are favorable opportunities for these agricultural enterprises. The labor is somewhat severe, and during the summer months confining, but while some male help is needed, this is an employment, which, if well managed, will yield excellent returns. The succession of early vegetables, strawberries, raspberries, black-berries, cherries, green corn, tomatoes, beets, cauliflowers, early potatoes, cabbages, plums, grapes, peaches, pears, and early summer and autumn apples, insures constant employment, and keeps both mind and body active and alert. To those who are appalled by so long a list of products, the cultivation of the small fruits only furnishes a pleasant and recreative employment.

The keeping of bees, the rearing of silk-worms, and the care of some of the more fanciful varieties of domestic fowls, and pigeons, guinea-hens, ducks, geese, turkeys, and rabbits, all furnish employ-ment which is both pleasant and profitable.

Horticulture and floriculture, as well as the management of a nursery of young trees, are employments which might be in the hands of women to a much greater extent than they are. At present, very few women cultivate flowers for any other purpose than their own pleasure, or the gratification of their friends; but there is nothing so abstruse in the arts of the florist and nursery-man, and nothing so severe in the labor required,

7*

as to put either beyond the reach of a resolute woman, and the business is one peculiarly healthful and refining in its character. If the enterprise is conducted on a scale sufficiently large, the collection and packing of flower-seeds is a branch of the business which will afford great pleasure and profit. An enterprising, intelligent woman, with some capital, who would qualify herself for this business and engage in it, on a large scale, might make her own fortune and afford a pleasant and remunerative employment to a large number of her own sex.

In the practice of some branches of chemical technology there is nothing necessarily beyond a woman's ability, though the work would be hardly agreeable to most women, involving as it would, a necessity for a dress approximating to that of a man, to avoid the perils of the flowing dress and readily combustible material usually worn by women. The protracted and severe study, and the constant laboratory practice required to keep pace with the rapidly increasing volume of discoveries in organic chemistry, would deter most women from attempting to enter upon the practice of general applied chemistry.

In the fine arts, especially in painting, sculpture, and music, a few women have distinguished themselves; and if the opportunity had been afforded them, or they had possessed the same resolute will, probably a considerably larger num-

CULTIVATION OF SMALL FRUITS.

ber might have done so. In the reproduction of
actual landscape, or the portraiture of animals,
even in those minute points which indicate the
skill of the artist, they have been admirable,
and their statues and busts of eminent men, living or dead, have been, in some instances, remarkable for their faithfulness and spirit; but in
general they have shown very little creative
power. Rosa Bonheur's " Horse Fair," and her
other pictures of animal life, entitle her to rank
with Sir Edwin Landseer, in this department of
her art. Yet she has never ventured, as indeed
she had no occasion, into the ideal world for the
subjects of her paintings. There seems to be no
good reason why this creative faculty should not
be developed in women, except, possibly, that in
their mental constitution, the inventive or creative power is weaker than in men. In music,
there have been women-singers of extraordinary
power and skill, female pianists, harpists, vio-
linists, organists of remarkable ability; but
very few composers, and generally those of only
the second or third class. In their several departments of musical art, the names of Jenny
Lind (Goldschmidt), Julia Grisi, Catharine Hayes,
Anne Seguin, Anna Bishop, Madame Laborde,
Madame Parepa Rosa, Adelina Patti (Caux), Clara
Louisa Kellogg, and others, will always be remembered for their powers of vocalization, and a still
longer list of instrumental performers of very high

rank attests the ability of women to attain to the highest plane of musical art.

It is surprising that with voice, ear, and hand so fully and delicately attuned to the highest musical excellence, there should never have been a Mozart, a Haydn, a Handel, a Beethoven, a Mendelsshon, or a Rossini, or even a composer of the second rank, among the women devoted to music. Musical composers there have been among them indeed, and some whose melodies possessed rare sweetness, and considerable vigor and originality; but none who have won to themselves an undying fame. These may, it is true, be among the wonders of the future. To women who possess the natural talent for becoming professional singers or players, and are willing to go through the severe and protracted study required to attain excellence, the musical profession offers fair rewards. As most of the eminent female vocalists have sung in opera, this naturally brings us to speak of the stage as furnishing an occupation for women.

There have been, in the past hundred years, a very considerable number of estimable women who have been connected with the dramatic profession. For the most part, women of high character and aspirations have preferred tragedy, as more dignified in character, and affording a better scope for their powers than any other department of the drama; and a calling which has been graced by such eminent names as Mrs. Siddons, Mrs. Fanny Kemble, Charlotte Cushman, Ristori, Rachel, Mrs. Charles Kean, Mrs. Mowatt, Mrs. Lander, and others hardly inferior in reputation, may perhaps fairly claim a right to be considered among the appropriate occupations for women. And yet, when we consider how numerous are the temptations to which the actress is exposed, how dissolute the society by which she is surrounded, and how great the peril, both to her good name and her eternal interests, we can not recommend any woman who has any regard for her own reputation, to endanger it by entering upon an actress's career. In all departments of theatrical life there have been, we doubt not, good and true women; we can even conceive it possible, that among the ballet-dancers, there have been some, whose purity of life was in strange contrast with the performances which formed a part of their daily duties; but we only echo the opinion of one who herself has borne an active part in theatrical life, when we say that in the present condition of the drama, no pure-minded woman has a right to imperil her reputation and her hopes of heaven by entering upon a theatrical career. The atmosphere of the theater is, at the present day, wholly corrupting, and it is impossible for any one to enter it without receiving a moral taint, which, like the poisoned breath on the polished steel, will corrode the heart, and impair its purity forever.

The stage, then, is not among the fit occupations for women, nor will it be, till that time shall arrive when it shall indeed become what it has often been styled, but never really was, " a School of Morals."

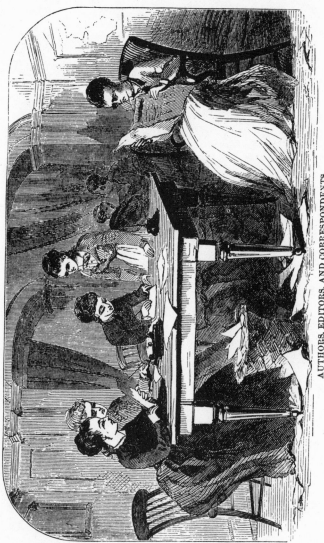

AUTHORS, EDITORS, AND CORRESPONDENTS.

CHAPTER XI.

We come next to consider the literary occupations of woman, aside from those of the teacher and other professions. The number of women who are engaged in authorship is increasing, but they are mostly occupied with one or other of three classes of works, novels, juvenile books—usually also fictions—and poetry. These three classes include a little more than two-fifths of all the books published in any given year, but the proportion of those written by women to the whole number of works of which they are authors, is certainly seven-eighths. Occasionally a woman ventures into the domain of history, and with tolerable, though not perfect success, for impartiality is an important requisite for a historian, and no woman has yet undertaken to write history, certainly not in England or the United States, who was not, to some extent, a partisan. Biography is more to their liking, and some of the most successful biographies of modern times have been written by women. In metaphysical science few women have ventured, and never, thus far, with such ability as to encourage others to attempt it. In political economy, a few women of our century have done themselves honor. In physical science, especially in astronomy, physical geography, botany, and zoology, they have done well. In criticism, either in art or literature, there are not more than one or two names of any eminence.

The classics seem to have very little charm for them, only two women of any note as authors in the present century having attained such a mastery of them, as to warrant them in writing any thing worth reading on the subject, to wit: Elizabeth Barrett Browning, and S. Margaret Fuller (D'Ossoli). Nor are there any female writers in the English tongue who have discussed with marked ability the classical works of either English or continental literature. The general distaste of the sex for mathematical studies has prevented them from attaining any distinction in statistical works.

As novelists, women often manifest signal ability in description and narration; occasionally considerable ingenuity in the conception and management of the plot of the story; and if they describe from the life, their characters sometimes stand out with a marvelous distinctness, and to the superficial critic, seem veritable creations; but the great defect of all their novels is, that the real creative faculty is wanting; that they can only describe what they have seen, and substantially only in the relations in which they have seen it. To this deficiency it is to be attributed that among all the female novelists of modern times (over one thousand in all), there is not one who can claim to rank, in permanent reputation, with several of the great novelists of the other sex.

As writers for children, women are entitled to a high, perhaps the highest rank. We certainly can recall no names of male writers at the present day, who have been more successful in writing for the young, than any one of a score of women in England and America, whose books are, and will be, among the most precious treasures of young hearts.

In the realm of poetry, women have attained to a fair, yet not to the highest success. The creative faculty is, so far, wanting for the production of any of those grand epics, of which that century is but too happy which can reckon *one* among its treasures. Mrs. Browning has made the nearest approach to being a great poet of any woman of modern times. In lyric and sentimental poetry, we can not reckon woman inferior to the other sex; but many of the so-called " collections of poems," from male as well as female writers, indicate rather facility of versification, a poetical feeling, and a considerable acquaintance with poetical literature, than any real poetic talent; and even those who are not wanting in poetic conception, too often, by a culpable carelessness and inattention to the elaboration and artistic finish of their poems, deprive them of much of their value.

We can not, however, reckon the writing of poetry as one of those avocations by which woman can earn a livelihood. Poems, the publishers say, do not sell, except in rare instances, and they will seldom run the risk of publishing them, unless the author will guarantee the expenses. At least four-fifths of the volumes of poems by female writers first published within the past five years, have proved heavy pecuniary losses to their authors or publishers. Novels are a little more profitable, but very few of them, unless by well known writers, pay for the labor expended on them. Of late years, women have become, very largely, contributors to our magazines and periodicals, either as essayists, critics, writers of short stories, or novelettes, or of serial novels, generally published subsequently in book form. In one or other of these ways, a considerable number have received a fair compensation for their work. Much of this writing, it is just to say, is of very fair quality; not of the highest, for magazine writing is apt to be a little slipshod. Some of it, especially that for the weekly family papers, is mere trash, only to be measured by the yard, and really worth less than the pure white paper which it mars and blots. We are not prepared to say, however, that the part of these papers written by women is worse than that contributed by men—

both are bad enough, and unworthy of their authors.

A considerable number of women have of late years became editors or managers of monthly, fortnightly, weekly, and we believe, in one or two instances, daily papers. We can not honestly congratulate them on their success. A few of the monthlies have been moderately well edited, but generally, where a woman has been the sole editor, the periodicals have been failures, both in a literary and financial sense.

At first sight it seems difficult to account for this; for many women undoubtedly possess some of the qualities requisite for successful journalism: quickness of perception, the power of ready and rapid composition, and the faculty of discerning the important issues to be discussed; but they fail oftenest in their lack of logical power, and terse, condensed argument, and in the want of discrimination in regard to the articles of others selected for publication. Women are often merciless critics, but their taste in selection is not always as correct, as their criticism is severe.

Where, on the other hand, the two sexes are united in the conduct of a periodical, especially one of higher literature, they have generally been more successful than either would have been alone. At the same time, the experience of most of those who have been associated with women in literary enterprises is, that many of them are

given to carelessness in the performance of their
share of the duties, to shirking the difficult parts,
and to diminishing somewhat the full quota of
work to which they are pledged. We do not
believe that all, perhaps not the major part of
literary women would do this, for many are truly
conscientious; but too often, a woman engaged
in literary pursuits, is a little more prone to shelter herself under the privileges of her sex, than
women in other avocations. We need not say
how prejudicial this general reputation is to the
real interests of literary women, nor how often it
causes their rejection from positions for which
they are eminently qualified, if only reliance could
be placed on their faithful performance of the
duties required. The late Mrs. Sigourney was
an eminent exception to this class. Whatever
pledges she made, either as to the time of com-
pletion, the quality or the quantity of her literary
work, were fulfilled to the letter, even at the
greatest personal inconvenience. She was the
soul of honor and conscientiousness; we wish as
much could be said of some living literary women.
The literary labor of women who are employed
either as editors or contributors to literary periodicals, is generally compensated as highly as that
of men in similar circumstances.

We have already spoken of those women who
are employed in the government offices. There
can be no question, that if the Civil Service bill

were passed, and the qualifications of both male and female clerks subjected to a rigid examination, as large a number of competent women as of competent men would be found for the service; and if, as in most instances would be the case, they could accomplish, without injury to their health, the same amount of labor as the men, they would undoubtedly receive, as they ought, the same salaries as the men of the same departmental class. The very considerable number of incompetents among the present women clerks in Washington is no indication of the inability of women to fill these places with first-rate ability; for those who were not fit for the place, were not appointed on any grounds of fitness, but simply to satisfy the demand of members of Congress, and others, who insisted on a place being made for their favorites. There is nothing in most of the government clerkships, which an intelligent and well-educated woman may not do as well as a man.

Turning to other employments not of a strictly literary character, yet requiring considerable education for their proper performance, we must confess that we see no good reason why women should not be employed as clerks and tellers in banks and private banking-houses. We might go further, and say tht there are women who possess the financial ab lity to fill the posts of cashier and president, better than they are filled in half the banks in the country. We are not aware that they have been employed in the subordinate positions to any extent; but they certainly might be to advantage. Rapidity and accuracy in counting money, the ready intuition which discovers counterfeits, by the feel, or by a glance, and the quick detection of forged paper, are all qualities in which woman can, from her greater nervous activity, her more delicate touch, and her keener instinctiveness, excel man. That she can become as expert in accounts as a man, has been abundantly proved; and in other qualifications of a moral character she surpasses most male applicants for such position. In money matters, women are generally more trustworthy than men; they have not the same temptations, of drinking, gambling, evil associates, and stock speculations, as young men, and would generally apply more closely to their business.

For the sake of the banks and bankers, then, we should advise the discharge of the greater part of their clerks, and the substitution, as fast as they can be qualified for the places, of competent young women of high character, at the same salaries. We believe the work would be better done, and that there would be a far smaller number of defalcations and breaches of trust to report.

The same arguments will apply with equal force to their employment in life and fire insurance offices, where they would do the work much better than it is now done, and with fewer frauds and embezzlements.

There is another side to this question, however. While the advantages to bankers and underwriters, of their employment would be very great, the advantage to the women themselves might be slight. All these confining employments, requiring the brain to be constantly kept intensely active, are very injurious to health; and it is a question whether the very delicacy of structure, which would render woman so valuable in situations like these, would not speedily induce impaired health, and cause her to fall a victim to overwork. A continued strain of this sort tells more severely and fatally upon woman than man, and overwork, in our banks and insurance offices, is killing far more men than we can afford to lose.

We can not, therefore, as a true friend of women, commend these situations to them, though we have no doubt of their intellectual and moral competency for them.

In our Western cities, and to some extent in New York, women well educated for these positions are becoming the cashiers, book-keepers, and confidential clerks of large wholesale houses. That they perform their duties faithfully and well, is the universal testimony of those who have employed them, and though they have generally been employed at a lower salary than male clerks, cashiers, &c., of no better qualifications, we have yet to hear of the first defalcation among them.

Their employment as clerks and saleswomen in retail stores, especially those engaged in the sale of drygoods, fancy goods, laces, silks, fringes, &c., as well as in toy, confectionery, flower, bakery, and tobacconists' shops, has been so common for some years past, that no one doubts their capacity for such work. It has been said, indeed, that they lacked the physical endurance needed for an occupation which required them to stand so many hours; and some have complained that they failed in tact in dealing with their customers—that they were very apt to make errors both in the quality of goods and in making change. But these objections, however valid they may be against individuals, weigh very little against the ability of the sex for trade. That many of them are equal in physical endurance to the other sex can not be denied; and the other shortcomings only prove that the individuals objected to had not been trained for their work, and were not competent to perform it properly. In general, women make more sales than men, in retail stores where both are employed, and though many customers prefer to deal with men, since they find it easier to decline purchasing from them when they wish to do so, yet a woman will be more sure to effect a sale to a customer whose mind is undecided, than a man

Of late years, women have been qualifying themselves for telegraph operators, and prove very successful in that calling. The popular proverb about a woman's not being able to keep a secret, whether true or false, does not now apply in this business, since nearly or quite all the messages in which secrecy is important, are conveyed in cipher, and are as unintelligible to the operator as to outsiders. Moreover, if a secret of any moment is confided to the telegraph without being put in cipher, some male gossip is quite as likely to let it out as the woman.

Another calling in which a considerable number of women find a livelihood, is copying, or writing from dictation. There is a large amount of copying to be done in the law offices, offices of patent solicitors, and in the transcribing of badly written manuscripts intended for the press. There are, also, many gentlemen who, from the illegibility of their penmanship, or from other causes, require an amanuensis, or private secretary, as we believe it is the fashion now to call them. Women secure much of this work, and if their handwriting was more clear and legible, and they were more generally and uniformly accurate in spelling and punctuation, they would obtain nearly the whole.

.Photography, in its various branches, is an art in which a few women have engaged with great success, and more might do so with advantage. Women have not, we believe, contributed any new

8

discoveries of importance to this art, but their manipulation, when they are thoroughly familiar with the business, is superior to that of men. Of course, a fair knowledge of practical chemistry is important in this pursuit. The coloring of photographs, a business requiring delicacy of touch, taste, and artistic skill, is very largely in the hands of women.

For a few years past, large classes have been instructed in most of our large cities in the arts of drawing and engraving on wood. A few succeed well in the drawing, and a still smaller number in the engraving, while the rest never acquire the skill necessary to enable them to do good work ; not, their teachers say, from any lack of natural ability, but because their minds are not on their work. There is ample employment at remunerative prices for every woman who can engrave skillfully on wood, or who can draw well upon the block, and there would be, were their numbers ten times increased ; but the skill required can only be attained by close and constant attention for some years. In other branches of the engravers' art, women have succeeded, and might do so again, if they would qualify themselves for their work.

From engraving the transition is natural to printing, and in this business there is a field for the larger employment of women. They have been, almost since the invention of power presses, employed as feeders, and have been very skillful

in their work. Of late years they have been acquiring a knowledge of type-setting, and now the
compositors on many newspapers, and in a considerable number of book and job offices, are
women. Mrs. Dall, writing in the autumn of
1867, estimates the number of female compositors
in the United States at 12,000. In this business
they are, on the average, more accurate than,
though not quite so quick as, men. When employed
on piece-work, *i. e.*, working at so much per thousand ems, they make very good wages. Work on
the hand or treadle presses usually requires more
strength than women possess. Recently, a Women's
Typographical Union has been formed in New
York, and embraces most of the female compositors.
It will secure for them fair compensation for their
work.

Another branch of business for which women
are especially adapted, but in which they are seldom engaged, is the sale of railroad, steamboat,
horse-car, and ferry tickets, and generally of
tickets to lectures and places of amusement. This
work does not require strong muscles, but only
readiness at figures and skill in judging of money,
both matters in which women can become experts
as readily as men.

We do not believe that women as often possess
the capacity for conducting great manufacturing
or commercial enterprises as men; in part, perhaps, because they have not been often trained to

the work; but there is abundant evidence that some women do possess this ability. We know that a young, beautiful, and accomplished woman in Western Massachusetts, whose husband was President and chief business manager of a very large paper manufactory, when he was cut off in the prime of manhood, took his place, and has now been for some years the active and capable manager of the business. We know that in the largest manufactory of fire-arms in the world, the widow of the founder of the establishment is the largest stockholder, and is constantly consulted in its management. A large machine-shop in Delaware, doing a successful business, is managed by the daughter of its founder, an intelligent young woman, who for some years worked constantly at the bench, and now can do as large a day's work, and do it as well, as any of the men in her employ. One of her sisters is also among the most skillful workers in the shop. These are only single instances, rare ones, perhaps, of the occasional ability of women to conduct large manufacturing operations. In commerce and trade they have oftener engaged, and with signal success in many instances. For many years, in Philadelphia, there was a prominent book-store and publishing-house, having the simple sign " S. HART & SON." Of the many thousands who dealt there, very few knew that the " S." stood for Sarah, and that this was a firm in which a mother and son were the partners. Mrs. Hart commenced business in this firm when her son (Abraham Hart, subsequently an extensive publisher, owner of coal mines, and millionnaire) was but sixteen years of age, and took an active, and long a controlling interest in the business, until failing health compelled her retirement. But larger enterprises, commercial, mercantile, and financial, than this have been and still are in the hands of women. Miss Burdett-Coutts is as successful in her business operations, the conducting of her great banking-house, and the management of her vast estate, as she is liberal and noble in the dispensing of her princely charities. In Paris, and indeed on the continent of Europe generally, some of the largest commercial houses have women at their head.* In New York, in some instances, where the experiment has been tried of a joint management of a mercantile business by husband and wife, and has failed, its subsequent management by the wife alone has proved successful. The number of women engaged in business in their own names in all our large cities is already great, and is constantly increasing. Few of them, as yet, engage in wholesale trade, but those few, as well as the retailers, have generally been successful.

Rev. Dr. Malcom, who about thirty years ago

---

* The name of Veuve Clicquot (the widow Clicquot), one of the largest manufacturers of champagne, will occur to many of our readers.

traveled extensively in India, Burmah, and Siam, says that in Burmah the women are the sole merchants and traders, and that they always accumulate property. They act invariably, he says, upon the cash principle, buying only what they have the money to pay for, and giving no credit. More than one of the merchant princes of England and of the United States has given to a favorite daughter a thorough business training, and has subsequently found his account in this instruction, when her clear intuition has enabled her to foresee and suggest a means of escape from threatened disaster, or to discern in the immediate future a wave of prosperity, for which, but for her, he would have been unprepared.

But while admitting the business ability of women, we do not believe that mercantile life exerts a favorable influence on their characters. The assurance, coolness, keenness, and hardness, which are almost inevitably developed in the merchant, and more distinctly, perhaps, in the retail trader, than in the wholesale dealer, stamp their impress more deeply upon the heart of woman than man, and in this rough attrition with the world, too often the down is rubbed off the fair and luscious peach—the delicate blush of maiden modesty gives place to the calm, cool, self-possessed expression of a woman who has become hardened to the stare, and indifferent to the opinion of those with whom she is brought into contact. The change is not alone in the seeming. The woman has become hard and worldly, and desirous of gain, and she is more of the earth, earthy, than she would have been in her home, or in some pursuit which did not call out so fully the more groveling elements of her character.

We come next to consider those employments, which, while they are undoubtedly feminine in their character, are sadly overcrowded, and hence, in many cases, do not yield an adequate livelihood to the sad and worn toilers in them. Embroidery, though an art requiring long and patient training, and in some of its varieties the exercise of much skill, is wretchedly underpaid; in part because the workers are brought into competition with the convent work of Mexico, South America, and the continent of Europe, which is very cheap, because the labor of the nuns is unpaid; and partly because this trade is mostly in the hands of Jews, who manifest great skill in obtaining needle-work at a very low price, and selling it at a very high one. It is almost impossible for the most rapid embroiderer to earn enough at her very trying and wearisome work to support herself in any comfort. How must it be, then, with those less skillful?

Other branches of skilled needlework pay better. A really good needlewoman can usually make a fair livelihood by her needle, either as milliner, dressmaker, or tailoress. And, though in our cities, the great increase which has taken place of late in the production of ready-made goods, of women's as well as of men's wear, has somewhat reduced the price paid for fine sewing, yet the more abundant supply of this description of work in part compensates for this. The trade in women's goods is now in the hands of men of a higher class, who are disposed to deal more fairly by the women they employ than the shirt-makers, and ready-made clothing manufacturers of goods for men's wear, have hitherto done.

But as we leave the class of skilled needle-women, and come among those who have the ability only to make up in the plainest and cheapest way the slop-work of the low-priced shops, we find again a fearful amount of overcrowding. Shirts and vests, overalls, and cheap linen coats made up at from fifty cents to one dollar and twenty-five cents per dozen, the sewer finding thread and needles, do not furnish employment so lucrative that we should suppose there would be much competition for it, and yet let any dealer advertise for hands, even at these pitiful prices, and he will have hundreds of women applying for work before twenty-four hours have passed. It seems impossible to keep soul and body together on such a pittance, even by the most active and unflag-ging industry, and yet we know that not a few do manage to exist, we can not say live, on the few pennies earned by incessant toil. Poor creatures, they believe themselves bound down to this single form of industry, and their struggle to win an existence for themselves and their little ones by it, really rises to the dignity of heroism.

In this kind of work, or rather in that a grade or two above it, which would otherwise come into the hands of these poor toilers, women in the country and in towns adjacent to our large cities, unconsciously often, do their poor sisters of the city a great wrong. The stout, healthy farmers' daughters, or the wives and daughters of well-to-do mechanics in the country villages, finding themselves not fully employed, at some seasons of the year, take large quantities of this slop-work to make up at their homes, and board and home not being taken into the account, they are able to make considerable additions, even at these wretchedly low prices, to their spending money. If they once realized that every piece of work made up by them not only reduced the price paid to the poor sewing-woman in the city, but often deprived her of work, they would turn their attention to other and better ways of earning a few dollars. Still, the beggarly price paid for this class of work is in great part due to the fierce and excessive competition of this great body of sewing-women for work. The unskilled laborer is said by political economists to be the most helpless, and the least provident of all classes of

8* M

society; yet even the unskilled female laborer, the charwoman, the cleaner and scrubber, the *chiffonnière* and the scavenger, fare better than these half-skilled sewing-women. Yet, if they but knew it, three-fourths of them might have good homes, comfortable food, beds, and air, and fair wages, if they would go into domestic service, either in city or country. The life they are now living is more abject, involves infinitely more suffering, and exposes them to sorer temptations than they would experience in service, and it is not counterbalanced by any enjoyment or liberty which the servant-girl does not have.

The sewing-machine has been, in some aspects of the case, a great blessing to woman; in others, an injury. The enormous increase in the amount of needle-work required in this country within the past fifteen or twenty years, has rendered its use indispensable, and while the number of operators has increased, they have been able to earn much better wages with the sewing-machine than they ever could have done without it. Skillful sewing-machine hands, can, if in full work, earn from seven to twelve dollars a week, and a few, possibly, even more, and they will tell you, generally, that they do not work any harder, perhaps not so hard, as they would have done with the needle, had there been no sewing-machines.

But here comes in the operation of that law which is constantly reminding woman of her weaker physical nature, and which, in this case, demonstrates the injurious effect of the sewing-machine. It has been definitely ascertained, that not one woman in a hundred can work steadily on the sewing-machine for three years, or four years at the furthest, without a complete prostration and shattering of the nervous system, so severe as to terminate either in protracted illness, helplessness, or death. The higher wages, the greater comfort in living, and the feeling of independence, are purchased at a fearful cost. The improvements in the manufacture of the machine, securing greater ease of motion, more speed, and less frequent delay from breaking the thread, imperfect tension, &c., may do something toward protracting the period in which they can be used by one operator; but the fact that, where the machines are driven by steam power, and it is only the sewing which the girls are required to direct, they break down almost as soon, shows the severe effect of this kind of work upon the delicate nervous organization of woman.

When we come, finally, to the class of unskilled, or but slightly skilled female laborers, we find a helpless class, indeed, and one more helpless from the exposures and hardships of their occupations; in prosperous times earning a scanty and precarious livelihood by their toil, and in times of business depression, almost wholly without employment; yet this class, with their lower intelligence, are less sensitive to the misery of their position, and accept alms without hesitation, and in the cities and large towns come to regard the city aid for the poor, or the almshouse itself, as their natural refuge, subsiding into it without any feeling of degradation, on the approach of winter. This ready acceptance of the pauper's life and fare is not a characteristic of our women of American birth and descent. However deeply they may have sunk in poverty, the poor-house is their dread, and they will often struggle almost till the agonies of death are upon them, to avoid so sad a fate. But the women of the lower classes of foreign birth or parentage have none of this feeling. To them, it seems the most natural thing in the world, that if they are not able to support themselves, the community should support them, and their easy confidence that it will, often saves them from much of that sorrow, which, to a sensitive heart, is almost unendurable. The great influx of immigrants from Europe has introduced a very considerable number of avocations for women of the peasant classes, which are still, and it is hoped may always continue to be (if they are to be followed by women at all), practiced solely by women of foreign birth. Among these are those of the *chiffonnières*, or rag and bone-pickers, scavengers, swill-gatherers, collectors of broken victuals, hucksters of small wares, costermongers or vegetable peddlers, &c., &c. It seems such a profanation, such an outrage on all our ideas of woman, to see her engaged in such employments, that we have often turned away with a shudder, as we have seen some poor old creature bent down under her load of bones, papers, rags, and trash, and exploring each box or barrel of garbage for new treasures. We could not imagine a countrywoman of ours engaged in such work.

CHAPTER XII.

THE dangerous and the criminal classes, to which all writers on ethics assign the vicious and depraved portion of all large communities, comprise, in the criminal division, not merely those who have been arrested and punished for crime, but the bold villains who, though constantly preying upon society, have as yet gone unwhipped of justice. Among the dangerous class are included petty thieves, vagrants, the uncared-for children of the streets, and those of a lower grade—roughs, rowdies, gamblers, habitual drunkards, and prostitutes of all ranks. These persons are all dangerous to the well-being of society, because they subsist on the product of their crimes, or are constantly engaged in practices which are hostile to good order and the interests of community.

It is with but one section of this dangerous class that we have to do in this work. No treatise on the condition and rights and wrongs of women would be complete, which failed to consider the condition of fallen women, and the causes which have led to their ruin. It is a sad and terrible thought that, taking not only our great cities, but our manufacturing towns and villages, our sea-ports and our commercial centers, of the women between the ages of fifteen and thirty, one out of every twelve (some very careful statisticians say, one out of every ten) is a thing of shame. And this in an enlightened, Christian nation, in the latter half of the nineteenth century, and despite all our efforts to promote purity and holiness! To what causes shall we attribute a state of things so deplorable? The question is a difficult one, yet it admits, we think, of an answer which will indicate most of the influences which induce prostitution.

We may remark in the beginning, though that is but a small consolation, that this vice is no more prevalent here, but somewhat less so, than in Great Britain or the continental States of Europe. In some of the continental States, especially in the south of Europe, among the lower classes, illicit love is the rule, and chastity the rare exception. We are not arrived at, we do not even approach, this depth of degradation, though the great influx of European immigrants of the lower classes has had its ill effects on the families of the poor in our large cities and manufacturing towns.

All the testimony, and it is voluminous, on the subject, indicates that the prevalence of this evil is not due, to any considerable extent, to inordinate or uncontrollable passion on the part of the sex. In the profligate and degenerate days of the later Roman empire this may have been, as Roman satirists alleged, a cause. It certainly is seldom one now.

Yet the minds of the young are corrupted, and the barriers of virtue weakened to a greater extent than most parents are aware, by the circulation, in secret, of vile books and prints in a large proportion of our female seminaries.*

But, aside from these minor sources of evil, the most prominent causes are not far to seek.

The fashionable mode of education has much to answer for in this regard. Developing the love of display as the chief end to be gained, teaching directly or indirectly the practice of deception, imparting little or no useful practical knowledge, and stimulating the love of admiration rather than the love of right, it fits the graduate to regard self-indulgence, physical indolence, the love of dress and show, as the prime objects for which a woman should live, and deception as perfectly justifiable.

---

* We have not, perhaps, in the text, expressed so strongly as we should, our deep abhorrence of this Satanic method of corrupting the youth of both sexes. We have it from undoubted authority, that there are very few academies, female seminaries, high schools, or boarding-schools in the country, in which these abominable books and pictures are not industriously circulated, sometimes by emissaries of the wretches who publish them. Recently the publication of vile newspapers, illustrated with great skill, but with the worst purposes, has been made an additional means of corrupting the young. That these evil seeds do often spring up and bear fruit, in the ruin of young people of both sexes, in soul and body, we have abundant and distressing evidence.

To young women thus educated, when adverse circumstances have driven them from the life of ease they had planned, the siren voice of vicious pleasure offers an indolent, easy life, ample opportunities for display and costly apparel, gems and ornaments in profusion, as the price of their virtue. Pressed by temptation at the very point where they are weakest, they yield, after a brief struggle, and enter, covertly at first, perhaps, on a life of sin.

The culture of the intellect, the harmonious development of its great powers, is a boon to humanity; but that education which does not strengthen the moral nature, and bring the conscience as well as the intellect into full activity, is a curse and a bane; and it is a question which every. parent should ponder, whether much of the so-called fashionable education of the day, does not to all intents and purposes ignore the moral nature of the child.

But while the ranks of fashionable vice are largely recruited from these graduates of a false system of education, who, after a brief and bitter experience of the hollowness and wretchedness of a life of sin, sink down to a lower depth of degradation, and thus make room for others of their own class to enter upon the downward road, considerable numbers are led to begin a life of shame from other though somewhat similar motives.

The country girl, whose great ambition it has

been to become a resident of a great city, and who has come thither on the promise of employment, with a fresh, young, and perhaps handsome face, is cast among associates of doubtful or positively evil character, and if she has a love of dress and display, and perhaps, also, a dislike for hard work, she soon hears, how "a single smile may bring her better fare and finer dresses than a month's wages," and though, at first, her soul revolts at the thought of the horrible price of such finery and ease, yet, as the love of dress urges its claims, she begins to parley with the temptation, which comes at first in its most innocent form, and yielding by degrees, she falls—a victim, like her more fashionable sister, to the love of display.

There are some, doubtless, though the very careful statistics which have been collected on the subject do not indicate that the number is large, who have succumbed to temptation under the pressure of starvation; but of those who have maintained their virtue up to this point, the greater part, by far, have nobly preferred death to dishonor. It is, we are well aware, a common occurrence for abandoned women to attribute their fall to this cause, but their habitual untruthfulness makes their statements less probable, and the investigations made by Dr. Sanger, Dr. Ryan, and others, prove that in many cases these stories were merely told for effect. That in some instances a young mother has sacrificed herself to procure food and clothing for her child; or daughters, to procure comforts for an invalid mother; sisters, for a sick and dying sister, is probable: but if the ranks of vice received no recruits but such as these, our great cities would soon become marvels of morality.

Many are doubtless victims of the seducer, who tempts as often by the promise of luxury and ease, as by the promise of marriage. Very many lost women become themselves tempters, and lead others to ruin. Procuresses and publishers of vile books have been known in some instances to send young girls, already ruined, to fashionable boarding-schools and female seminaries, as pupils, to infuse poison into the minds of their associates, and in more than one instance those engaged in this nefarious traffic have entered Sabbath-schools, procured situations as teachers, and used their position to drag innocent souls down to perdition.

This terrible evil does not seek its victims alone in the ranks of the unmarried; very many wives, in city and country, fall a prey to the tempter, and the houses of assignation which abound in our great cities offer a covert to thousands of "silly women, laden with sins, led away by divers lusts." The fatal facility of divorce greatly increases the number of women who lead an abandoned life; the boarding life in the great hotels of the city is full of perils to young wives;

and those who have been prompted by love of ease or dislike of care, to the fearful crime of the murder of their unborn babes, have already trodden the downward road so far that their falling into this sin also, is hardly matter of surprise.

The concert-saloons, dance-houses, and low dens, are largely supplied from young female emigrants, who had lost their virtue in their own country, or were ruined, as so many are, on board ship. That the supply from all these sources is not always equal to the demand, appears from the fact that a noted New York procuress, last year, advertised in an English paper for fifty English governesses, for whom she promised to find situations on their arrival here, but whom she intended to use as fresh victims for her diabolical sacrifices. Whether she was successful in luring any to ruin is not known. Horrible as is every thing connected with this loathsome subject, the worst remains to be told. In our manufacturing towns and cities, a large proportion, some say a majority, of these daughters of shame are girls between the ages of ten and fifteen years; mere children, yet lost to virtue, to their families, to society, to God.

The people of Canaan—and the Israelites, at some periods of their history, following their example—passed their children through the fire, in the worship of Moloch—but what were the tortures they endured in the arms of that red-hot, brazen image, to the writhings of these lost souls in the agonies of the world of woe ?

It has long been a question with the moralists, whether the course pursued by virtuous women toward these erring, fallen ones, was in accordance with the spirit of the Gospel. Other sinners, great criminals even, if they repent, are forgiven, and, on evidence of their full reformation, are often restored to society and to the privileges they had forfeited by their misconduct ; but to the fallen woman, until recently, there was, in the view of women, no place of repentance or forgiveness, neither in this life nor in the life to come. Her doom was sealed.

In defense of this course on the part of virtuous women, it was urged that the sin against chastity was a graver, deeper sin, than any other ; that the white robe of innocence once soiled, could never again be restored to its former purity ; that the stain was too deep ever to be effaced.

It was claimed, also, that womanly purity was so delicate a thing, that the slightest breath would injure it ; that any contact with the impure, even for purposes of mercy, marred its immaculate whiteness ; and that there was no safety for woman, however pure and holy, but in shunning all manifestations of sympathy or pity for the fallen.

To such an extent has this view been maintained, that a mother has been known to drive from her door a once beloved daughter, who, penitent and perishing, came to seek forgiveness and hope from the mother that bare her; sisters, to turn coldly and haughtily from a sister once dear, who implored them, for Christ's sake, to hear and help her; and even a daughter has been taught to shun a mother who had once cherished her tenderly, but who had since sinned and repented.

But is the purity of a virtuous woman so much more spotless and precious than that of the Divine Redeemer, that she should hesitate, for fear of soiling her purity, to follow where He has led the way?

To Him "the woman of the city, that was a sinner," but who sought with deep, penitential sorrow, relief from the burden which crushed her, did not apply in vain for pardon; and while proud Pharisees and scornful Sadducees turned away in contempt, and with bitter hatred, from these daughters of shame, who were, perhaps, after all, no greater sinners than themselves, He declared, in "words such as never man spake," to the truly penitent, that their sins were forgiven. It is matter of rejoicing that so many women of the highest character and the most unsullied reputation, have of late, both in Great Britain and the United States, sought to rescue their fallen sisters in the spirit and temper of their Divine Master. Abhorring the sin, they are yet tender and kindly pitiful toward the repenting sinner; and their success has been in proportion to their zealous and patient labors. More than two thousand of this class, hitherto considered so utterly hopeless, have been reclaimed and restored to society within five years past. To them the dark and sinful past will ever be a bitter remembrance, and its shadows will darken, as its impurity has fouled, the sweet, bright current of an innocent and joyous life; but they are no longer tempters to sin, but, having themselves suffered, seek to pluck others from the fire; and, in many cases, their humble, penitent life has restored them fully to the confidence and friendship of their sex.

In some cases, as in the midnight meetings, and occasionally in the management of the Magdalen asylums, good men have participated in this work; but, for the most part, women have achieved the greatest success in it.

Asylums for the reformation of abandoned women are not, it is true, a new thing; they have existed in Europe for two hundred years or more, and in the United States for forty, but have not generally appealed so directly to the hearts and sympathies of the fallen women, as to bring many of them to repentance and thorough reformation. The asylum has been, to some extent, a prison; the treatment, formal, stern, and forbidding, and the poor women, instead of being encouraged to banish from their minds all recollection of their life of shame (to which no allusion should be allowed), and exhorted to begin, in humble trust in a

Saviour's love, a new life, were daily reminded what terrible sinners they had been, and what mercies they enjoyed, in being permitted, vile as they were, to be under the care of those who were so much holier and purer than they could ever hope to be.

This was, in many instances, the old system, and there need be no wonder that it very generally failed. The design of the managers was good, but they approached their work in too Pharisaic a spirit, and in utter ignorance of the laws which govern mental and moral action. The constant reminding of a sinner of his misdeeds, and their heinousness, will either depress unduly, or harden the partially penitent offender; and the contrast drawn between the impurity of these poor fallen women, and the immaculate virtue of those around them, could only breed a feeling of despair on their part; while the reflection on their past life, under these depressing circumstances, would tend only to recall its fleeting pleasures, and tempt them, viewing themselves as irrecoverably lost, to return to the life they had struggled to abandon. Very painful is it to read in the annual reports of many of the old Magdalen asylums, that so many—often nearly one-half—of those discharged as reformed, had returned to their evil courses again.

Very different, and very much wiser, is the course now pursued in the reformation of the fallen

The door of the "Home"—expressive word, as indicative of the changed method of treatment,—as it closes between them and the street, shuts out their past life of sin, to which no reference is ever made, and they are treated just as other young women needing employment and mental and moral training would be; employment is furnished them as soon as they are able to undertake it, and while they are made to feel that every thing around them is pleasant, and breathes the spirit of love and kindness, they are yet taught that labor, and often protracted and weari-some labor, is the prerequisite to an honest life. Every thing which can recall the incidents, the gayeties, or the terrible wretchedness of their past life, is carefully kept out of their way. Kindly, sisterly advice is given in regard to their reading, during the time they have for that purpose, and no harbor is given to sensational stories, either in newspapers or books. The efforts to bring them under the influence of religious principles are not made in any Pharisaic way, but the kindly voice of a sister speaks of the love of Christ, of his compassion and tenderness, and gently leads the erring one to trust in a Friend so sympathizing yet so powerful. The women thus reformed do not relapse into evil ways.

And yet it must be acknowledged that, of all classes needing reformation, abandoned women are the most difficult to be successfully reached and

9   N

permanently benefited. The difficulty exists, to a great extent, in the mental and moral characteristics of the women themselves. Some of them have been brought up from infancy in an atmosphere of vice; they have never known what purity was; and their whole thoughts, and the language they use, have become so depraved, that even the most harmless words have to them an evil suggestiveness. For this class, there is a complete renovation of the entire mental as well as moral faculties necessary; and they are so utterly devoid of truthfulness that it is very difficult to ascertain when they are really changed.

But the greater part of these women are girls whose vanity and love of dress and display, indolence and giddiness, have been their ruin. Generally in these, there is no fixedness of purpose, no perseverance; they are impulsive, and while the fit of disgust at their former life is on them, they resolve to reform, and continue in their purpose, till some temptation, or some refluent wave of remembrance of their old career, carries them off again into the vortex of destruction. Very few of these have the moral courage necessary to enter upon and steadfastly pursue a new life. The almost universal practice of indulgence in intoxicating liquors, which these women say they find indispensable to drown recollection of their happier past, is also a powerful obstacle to their reformation.

Those emissaries of Satan, the procuresses, are ever on the alert to draw back to perdition those women who are struggling up out of the depths to life and hope, and evil men are ready to help them. As a general rule, therefore, these reformed women are safest when far away from the scene of their temptation and fall, and amid the quiet and retirement of the country; but, alas! the country is none too pure, and the Serpent who tempted our first mother, amid the beauty and glory of Eden, has his representatives even amid the fair landscapes of the country, and the quiet and peace of rural homes; and finding there the dove, whose plumage has once been soiled, and whose wings are drooping, they pounce upon it, and too often lure it back to sure destruction.

It is not within the power of human legislation to change the human heart, or to suppress the fires of passion and sin in the minds of the depraved; but much might be done by judicious legislation to diminish the carnival of lust, which threatens to destroy our nation. The existing laws against the publication and sale of vile books, prints, newspapers, jewelry, &c., might be enforced more rigidly, and the great sources, as well as the tributary rills of this villainy, be broken up; the acting of obscene plays, whether in opera, opera bouffe, or the ordinary drama, prohibited; other laws might be enacted, making the keeping of a house of ill-fame or assignation a felony, punishable both by fine and imprisonment; punishing the leasing or selling a house or furniture for such purposes by fine and forfeiture; punishing seduction, especially of girls under twenty-one years of age, with great severity, and making the finding of girls under eighteen years old in these houses *prima facie* evidence of their abduction, and so punishable by fine and imprisonment. Such statutes as these could be enforced even in our largest cities, for this foul and loathsome disease on the body politic, this so-called "social evil," is making its blighting influence felt in all ways upon the physical, intellectual, and moral life of our people, and it must be crushed out, or it will bring upon us swift and sure destruction as a nation.

After legislation and the vigorous administration of the law has done all it can to suppress this vice, there will still remain enough of evil which the law can not reach, to give ample employment to most devoted reformers, and to make the prospect of a millennium remote.

CHAPTER XIII.

THE rapid review we have given of occupations now open to women, will, we think, convince any candid mind, that whatever may have been the case in the past, there is now no lack of employments for women, and that in one or other of them, a single woman (either unmarried or widow) of good health and fair intelligence, should find no serious difficulty, if she is industrious, in earning a livelihood.

There is this difference to be noticed between most of the employments of men, and the greater part of those of women, that the former require a longer and closer apprenticeship than the latter, and hence that there is greater difficulty in a man's changing his business, than in a woman's entering upon a different employment. A man who has learned the trade of a mason, finds it 'difficult, if not impossible, when work is dull in his trade, and he can not find an engagement, to take up the business of a house-joiner, a blacksmith, or a tailor. But a woman who has been an operative, for instance, in a hoop-skirt factory, can, with but slight training, find employment equally profitable in the manufacture of undergarments, in a ready-made clothing establishment, or in a printing-office as press-feeder. This is not due so much to the greater facility of adaptation of women to varied occupations, as to a certain family resemblance, which very many of the occupations of women have to each other.

There ought not to be so much difficulty in finding employment for all women whose circumstances require it, as for men, for another reason : if we deduct boys under fifteen, and old men too infirm for work, nine-tenths of the remainder of the males in any community have, or require some employment, some business which they follow with considerable regularity, and on which they place more or less dependence for a livelihood.

In the case of women, after deducting the two classes named, girls under fifteen and old women too feeble to labor, we must deduct also the great body of married women, whose employment, with occasional exceptions, is the care of their families and households, and that other very considerable class who scorn all labor or toil except that of dressing themselves for public inspection, and walking, riding, or shopping. Leaving these two classes out of the account, and we find not more than forty per cent, at the utmost, of women of adult age requiring employment.

In the more than one hundred distinct occupations in which women have engaged in this country with success, there certainly should be, and there is, a sufficiency of employment for the comparatively small number who need it, and in one or other of these so readily interchangeable, there ought to be no difficulty, in almost any season, in an intelligent woman, in tolerable health, finding business; while men, in many of the mechanical trades, are very much at the mercy of the financial condition of the country. When money is scarce, business dull, and materials high, the builder will not erect houses, and, consequently, the mason, the joiner, the painter, and the plumber, are thrown out of employ; when the publisher finds no demand for his books, and hence suspends publishing, the papermaker, the compositor, the pressman, the bookbinder, and the packer, are out of work. These vicissitudes of trade do not so much affect the employments of women.

"But," the ultra advocates of women's rights reply, "all this talk of what ought to be, does not alter what *is*. Everybody knows, or may know, that every year many thousands of women in our great cities are reduced to the verge of starvation for the want of remunerative employment. What will you do with that fact?" Softly, fair friends. Your "many thousands," under the careful and rigid scrutiny of the visitors of the associations for improving the condition of the poor, and the city authorities, dwindle to a few hundreds, and of these the greater part lack employment for one

of two reasons : either that they are in too feeble
health to be able to work, or that they are too
indolent or weak-minded to desire it.

Infirm health is a great misfortune, especially
to the poor, who must depend upon their labor for
their daily bread. It is bad enough when the
father of a family is prevented by illness from
earning the means of supporting his family; it
is worse when the poor widow is afflicted by it,
and can not do work enough to supply with food
and clothing the little ones whose only earthly
resource she is. For all such, we feel the profoundest sympathy, and would willingly extend to them
our aid, as far as possible.

But the laws of trade are inexorable. If man
or woman is too ill to do the work they are accustomed to do, the work must be done, and, except in
rare instances, the pay received, by those who are
able to do it. So obvious a law of political economy as this can not be subverted, however hardly
it may bear on the infirm. For them, some other
provision must be, and generally is, made.

Take the other class, those who are in sufficiently
good health to be able to work, but who, nevertheless, fail to find employment. We have said, that
in most cases, this failure was the result of indolence or weak-mindedness. This may seem to be
censorious, but it is true. At four different periods, within the past twelve years, benevolent
persons, connected with either the public or pri-

vate charities of New York City, roused to anxious concern for the welfare of the unemployed poor, and especially of unemployed poor women, by the statements made in the public prints concerning their sufferings, have attempted extraordinary measures for their relief. In each case there has been no lack of funds to carry out any desirable measure of relief; for the citizens of New York do not lack a charitable spirit.

The complaint made was, in each case, that they could not find work; that they were willing to do any thing, and to go anywhere, if they could find employment which would sustain life. The first instance to which we refer occurred in the autumn and winter of 1857, after the terrible financial panic of that year.

Several of the charitable organizations of the city, deeply impressed with the apparent suffering of the season, and finding that employment in the city could not be had for all, offered to take, at the cost of the societies, as many single women as desired to go to the West, and procure good situations for them; stipulating, of course, that they should have testimonials of good character from their pastors, or other persons of known respectability. Greatly to their surprise, very few applied for the opportunity of going; and when those who had been complaining of the want of employment were questioned as to their reasons for not exchanging starvation and wretchedness for comfort, their

9*

reply uniformly was, that they thought they could get along somehow; they didn't want to leave the city. Their "getting along somehow," consisted, in most cases, in receiving pauper-relief from one, two, or three sources; and, in some, unquestionably the wages of unrighteousness. The few who did go, were hardly better than those who stayed. Most of them, though presenting certificates of good character, had already fallen, and, though excellent situations were obtained for them, within six months the greater part were found in brothels in the Western cities, one of them having actually established a house of ill-fame, and employed several of those who had gone West with her.

The subsequent experiments of 1861, 1866, and 1869, were too similar to need repetition. In all instances, women bound by no strong ties to New York, and, according to their own representation, starving there, very generally refused to leave the city for comfortable situations in the country, and very often also refused situations in the city or its suburbs, on the frivolous grounds that the work was too hard, or it was too far off, or that they preferred a different class of work. This was the result of hundreds, and in some instances thousands, of applications. Is there not reason to think that, in these cases, either indolence or weak-mindedness was at the bottom of their refusal to accept work?

There are cases, doubtless, of married women,

or widows with small children, and, perhaps, of single women who have parents or young brothers and sisters dependent upon them, who find, in some seasons, difficulty in obtaining the sort of work which they are capable of doing; but these are, almost without exception, those who are unskilled, or only half-skilled laborers; and with these, as with the same classes of the other sex, there must be always periods when there is little or no work. Their only resource is to acquire a higher degree of skill, or sufficient knowledge to enable them to rise to a better grade of work, for which there is always a greater demand and fewer laborers to supply it.

It is hard to say it, perhaps, but it is the truth, that this class of unskilled or but partially skilled laborers, of both sexes, owe their abject condition, in great part, to their own ignorance, heedlessness, and unthrift. It is true, that sickness, either of the bread-winner himself (or herself), or of some of the family, may occasionally aggravate their misery; but even this is often but another result of their thriftlessness. It is really but little harder for a young man or young woman to acquire a trade or learn a business which will give them a good livelihood, and in which their services will always be in demand, than to jog on, doing the lowest kind of drudgery, and receiving the very lowest wages, even in prosperous times, because of the competition which is fiercest in the lowest kinds of work, from the great numbers who do not know how to do any other; in dull times, the competition grows more intense, as the work is less abundant, since the number of mouths to be fed is not diminished, and the scarcity of employment leads to underbidding, till wages are too low to sustain life. These very low wages compel this class of the very poor to shelter themselves in the closest, filthiest, and most unhealthy tenements that can be found, because they are unable to pay the rent of any better rooms, and often they are obliged to herd together, all ages and both sexes, in a way which a decent herd of swine would resent. There follows from this, sickness, physical prostration, and a moral degradation which sinks them still lower in wretchedness.

Now, in this condition of affairs, there is very little chance of improvement. Legislation can do nothing to improve it, for there is no possibility of regulating the price of labor otherwise than in accordance with the laws of supply and demand, and any attempt at fixing a minimum price for any description of work, would inevitably result in wide-spread disaster; it is impossible to increase, to any considerable extent, the amount of work which unskilled or partially skilled laborers can perform, in times of financial depression; indiscriminate charity only defeats its own purpose, by pauperizing a large class, capable, ordinarily, of supporting themselves in some sort, and even the most skillful administration of relief increases so enormously the number of the dependent class, that (as Great Britain has found of late) it threatens to swamp all the smaller tax-payers. The multiplication of lodging-houses, and good, but low-priced tenements for the poor, which has been attempted on a large scale in London, and to some extent, in Boston, New York, and Philadelphia, benefits a class of the poor, but not *this* class; the lower grades of the skilled laboring classes, not having lost all ambition, secure these tenements, and gradually begin to better their condition; but this class will continue to occupy their miserable kennels, even at the same rent which the others pay; or if, which is very rarely the case, they do occupy one of these better tenements for a little time, they soon render the rest uninhabitable by their untidy and degrading habits, and their morbid dread of cleanliness and pure air.

There seems to be no resource for them, except by some process of education and reformation, by which their capacity for a higher and better paid class of work can be increased; and the greater part of them, it is to be feared, are too old to learn.

There is great complaint among the ultra-advocates of women's rights, of the low rates of wages and compensation for labor allowed to women.   Some of these complaints are just, while others are grossly unjust. In the lower grades of skilled labor, and in all unskilled labor, women's wages have been, and still are, much lower than those of men engaged in the same classes of employment. The discrimination has been greater than it should have been, but the causes of it were these : that women possessed less physical strength than men, and consequently could not perform as much, or as severe labor in a given time; that generally they were less skillful in their trade or business than men, and consequently did not do their work so well; that they did not give their whole minds to their work, but were occupied with other thoughts and objects, and hence made more blunders, involving losses to the employer; that in those kinds of work where the supply of labor was equal to, or greater than, the demand for it, women, for the sake of procuring work, would underbid each other, and thus reduce the price of labor by a disastrous competition; and finally, that those employers who offered the lowest prices had the most applications from working-women, and, owing to the low prices they paid for work, could undersell their competitors in the market, who paid better prices to their employés. That some of these reasons indicate hardness and lack of sympathy on the part of some employers is undoubtedly true; but we must take men as we find them, and must remember that all trade and business is governed by certain absolute laws, and that one of the most inexorable of these is, that where the supply of any thing (labor as well as any thing else) equals or exceeds the demand, the lowest price at which it is offered will, other things being equal, be the ruling price.

Yet, except in the case of unskilled or partially skilled labor, the women have the remedy for this in their own hands. In most descriptions of manual labor, a woman's work is not worth quite as much as a man's would be, where the payment is to be made by the day or the week, for the same reason that a boy's work, though it may be as well done, is not worth as much, viz. : because the greater part of this manual labor requires, for the accomplishment of the greatest amount in a given time, greater physical strength than either the boy or the woman possess. Where the work can be done by the piece, if it is as well done, it should receive the same pay. The same rule should apply to clerkships and the like employments ; where the work performed is the same, and as well done by one sex as the other, the pay should, in justice, be the same. Inasmuch, however, as there exists in the minds of many employers a prejudice (unfounded, we admit) against the employment of women in places of trust and confidence, it is worthy of a question whether some slight concession in salary, sufficient to turn the scale and secure them the position, might not be advisable, at first, as a matter of policy.

The remedy which we would have women employ to prevent the reduction of the wages of skilled working-women, is that which male mechanics have tried with such success for a few years past—that of trades-unions or associations, which should regulate the prices to be required for work in their several employments, and provide for the support of those thrown out of employ when it was necessary to resist an attempted reduction of wages.

The great obstacles to the increase of women's wages have come from themselves; their ruinous competition, their underbidding, and the taking of work at low prices by women in the country, to occupy their spare time. Trades-unions would remedy these evils to a great extent, if women would unite in them and be true to each other.

Co-operative societies and organizations might also do much for them, if rightly managed; the cost of food and of clothing, the two great items of expenditure among the poor, and especially with poor women, would be greatly reduced thereby.

Finally, the material comfort of working-women would be greatly promoted by the increase of their practical education. In the lower grades of intelligence and skill there are always crowds and intense competition; as the working-woman rises higher in the scale, and becomes capable of better and more skillful work, the wages increase, and the competition decreases, till at last she reaches a point where the supply of labor is not equal to the demand, and can sell her labor at her own price. In most of the higher grades of employment the salaries of women are nearly equal to those of men, especially if we take into account the greater strength, and more uniformly good health of men.

Teaching is frequently spoken of as an exception, and the reports of the superintendents of public schools in the different States adduced as proof. Yet here the difference is more apparent than real. In California, the wages of female teachers average the same as those of male teachers. In several other States they approximate very nearly; and in those States where the difference is considerable, it is usually due to the fact that women are employed, much more largely than men, in schools of a low grade, or as assistants, where the wages would be lower, without reference to sex.

Wherever women competent to fill first-class positions are employed in those positions, their salaries are generally equivalent to those paid to men under the same circumstances. In St. Louis, for instance, where a part of the High Schools have women for principals, and the remainder men, the salaries are the same for each. The rule

o

in teaching, as in every thing else, is, that first-class qualifications will command first-class prices.

In all these employments it is absurd to suppose that legislation could accomplish any thing in the way of regulating the prices of labor, or in any way ameliorating the condition of working-women.

We shall show presently, that the possession of the ballot would be equally ineffectual in producing any such result. We may add, now, that even were any considerable number of women to make politics a profession, those who did so would be drawn from the intelligent class, who have no difficulty now in obtaining a livelihood, and not from the poorer classes, who are the only ones who need relief, but who do not possess either the education or the skill to enter upon such a career. So far, then, as the appeal is made to struggling and oppressed working-women to demand the ballot as the panacea for all their woes, we must denounce it as utterly unworthy of those who make it, and, in fact, the merest demagogism. They can not be in any way benefited by it, and the leaders of this suffrage movement know it, or should know it, if they do not.

CHAPTER XIV.

BEFORE proceeding to consider the propriety of conceding the suffrage to women, it may be well to devote a little space to a history of suffrage, its origin and progress in past ages, and ascertain whether there is an inherent right of suffrage in any class or body of men or women.

In the early ages of the world's history, the patriarchal form of government, an evident outgrowth of the paternal, prevailed universally. The father of the family, and in process of time the patriarch of the tribe, was the supreme authority, and from his decision there was no appeal. Under this form of government, continued to this day among the pastoral and nomadic tribes of Asia and Africa, there was no thought of suffrage, and no occasion for it. By and by, when cities and towns began to be built, and the nomads became citizens having fixed habitations, some man possessing greater bravery, mechanical skill, or power of control than the rest, became the king of a given territory, and the people, awed by his superior qualities, gave him their allegiance, and obeyed his commands as implicitly as they had previously done those of the patriarch. In the

case of Nimrod, the kingly quality was his ability
as a hunter, and very possibly, also, as a warrior;
in the case of the first Hadad, king of Damas-
cus, it was his skill as a smith, the most practical of the arts of that time; in Saul, his gigantic
stature and his regal bearing.

These kings were absolute, as are most of the
Oriental monarchs to this day, and the people had
no means of redress from any injustice of the
monarch, except by revolution or a change of
dynasty.

As the ages rolled on, the chief men of some of
these nations began to claim a right of participation in the government, and finally obtained it, in
one way or another. Sometimes they formed a
council, or parliament, to which they required the
king to submit his more important measures, and
which he could only execute when a majority of
them sanctioned them; sometimes they only exercised an advisory power; at others, they became
subordinate rulers, and convened in council at
long intervals.

In Rome, the kingly power was abrogated, and
consuls, chosen by the senate (the assembled
body of nobles or patricians, who were nominally
selected and appointed by the quæstors), governed
under the general title of the Senate and People
of Rome. These patricians exercised some powers of suffrage in virtue of being the governing
power of the republic; but, really, they were

only so many kings, exercising a joint authority. Through all this period of consular and senatorial authority, the plebeians had no voice in the government directly, though the tribes, organizations of the people, who were invested under certain restrictions with the right of Roman citizenship, voted for tribunes, an inferior class of officers, who yet acted as checks on the power of the consuls and the senate. The privilege of citizenship, which conferred this limited right of suffrage, was highly prized; and where it had not been granted to a family for services rendered to the State, was often purchased at a high price. Until after the Roman commonwealth had begun to decline, even this limited suffrage was not by any means general among the male inhabitants. Great numbers had never been invested with the privilege of citizenship; the slaves, who numbered, at times, as many as five or six to one of the citizens, never exercised the right of suffrage, and for many years the freedmen (those who had been slaves but had been emancipated), did not share this privilege.

Under the later emperors, the soldiers were actually the governing power; they made and dethroned the emperors at their pleasure; and the right of suffrage, after it was given to the masses of the male population, was barren of any good influence, or any potential authority. They were ignorant, brutish, and careless of any thing except the public distribution of food and the excitement of the public games (*panem et circenses*), and they voted *en masse* for the demagogue who would promise them these in the greatest profusion. Thus pauperized and demoralized, the Roman voters only hastened the ruin of the empire, by their universal suffrage, and the voting places were the scenes of the most infamous crimes and outrages.

In some of the Grecian States, the experiment of general suffrage had been tried, with not much greater success. The *demos, i. e.* the people, who took part in voting, never comprised, however, a majority of the male population; yet it was a fickle, easily influenced mass, readily won to any enormity, cruelty, or injustice, by the artful harangues of the unprincipled aspirants for power. The form of government was almost constantly changing, and if by any chance, a wise and just man, such, for example, as Aristides, was elected to a high position, he was speedily deposed, by the jealousy of the fickle populace who had previously voted for him.

It is not strange that, with such examples before them, the people of Europe, in the Middle Ages, went back, with something like contentment, to a despotic and absolute government; and that they preferred the tyranny of a single ruler, to the variable whims of an excitable and fickle populace.

The first revolt from this was not in the direction of suffrage, but in the attempt of the feudal barons to wrest from the despot a portion of his power; and the necessity, on his part, for courting what were called then the common people, but were really what we now call the middle-class; the traders, ship-owners, and small but independent landholders.

It was long before any suffrage was thought of, except that of the nobles, or patrician class, in which were included abbots, bishops, who held large domains, and the higher clergy. The ballot, as a political institution of modern times, was first established, we think, in Scandinavia, though possibly some of the cantons of Switzerland might have voted in the small way, quite as early. In Hungary, it was in use earlier than in England, after the Norman conquest. Under the Saxons there was an assembly of notables (the Witenagemote), which was elected from the freeholders. Through all the countries of Europe, however, the principle has constantly prevailed, that the suffrage was only to accompany the possession of property. The argument has been, that it was only the man who possessed property which was liable to taxation, who had any claim to participate in the election of the representatives who were to act in voting, levying, and expending the moneys raised by taxation. In different countries there were differing views relative to the

amount of taxable property necessary to constitute a vote; in the Scandinavian States it was
smaller than elsewhere, but in all, until recently,
it must be real property, *i. e.* houses or lands.
Within the last forty years, in several of the
European States, the possession of personal property from which an income is derived, or the payment of a certain amount of annual rent, varying
in different countries, and in Great Britain, in
town and country, has been accepted, to some extent, as a substitute for the possession of real
estate.

There are instances in all these countries, where
single women, unmarried, or widows, possess large
landed estates. In Great Britain, these women,
possessing all the other requisite qualifications for
voters, except sex, have, in some instances,
claimed the right to vote, or, as was the case two
or three years since, petitioned Parliament to declare their right to the ballot. That, in a few
instances, during several centuries past, women
have voted on this ground is certain, but Parliament declined to sanction their use of the suffrage,
although their petition was respectfully received.

From the English point of view, we must confess that it is somewhat surprising that it should
have been refused. They had the qualifications
of voters, and it could hardly be claimed that
their property was fairly represented in Parliament by the votes of those of their male relatives

who might, or might not have a contingent interest in it; and voting in England did not necessarily require personal attendance at the polls, or at least, provision could have been made to avoid this, in the case of the limited number of female voters who would, at that time, have come under the provisions of the Reform law of 1832.

There must have been, in the minds of the British legislators, some reasons why they believed the privilege of voting on the property they possessed would be fraught with evils to these women, which would more than counterbalance any benefits which might be derivable from it to their property.

That these reasons existed also in other minds we know from the fact that there has been, and still is in England, a wide-spread feeling of dislike to the exercise of the suffrage by women, on the part of some of the most accomplished and intellectual women of the nation.

The author of " Woman's Rights and Duties," * herself a woman of high social position, and the most thorough culture, says, vol. I., page 390, of her work on this subject :—

" A question has occasionally been raised, and I believe by more than one writer, whether the right of voting be not unjustly withheld from women.

---

* " Woman's Rights and Duties considered with Relation to their Influence on Society, and on her own Condition." By a Woman, In two volumes. London: John W. Parker. 1840,

10

But it seems an almost conclusive objection to giving them the franchise, that by the very principle upon which it is bestowed, women are unfit for it, being always under influence. There are, no doubt, some cases of exception to that rule, but so there are to every other rule, by which persons are excluded from the right. Perhaps no other rule is so extensively true, as that women are under influence. But further, women have no *political* interests apart from those of men. The public measures that are taken, the restriction or taxes imposed on the community, do not affect them more than male subjects. In all such respects, the interests of the two sexes are identified. As citizens, therefore, they are sufficiently represented already. To give them the franchise would just double the number of voters, without introducing any new interest; and far from improving society, few things would tend more to dissever and corrupt it.

"But the disabilities or oppressions to which they are subject *as women*, could not be in any degree remedied by possessing the franchise. Interests of that description being exclusively female, would come into collision, not, as in other cases, with the interests of a class or a party, but with those of the whole male sex; and one of two things would happen. Either one sex would be arrayed in a sort of general hostility to the other, or they would be divided among themselves. Than the first, nothing could possibly be devised more disastrous to the condition of women. They would be utterly crushed; the old prejudices would be revived against their education, or their meddling with any thing but household duties. Every man of mature age would probably stipulate, on marrying, that his wife should forswear the use of the franchise, and all ideas connected with political influence, or the coarse and degrading contentions of the elections.

" If each sex were divided among themselves on particular questions, unprincipled men would endeavor to secure their election by creating female parties. Men of such character now disguise their personal interests, by affecting to adopt some measure popular with the mob, or suited only to the partial interests of some locality. They do not always desire to forward such measures; but they delude and corrupt the people by using them as pretexts. If women had the franchise, men would address themselves to the worst part of the sex, the most clamorous, and those least restrained by female decorum. The pretexts made use of to delude them would probably be injudicious, as measures, and condemned by the informed and reflecting of their own sex.

" It has been maintained throughout this work, that the interests of women can be served chiefly through opinion, though without denying that some legal enactments might also be required for certain special hardships. Can it be seriously imagined by any dispassionate woman, that those legal changes could be as well brought about by the power of now and then forcing an advocate into the legislature, as by their general influence in society, won through their own moral and mental deserts, and identified in men's minds with the influence which justice must always retain over their feelings?

"Conducted as elections now are—scenes of violence and tumult—women would be subject to every species of insult. It may be imagined that a remedy might be found for that; but what remedy would be found for the inflictions no law could reach or define, and which they would suffer at home for that exercise of their right which was opposed to the interests or prejudices of their male relations? Can it be supposed that the ballot would give any security? Surely not. Intimidation and bribery, already so mischievous, would be far more dangerous to the timidity and comparative poverty of women than they now are to men. And, educated as they are, their most honest decisions would be worse formed, even, than those of the other sex, defective as the political knowledge of the greater number is still allowed to be."

The force of this reasoning will be the better

appreciated, if we remember that at that time, in England, there was a strong pressure in favor of a limited female suffrage, and that it was this limited suffrage, based on freehold qualifications, and not comprising, probably, 30,000, or at the utmost, 40,000 votes in all, which she regarded as likely to prove so injurious to the women themselves. The same feeling has been manifested of late, on the subject, by women of high rank and position, who would have themselves been entitled to the suffrage, even before the passage of the recent Reform law, which, though still requiring a property qualification, has greatly enlarged the number of voters.

But suffrage in England, as in all the countries of Europe, rests on an entirely different basis from that which obtains in the United States. In the early history of this country, various qualifications were required. Among many of the colonies, at first, a religious test, more or less strict, was established. In the Quinnipiac, or New Haven Colony, no man could vote who was not a member of the church; in Massachusetts, Plymouth, Connecticut, and, we believe, New Hampshire, voters were required to be members of the parish, that is, nominally, and perhaps really, attendants upon the established church of those States (the Congregational), as well as freeholders. Maine and Vermont were not then distinct colonies. In Rhode Island they were only required to be freeholders. In New York there was a property qualification, and, for a time, a religious test, also. Pennsylvania required the freehold, as did Maryland and Delaware. Virginia only granted suffrage, with some vexatious exceptions, to those who were members of the Church of England, and were also proprietors. In the Carolinas the property qualification was high, and the number of voters small. In Georgia, from the beginning, there was a larger liberty, though a small property qualification was at first obligatory.

The principles enunciated in the Declaration of Independence, had they been understood as they now are, would have led at once to the establishment of universal suffrage, inasmuch as the assertion that "governments instituted among men derive their just powers from the consent of the governed," if it means any thing, affirms that the consent of all the governed, those possessing no property, as well as those having an interest in the stability and righteousness of the government, is necessary to the existence of a rightful government.

Taken in this sense, the proposition is not true of all governments, or of any one government now existing, or which ever did exist. As Dr. Bushnell has well said, "No fifth part of our own people, in fact, ever consented to the government, whether formally, or by implication. No new statute passed, ever had the consent of more than a very small fraction of the people. Minors, women, invalids, absentees, voters of the opposing party—take away all these, and how much of consent is left? If the major vote of such as have the ballot supposes general consent, then it must be by a legal fiction so great, that it would scarcely be greater without any vote at all."

Nor, can this affirmation of the Declaration be understood in that other sense often put upon it that, "the consent of the governed" implies the surrender of individual rights to society as a return for its protection; for this view, besides being directly opposed to the sentiment which the authors of the Declaration were seeking to impress upon the people, is wholly untrue in point of fact, since the rights and powers of society were not in any sense the powers of individuals.

In neither sense did it exert any considerable effect upon the colonies which adopted it; no material changes being made in their suffrage laws for many years after, and, when made, being the result of other causes and influences. It was, in short, one of those "glittering generalities" of which the late Mr. Choate was accustomed to speak, and which Mr. Jefferson was such an adept at incorporating into his appeals, protests, declarations, and addresses, to tickle the popular ear, and give utterance to an apparent truth, when really only announcing a plausible fallacy. For a variety of causes, and with a remarkable lack of perception of the ultimate results of their action, the suffrage has been granted to one class after another, until, in some of the States, there are now only women, minors, Indians not taxed, convicts, aliens who have not been naturalized, idiots and lunatics, and transient persons, who are not permitted to exercise it. In some of the States there still lingers the ghost of a property qualification; in others, there is an educational qualification, but so low as to be nearly worthless.

Under the pending (fifteenth) amendment to the Constitution of the United States, negroes and persons of African descent will gain the right of suffrage in those States where they do not already possess it; and, should the decision be made in our higher courts, that the Chinese and Japanese are citizens and liable to taxation, they will form a large addition within a few years to our voting population. That we have been injudicious in thus extending the privilege of suffrage, and should, if it were possible, restrict instead of further enlarging it, will appear, we think, when we have considered what suffrage is, whether it inheres in any class or classes of men, and from whence comes the power of conferring it.

CHAPTER XV.

In considering what suffrage is, we must first look at the constitution of society; for on this depends the necessity or propriety of suffrage. About the period of the American Revolution, the political ideas of Rousseau, Voltaire, Diderot, D'Alembert, and other European democrats, were promulgated, and exerted a powerful influence on the minds of the statesmen of the new republic, then just emerging from its colonial condition. Their theory was, in substance, that the perfection of human liberty and equality was to be found in the savage state, and that, in that condition, all human beings, or at least all men, were in a condition of perfect equality—no one possessing any greater rights than another; and that it was possible to rear a State which should have for its basis this condition of the perfect equality of all men; and, that this State being made up of the ag gregation of individuals, each of whom relinquished a portion of his prerogatives to the State, it thus acquired the power of government and control, through the consent of all the governed. This theory imbued the minds of our early statesmen, and led them to seek the establishment of a **new** republic on these newly-discovered principles but they soon found that their theories were impracticable, and contented themselves with stating them in general terms, while following in actual practice other, older, and sounder doctrines.

This theory contained two great fallacies, which it surprises us to know were not detected by the clear and vigorous intellects of those days, viz., that of considering the individual the unit of society, and ignoring the family, the true unit of both society and government, from the creation to the present time; and that of asserting the equality of all men, in any other sense than that they were equally human beings, when even those who uttered this declaration, would not have admitted that, either in civil, political, or social rights, the savage Indian, the degraded Hottentot, or the still more degraded Bushman, or Andaman Islander, was his peer.

The great truth, that the family, and not the individual, is the *unit* of all human society and of all government, has a wider significance than has generally been bestowed upon it;* for it follows, that both society and government being formed by an aggregation of families, and not of individuals,

---

* For an able and satisfactory development of this doctrine, see "The Law of Love, and Love as a Law." By Mark Hopkins, D. D., LL. D., President of Williams College, pp. 282, *et seq.*

The writer takes great pleasure in acknowledging his obligations to Rev. Dr. Hopkins, not only for his suggestions on this but on other subjects connected with this work.

the latter, as individuals, do not relinquish, and can not have any distinct rights, of which the government or community takes possession; and it also follows, that, in all governmental acts, whether voting, holding office, making or executing laws, arresting, trying, and punishing, or acquitting those charged with crime, those performing these various duties must act in a representative capacity,—doing these things for those whom they represent,—as guardians, trustees, or deputies. Applying this principle to the exercise of suffrage, it is plain that each family needs, at the utmost, but a single representative, its proper head and father, who represents the entire interests of the family, including himself, his wife, and his children, if he has any. Should there be adult sons, they may have a constructive right to a vote, since they are making preparations to become themselves heads of other families. Adult daughters can have no such claim, since, if they remain at home, they are sufficiently represented by their father; if they marry and leave their former homes, they can be represented by their husbands, the heads of new families. The case of single women, living in households by themselves, and possessing property, is exceptional, but might be provided for by another arrangement, of which we shall by and by speak. But society, as thus constituted, has the right, unquestionably, to limit suffrage still further, though with cer tain restrictions. It may require, for instance, that no head of a family, or prospective head of a family, shall become a voter till he has arrived at the age of twenty-one years; that no one shall exercise this right, who is under the influence or control of others; no one who has been convicted of crime; no one who is an idiot, or who is insane; no alien, who has not signified in such way as it may prescribe, his intention of becoming a citizen, or who has not resided a prescribed period in the country; no person who does not possess the ability to read the language of the country, and its fundamental laws. The justice and propriety of such requirements will be obvious to all; with the exception of the mental disqualifications, these conditions are all within the capacity of every good citizen to attain, either sooner or later.

But taking this view of the subject, society would not be justified in excluding a head of a family from the suffrage on the ground of his poverty, unless there had been a fully understood compact from the beginning of its organic existence, that there should be a fixed limit of property as the minimum, which should entitle the representative of a family to a vote; it would be still more unjustifiable, if the privilege of voting should be confined to those possessing landed estates only; or to those professing any particular form of religious faith; or to those of a particular color or race, when they possessed the other requisite qualifications.

There is another class of restrictions, whose justice will be evident to all. Where the votes of a community or State would decide the question of the propriety of declaring war with some other State or nation, it would be obviously unjust that those should turn the scale by their votes who could not do the fighting, or furnish the sinews of war; on a question of heavy taxation of property for some specific purpose, even were that purpose for the benefit of the majority of the community, it would not be just that those who had no property to be taxed, should, by their votes, overpower the tax-payers, and take their property from them against their will. Again, it would be unjust that those who have manifested and still entertain hostile sentiments toward the government, and desire its overthrow, should be permitted to vote.

There is still another question in regard to suffrage, viz., whether property and vested rights ought not to be represented, as property ? There are large amounts of property, especially in our large cities, in the hands of non-residents, aliens, minors, single women, and widows, which is taxed but not represented; there are, also, colleges, universities, and other institutions, trust companies, banking and insurance companies, and other corporations, which have no distinct representation, though obliged to pay taxes. In regard to the latter classes, it may be claimed, indeed, that they have their paid advocates in the municipal or legislative bodies, who attend to their interests, sometimes to the detriment of their other constituents; but there is quite as much reason for the representation of property, as such, as for the representation of families; and in the large cities quite as much danger of unjust and oppressive taxation of this unrepresented property, as of unjust and oppressive legislation in regard to families.

Various modes of remedying this evil have been suggested; one is, the permission of proxy votes for the unrepresented property; another, the admission of a certain number of representatives of this property and these vested rights, into the municipal councils and legislature; a third, the making the representation of property the ground of the election of one branch of the legislature or municipal government. Whether either of these plans would answer the purpose, is doubtful. In the only case, which specially concerns us in this connection, the lack of representation of the property of unmarried women and widows, the number is so small, that, except in the event of a distinct election of one of the branches of the municipal or State legislature by the property vote alone, they could not exert a sufficient influence in favor of any one candidate to put him under any especial obligation to protect their interests. They would be as safe, so far as their property was concerned, in the hands of legislators elected without their vote, but whose constituents they would be, and over whom they might be able to exercise a strong personal influence.

There would be also a reluctance on the part of educated and refined women to proclaim their possession of property by coming to the polls, associated as they must be there, with many men of the rougher classes, not numerous enough themselves to make their influence felt as a restraint, and subjected, as they would be, to discourtesy and insult.

It would be manifestly unjust to grant this property suffrage to one class of the now unrepresented property-holders, and withhold it from the others, who are equally sufferers from the want of it. If it be wrong that single women possessing property should not be allowed to vote, it is equally wrong that the property of non-residents, aliens, minors, and other classes, should continue unrepresented. Yet it would be a difficult matter to arrange a satisfactory mode of representing all these classes, which would give them any really potential voice in the imposition of taxes.

In thus advocating suffrage on the double basis of the family and of property, we are aware that we have advanced beyond the position occupied by many able writers on political science. Some contend that property alone should have the right of representation, or in other words, that those only should have the suffrage who have a property interest in the preservation of good government. It must be confessed that there is much force in this position. Whether it should be so or not, it is a well-known fact that the possession of property gives a man the strongest possible interest in the maintenance of a just and good government; and those legislatures chosen only by the votes of men possessing a freehold qualification, have been uniformly of a higher character, and more just and careful of the interests of all the classes they represented, than those who were chosen by a promiscuous rabble of voters, not one-third of whom had any interest whatever in the preservation of good government. "Manhood suffrage," as it is termed, the permission for every man, not an idiot, lunatic, or criminal (and these are not always excepted), to participate in the work of choosing our rulers, legislators, and judges, is not a measure which commends itself to good and thoughtful citizens. Why should an ignorant, drunken brute, who has no interest in the government, unless it is to enable him the better to escape the just reward of his crimes, a foreigner perhaps, and entirely destitute of any knowledge of our country, its laws, or its institutions, be permitted to participate in the election of a judge, a legislator, a governor, or a president? He has no property to be protected, no interests which will suffer from bad government, and he is influenced and controlled in his vote, by the keeper of the liquor-shop where he obtains his whisky, or by the demagogue in whose pay that liquor-dealer is.

Other political economists insist that that is the best government where there is no voting; that, given an able and just ruler, with an administrative council, composed of good men, intelligent, and desirous of doing right, and the right of petition bestowed upon the people, a government would be better administered, and all classes better cared for, than in a so-called free government.

There can be little doubt that, admitting these conditions, the community generally would be happier and better; but the risk that, when intrusted with absolute power, the ruler and his council might not be so just and upright as they were supposed (since the possession of irresponsible power so often results in tyranny and oppression even in men of the best intentions), is so great, that few would be willing to exchange their present freedom for it.

But that suffrage, either limited or universal, is the best means of electing or controlling the officers of a government, is not so certain, after all. Its machinery is necessarily cumbrous in a great State; its results uncertain, and liable to be influenced by demagogues and designing men, who seek control for their own evil purposes. Where it is universal, or what we term so, embracing about one-fifth of the entire population, viz., all males of adult age, except aliens, idiots, lunatics, and convicts, the vote of the lowest and most worthless vagrant, who is marched up to the polls to do the bidding of his political master, weighs just as much, and often neutralizes, the vote of the worthiest and most respected citizen. More than this, it has proved hitherto an impossibility, in our large cities, to prevent fraudulent voting, both in the way of the same voter casting his ballot at several polling-places, and of persons voting under false names, or when they were disqualified. It does not admit of a doubt that, at the last Presidential election, from ten to fifteen per cent. of the vote was fraudulent, in some of the States. The further extension of the suffrage would only aggravate this already terrible political evil.

The method of selecting all officers of government by competition, adopted in China, would seem to be, under proper regulations, decidedly preferable to that by suffrage. All persons who are desirous of attaining to any position in the State, enter, in youth, the public schools or universities, and are promoted, according to their attainments in literature, science, art, and morals, from one school to another, by rigid and careful examinations by papers; when, by successive promotions, they have reached the three highest schools of the empire, they enter into competition for any vacancies in positions under government, and from these are promoted still higher by successive competitions. The adoption of such a course for the selection of all our State officers, legislators, officers of the general government, &c., would secure men of high qualifications, and would not be liable to the same objections which exist to our more clumsy and corrupt method of suffrage.

Let us now briefly review the positions of this chapter, since their bearing is so important on the question of suffrage.

We have, we think, demonstrated that the *family*, and not the *individual*, is the unit of all organized society and government; that this being the case, there is no such thing as an *individual right of suffrage*, as no one individual, male or female, has contributed any thing or relinquished any right to society, which gives him or her a claim to a vote as an equivalent. That if suffrage is a right at all, it inheres in the head of a family, as the representative of that component of society; that it might, by a liberal construction, be extended, also, to the adult sons of the family, inasmuch as they are, prospectively, heads of other families; but not to the wife or adult daughters, inasmuch as, if they remain at home, they are represented by the husband and father, as the head of the household; and if the daughters marry, they are represented by their husbands as heads of other households. We have also attempted to show, that if there be any other right of suffrage than this, it must inhere in such *property* as is unrepresented by male heads of families, such, for instance, as the property of single women or widows living by themselves, aliens, non-residents, minors, and persons under the care of trustees, and perhaps, also, corporations. We have suggested several ways in which such property might be represented effectively, have shown that there were serious difficulties in the way of accomplishing such representation, and that in the case of women holding property, unless there were a separate branch of the State or municipal legislature, elected solely by the property vote, their participation in a general election would be unfair, and unproductive of sufficient advantage to compensate for its trouble and annoyances. We have also considered other theories of suffrage, and have shown what a cumbrous and imperfect measure it is, and how liable to fraud and abuse ; and have briefly described the method of competition by examination for office as practiced by the Chinese, as an available and desirable substitute for suffrage. The bearing of these several points on the question of woman-suffrage will be more fully seen as we continue the discussion of that topic.

CHAPTER XVI.

THE suffrage laws of the United States seem to have been based on no well-defined principle, but to have been the outgrowth of circumstances, without any clear comprehension of the character of the liberties they were granting. In some instances important franchises have been conferred on classes not qualified to use them judiciously, merely to appease a popular and unreasoning clamor. The suffrage, originally, in the older States, the privilege of freeholders only, was subsequently granted to those who performed military duty, and, in some States, to those who were members of a volunteer fire department, if of suitable age. It was next conferred on those who had served as volunteers in the war of 1812, the Mexican war, and later, the recent civil war, where they were not, on other grounds, voters. In a fit of democratic generosity, the freehold qualification was swept away in most of the States, and all white male citizens, natives of the country, or naturalized under United States laws, which required five years' residence and three years' declaration of intention, except convicts, lunatics, and idiots, were permitted to vote under certain restrictions of residence. A provision was made by the Constitution in regard to the Southern States, by which a Congressional district should be deemed to have the requisite population, when the white and free colored population were added to three-fifths " of all other persons " (the constitutional euphemism for *slaves*), to make up the necessary number to entitle the territory to a representative. Thus, in one sense, the Southern vote was increased by three-fifths of its slave population, although these cast no vote, and literally, none was cast for them. The late civil war abolished this method of increasing the congressional representation of the South, by abolishing slavery. A considerable number of former voters at the South were at first disfranchised in consequence of their participation in the insurrection, but by successive amnesties they were nearly all restored to their civil rights, and by the action of the constitutional conventions of the reconstructed States, most of them were permitted to vote and hold office again. The emancipated slaves had in many instances contributed all in their power to the success of the national government; nearly 300,000 of them had borne arms, and others in various ways had given aid and comfort to the national soldiers. It was proposed to grant them the suffrage as a compensation for their patriotic sacrifices; and so earnest and loud was the popular clamor to grant this privilege to all the adult men of color in the South, that an amendment to the Constitution was passed by Congress and ratified by the States, and provision made to this effect in all the new constitutions of the reconstructed States. The measure, though prompted by the best of motives, was injudicious; there was some reason for according the privilege to those colored men who had been in the Union service, either as soldiers, teamsters, or servants, though even they were scarcely qualified by their intelligence for the exercise of so important a right; but to extend the same privilege to all the plantation negroes, before they had acquired any knowledge in regard to the government, or were able to understand the Constitution, was exceedingly unwise. They were, of course, very liable to be influenced, in regard to their vote, by designing men, one of the worst evils of a free suffrage. It might be said, indeed, in partial justification of this measure, that they were generally very nearly as intelligent as the poor whites of the South, who already possessed the right of suffrage, but two wrongs do not make one right, and the remedy should rather have been the establishment of an educational test, and the refusal of the privilege to all, black or white, who did not come up to it.

But the popular heart was still unsatisfied, and now the cry was for the abolition of all distinctions of race or color, as a ground of withholding the privilege of suffrage throughout the Union. The amendment to the Constitution prescribing this will undoubtedly be ratified. So far as the negroes in the Northern States are concerned, the measure is not seriously objectionable, while such facilities exist for conferring the privilege upon ignorant and often degraded foreigners,—as the negroes are generally the better citizens of the two; but, with the near prospect of a vast influx of Chinese, mainly of the lowest class, who can, in five years at the most, become citizens and voters, we must think this further extension of the franchise should have been better guarded.

The advocates of universal suffrage in the United States have now only women and minors left upon whom they can confer the right; and there are those who argue that, having swallowed and digested every inch of the camel, we should not so carefully strain out the gnat.

To this reasoning we can not agree; if we have done wrong in the past, if we have conferred privileges on those who were unworthy of them, or who, if not unworthy, were not entitled to them, it does not follow that we should continue to err in the same or any other direction. If there is but little left to contend for, that little, if right, should be as valiantly defended as if it were more, since it is *all* that we can retain.

We are prepared, then, to consider the reasons why, in this country, suffrage should not be granted to women, as women; a different question, be it observed, from that which agitates the public mind in England, the question there being, whether the suffrage should be granted to some women, not as women, but as holders of property.

These reasons may be divided for convenience sake into four classes : those concerning the polit ical, social, intellectual, and moral relations.

Beginning with the political aspect of the question, we may remark, in the first place, that woman has no need of the suffrage, since she is already represented in the legislative bodies, whether State or municipal, as well as by the officers of the State and nation. The family basis of representation, which, however unwisely it may be extended, is the true basis, makes the husband and father the true representative of his entire household, and the intelligent American voter generally feels that the responsibility appertaining to this representative character rests upon him. The members of our municipal, State, and national legislatures forgetful, as they too often are, of other interests confided to them, or of duties required of them by their constituents, are seldom, we might almost say, never, unmindful of the wants and requirements of the women whom they represent quite as truly as they do the men of their respective districts. Whatever may have been the case in the past, it is certain that, at the present day, women makes no reasonable request of our legislators which

11   Q

passes unheeded; on the contrary, the danger is rather that of excess in their liberality in gratifying the wishes of woman than of denying her what are her just rights. In all directions in which it is in the power of a legislature to improve the condition of woman, she has but to ask to receive. This general sentiment of tenderness and regard for the sex on the part of men, both in high and in low station, is invaluable to women. It is their greatest protection and safeguard, and it would be the greatest of misfortunes to them were it to be, by any means, blunted and lowered in its tone.

But there is another power which women exert, independent of this general deference which they command, the power of personal influence, not only over voters, but over their elected representatives. An earnest, determined woman, possessing those graces of person or intellect, which fit her to influence and control men, can carry almost any measure on which she has set her heart, over every obstacle, in either the State or national legislature. Take the case of Miss Vinnie Ream, who is engaged in making a statue, for the Capitol, of President Lincoln. Miss Ream may prove a sculptor of remarkable ability, and her statue may be, when completed, the eighth wonder of the world, as a work of art; on this point we have no right to express an opinion, since it is not yet completed; but whether it be so or not, one thing is certain, that it was not the consideration of her extraordinary abilities as an artist which led to her obtaining this commission, for she had done nothing worthy of note, and of the few busts or figures in plaster which she had executed, the members of Congress, either senators or representatives, had generally no knowledge, and many of them were incompetent to judge, if they had seen them. No! it was her daring, young girl as she was, in proposing to undertake such a work; her determined personal canvass of the members of Congress for their votes, and the magnetic influence of her powers of fascination over grave and venerable senators, and intelligent representatives, which enabled her to procure an order for a statue, more liberal in its terms and more remarkable for its perfect confidence in the, as yet untried, ability of the artist, than any commission of the sort in modern times. Instances of this power of woman's personal influence in political matters are innumerable. Who has not heard of the beneficent efforts of Mrs. Husband, during the war, in procuring from President Lincoln the commutation of sentence, and often the pardon of, soldiers condemned to die under the barbarous military laws? Who does not know of the success of the infamous Mrs. Cobb as a pardon-broker during the late administration?

In the second place, the exercise of the suffrage by woman would be an attempt to make suffrage individual instead of representative, and so against the natural order of things. The other extensions of the voting privilege, to which we have referred, however injudicious they may have been, did not materially interfere with its representative character, as based on the family as the *unit* of society; but this would inaugurate an entirely different principle; the right of the individual, as such, to participate in the government, a claim incompatible with the organization of society, and subversive of its best interests. In all large communities and States, the principle of representation must obtain in the government. The executive represents and is responsible to, not merely the party which elected him, but the whole people of the State or community. The member of Congress, or of the State legislature, represents all the people of his district, and it is his duty to further their interests so far as is compatible with justice; and every voter who casts his ballot, represents, on an average, five people who do not and can not vote. Abrogate this principle of representation, and let each voter represent only himself or herself, and you loosen the bond which holds society together; the male voter will say at once : " I have no need to consider anybody's interest but my own; my wife, my sister, my daughter, may desire to see a certain man elected, or a certain measure voted for, which will prove beneficial to their interests; but they must vote for it themselves; I shall consult my own interests solely." The representative elected by the votes of those who exercise the suffrage solely for the gratification of their own whims, will cease to regard his representative character as essential; he has no longer to look upon the families of his district as his constituents, or to feel a responsibility to them. They are merely an aggregation of individuals who cast their votes for him, because he was nominated, and not because they expected to hold him accountable for his acts, and he must make the most of his opportunity, for he may not have another. Hence will come rings, corruption, public plunder, and subserviency to great corporations, to an extent far beyond that which has already awakened the indignation of the public.

In the third place, by woman suffrage women will gain nothing, while they will lose much. From what we have already said, it will be seen that they will lose all the advantages which they now possess from the representative character of the suffrage, all that chivalric regard for their interests, which now prompts our legislators to grant all their reasonable and some of their unreasonable requests, as a matter of course; all that their personal influence is now able to effect, and all that is gained now from family, in the place of individual interest in the ballot.

Women would be, in almost all communities, a

minority at the polls; there would be so many who could not, and so many who would not, vote, that it would be remarkable if their vote ever exceeded that of men. It would hardly be possible that, in any case, even in matters concerning their own interests, they would all vote alike. They would be likely to be divided, as their husbands, brothers, and fathers were between the two parties, perhaps unequally, but never to such an extent as to enable them to rule or control either party. Generally, they would have to vote for men, often for men whom they greatly disliked, for legislators, or State, or national officers. They might, and doubtless often would, contribute to place in power some unprincipled demagogue, but very rarely would they be able to rally votes enough to succeed in electing an upright and honest man; they might, at times, be allowed, as a special favor, to elect one or two of their own sex to the legislature, or to some petty office; but such an election would prove any thing but a favor to the unfortunate candidate; in a hopeless minority, so far as any action in relation to her sex was concerned, all her prestige as a woman gone, without influence or position, yet expected to do for her sex what chivalry had previously prompted men to do, it would be strange if the poor representative of women's suffrage did not very early resign her seat, in an uncontrollable fit of home-sickness.

Naturally enough, the measures which concerned women would be referred to them in a legislature in which there were a few (there never would be many) female members; but their power to effect their passage would be infinitely less than if they were not members of the legislative body. In such a body, and as a member of it, the most eloquent of women would find her oratory out of place, and her pleas would fall cold and dead. All legislation in the interests of women would be paralyzed, and their progress in the attainment of their legal rights arrested, and postponed for a full half-century.

In the fourth place, there is no possible plea in justification of woman's intrusion into the realm of political action. The admission of some of the classes which have latterly received the privilege of the suffrage might be justified as an act of self-defense; the foreigner, after a certain period of residence and naturalization, might plead in favor of his admission to the suffrage, that he had property to protect, that the attitude of the native-born citizens toward him was one of hostility, and that he must have the ballot for his own protection. In like manner, the men of color might ask for the suffrage to protect them from the encroachments and oppressions of the whites, and the disfranchised citizens of the South might seek it to save them from apprehended aggressions on the part of the blacks.

But the relations of men and women can never be, to any extent, such as under ordinary circumstances to array them in hostility to each other, or make one fear the aggressions of the other.

Mother, wife, sister, or daughter; one or other, and perhaps more than one, of these relations every woman holds to the men around her ; and, if he would, man can not make any laws or take any measures seriously detrimental to their interests They are bone of his bones, and flesh of his flesh and if he is made their representative and trusted to act for their interests, he will, from the sheer selfishness of relationship, do his best for them. But separate the two sexes; let man understand that woman is determined to stand for herself, and neither desires nor needs his assistance, and how soon would an antagonism be engendered, which many waters could not quench. All such interference with the laws of nature, and the relations in which the All-wise Creator has placed his creatures to each other, can only be productive of evil and misery.

In the fifth place, the exercise of the privilege of suffrage would not be, and, in the nature of the case, could not be a remedy for any one of the wrongs or evils from which women now suffer.

We have all heard of the pope's bull against the comet, and we remember how the comet kept on its way undisturbed by the fulminations of his holiness.   The comet moved in obedience to natural laws, over which the pope's missives could have no control. Precisely similar is the case of the principal wrongs of which women complain, and which are, undoubtedly, real wrongs: low wages—we might say, starvation wages—too many hours work in the day, want of employment, over-crowding in many branches of business, and, perhaps, also, more stringent enactments against broth-els, seduction, &c.

In a former chapter we have shown that the evils complained of in regard to employments were not, in any respect, subjects for legislation; that the laws of supply and demand must regulate the prices of labor as of every thing else, and that they must be remedied, if remedied at all, by an increase of intelligence which should lift up a con-siderable number to a higher plane, where the demand was greater than the supply; by trades-unions, which would enable women to control the price of their labor; by the suppression of the practice of underbidding, both by the poorest class of partially skilled working-women in the cities, and by women in the country, who, having homes and food furnished, undertake this kind of work to supply themselves with a little pocket-money; and by co-operation, which should enable them to obtain food and rents cheaper, and, perhaps, to be-come their own employers. It is obvious that the suffrage is not required for any of these purposes. As to the legal enactments sought, is it not plain

11*

to every thoughtful mind, that the probability is a thousand-fold. stronger of obtaining the desired legislation speedily, by appealing to existing or soon-to-be-assembled legislatures, and asking for the enactment of such statutes as are needful, on the ground of good order, good morals, and the moral and social rights of women, than by attempting, what would prove a perfect failure, the election of a sufficient number of women to any legislature, to pass, by their votes, the desired enactments?

The arguments which we have adduced will, we believe, be sufficient to show the inexpediency of women's suffrage as a political measure.

CHAPTER XVII.

THE objections to woman-suffrage on social grounds are numerous and important. If women are to vote, they must either be conversant with the political questions of the day, and able to form an intelligent opinion on them, or they must vote under the leading and guidance of others, and thus become the dupes and prey of selfish and unprincipled politicians. In the one case they will become partisans; zealous, earnest, indefatigable in their way, but, alas, too forgetful of that womanly modesty and grace which is the highest ornament of womanhood. If now it should happen, as it often would, that the wife should, from conviction or from prejudice, adopt the views, principles, and candidates of one party, and the husband those of another, and both were positive and decided in their opinions, what bickerings, what acrid debates, what bitter feelings would be engendered in the family circle! How unseemly would be such contests in the presence of their children, if they had any! And, how often would it break up the peace of families, and lead to separation, or, at least, to permanent estrangement! Again, as Dr. Bushnell has well observed: "The struggle (of a great

political campaign) is a trial even for men, that
sometimes quite overturns their self-mastery, and
totally breaks down the strength both of their
principles and their bodies. And yet if we en-
large the contest, as we must when we bring in
women, it will be manifold more intense than now.
Hitherto, it has been an advantage to be going
into battle in our suffrages with a full half, and
that the best half morally, as a corps of reserve,
left behind, so that we may fall back on this
quiet element or base several times a day, and
always at night, and recompose our courage and
settle again our mental and moral equilibrium. Now
it is proposed that we have no reserve any longer,
that we go into our conflicts taking our women
with us, all to be kept heating in the same fire for
weeks or months together, without interspacings
of rest or cooling times of composure. We are
to be as much more excited, of course, as we can
be, and the women are, of course, to be as much more
excited than we, as they are more excitable. Let
no man imagine—as we see to be the way of many
—that our women are going into these encounters
to be just as quiet or as little nerved as now, when
they stay in the rear unexcited, letting us come
back to them often and recover our reason. They
are (to be) no more mitigators now, but instigators
rather, sweltering in the same fierce heats and com
motions, only more fiercely stirred than we.
What we take by first-hand impulse, they take by

PRESIDENTIAL CAMPAIGN DEMONSTRATION.

exaggeration. And, accordingly, it will be seen, that where we are simply at red-heat, they are at white; that where we deprecate, they hate; that where we touch the limits of reason, they touch the limits of excess; that, where we are impetuous in a cause, they are uncontrollable in it. We know how, as men, to be moderated in part by self-moderation, even as ships by their helms, in all great storms at sea. For the other part, we had women kept in moderation by their element, even as ships in harbor lie swinging by their anchors; but now we get even less of help from them than they do from us. I do not mean by this, that women do not show as brave self-keeping often as men, but that going more by feeling than men, they feel every thing more intensely, and with more liabilities to excess. They make more of their idols, too, than men do, raise more false halos about them, and even have it as a kind of virtue to bear defeat badly in their cause. Hard pushed by adversaries, they almost certainly count them personal enemies. It is not that some hysterical, over-delicate women are prone to such exaggerations of sensibility, but that, like our Southern women, or the tough city mothers of Sparta, they too commonly allow their passions to get heated, and call it their righteous sentiment. To conceive our whole popular mass, both male and female, seething at once in the same vortex of party commotion—ten women taking hold of one man, to at once possess and dispossess him in their higher key of excitement—is no pleasant thing to contemplate. But the specially sad thing of it is, not that men will be heated and put to a strain, and made coarse, possibly violent, but that women will be. Men are made to be coarse, after a certain masculine fashion, but there is no such masculine fashion for women."

These storms of passion, which must come very frequently in the life of every woman of the educated class who gives herself up to politics, can not pass without leaving their sad traces both on her social character, and on her countenance. There is no hatred so implacable, especially with women, as a political hatred, no bitterness so intense as that which is gendered by political strife. How fearful must be the effects of this upon neighborhoods, where old friends will no more speak to each other, but pass those whom they formerly loved with a scowl of hate, or a look of contempt, and where often they will seek the injury of those once dear to them as the apple of their eye.

That we are not exaggerating these results, will be evident, if we recall the conduct of women of the highest social position in the South, during the late war. Women there did not vote, it is true ; but they became fully absorbed in the political questions at issue, and entered into them with such a violent spirit, that those who had formerly been the most gentle and amiable of their sex, manifested a temper almost fiendish in its bitterness, and this, not only toward the soldiers and the people of the North, against whom it might be supposed that their wrath would be most naturally directed, but they were even more bitter and vindictive toward Southern men and women who espoused the side of the Union. Women, formerly gentle and refined, gloried in wearing charms, rings, &c., made from the bones of the hated Yankees slain in battle, or murdered by guerrillas; they often expressed their desire, which some of them put in practice, to kill some of them for themselves, and the Southern gallant could bring no surer passport to the affections of the woman whom he sought to win, than the evidence that he had killed a Yankee.

Toward Southern Union women, this bitter hate manifested itself in all possible ways. We have now in mind the sufferings of a noble Christian woman in one of the Southern cities, a lady whose wealth, culture, refinement, genial manners and large-hearted liberality, had enabled her to maintain for years the highest social position. To be on terms of intimacy with her, had been long a privilege for which the best families of the city were ready to strive; but at the beginning of the war she was unflinchingly loyal and Union-loving; and very soon all her old friends, with but two or three exceptions, fell off; her house, once thronged

with visitors, was now deserted; as she walked
along the streets, her former friends passed her
with averted gaze or carefully drew aside their
clothing, lest it should be tainted by contact with
her; scurrilous and abusive notes, penned by
female hands, were constantly sent to her, and
attacks upon her character and reputation of the
most cruel nature were made by female contributors to the public prints. The fences and walls
of her dwelling were covered, night after night,
with the most outrageous abuse, and her life was
more than once in peril. She persisted, however,
in her tender care for Union soldiers, sick, wounded, and in prison in the city; but even since the
war, the old hatred ever and anon breaks out, and
of all her professed female friends before the war,
she can now scarcely number one whose attachment has been unfaltering. And this was but one
instance of hundreds occurring throughout the
South.

Does the picture disgust and shock you, fair
sisters? Remember that human nature (and
woman nature) is much the same everywhere, and
that under the influence of ungovernable political
passion, in the heated contests that are coming,
you, too, much as you may now loathe the thought
of such a thing, might be betrayed into similar
excesses. Hazael (2 Kings, viii. 7–15) was horror-
stricken when Elisha told him of the terrible
cruelties he would commit, and exclaimed, un-

doubtedly in the honesty of his heart, "Is thy servant a dog, that he should do this thing?" And yet he was even more brutal and cruel than the prophet had predicted he would be. Nero, according to Roman historians, was, in his youth, of so gentle and amiable a disposition, that he wept and shrunk back from signing the death-warrant of a notorious offender; yet such was his subsequent career of cruelty and crime, that his name has become the synonym of infamy.

The effect of these terrible excitements, these whirlwinds of passion, upon the general temper, can not be other than evil. The human heart thus torn and rent by the tempest never regains its former serenity. The temper will be fitful, and at intervals of constantly increasing frequency; outbursts of passion will occur which will cause intense suffering to all around them, as well as to the unhappy victims of passion themselves. Walter Savage Landor, the poet and essayist, united to an almost womanly tenderness and gentleness this tendency to be betrayed into fits of ungovernable passion, and with increasing years these paroxysms grew more frequent, till he became a terror to all his friends. Nor will this life of intense excitement, with its coarse and brutalizing influences, be less marked in its effect upon the face, the air, the voice, and the manner, of the women who have been subjected to it. As well might we expect the oak, scarred and blighted by the lightnings of heaven, to show no traces of the thunderbolt's course, as that faces, once fair, but so often visited by the fiery storm of passion, should retain no marks of the tempests that have passed over them. The face of an actress, especially of a tragedian, speedily shows the traces of the passion she has successfully simulated, and it requires all the resources of the cosmetic art to prevent them from becoming so manifest as to impair her capacity for her profession. How much more difficult will it be to hide the wave-marks of real passion !

The charm of beauty, that grace of features which we call *fair*, will disappear very speedily under the cares and violence of political strife, and women will acquire a bolder, and, at the same time, a more care-worn expression ; they will have a sharper, more wiry voice, modulated upon a higher key, and that " lean and hungry " look which has been the characteristic of politicians since the time of Cassius.

The blush of modesty, the timid, half-frightened expression which is, to all right-thinking men, a higher charm than the most perfect, self-conscious beauty, will disappear, and in the place of it we shall have hard, self-reliant, bold faces, out of which all the old loveliness will have faded, and naught remain save the look of power and talent, blighted like that of a fallen angel.

Were women to vote, they would feel a necessity to have political papers of their own, devoted to the feminine side of political life, and these, of course, of differing politics to suit the differing tastes of their patrons, and, of course, edited by women. Our present political papers, in the heat of a party conflict, are none too decorous; their gross personalities, slanders, and diatribes on the candidates and their supporters, often make a man of any sensibility regret that he ever learned to read; but, judging from the few political papers hitherto edited by women, as well as from the tendency of the sex, when enraged, to indulge in the most severe and abusive language, we may safely conclude that the worst specimens of the political newspaper hitherto, would be models of decency, when compared with the sheets which would then grace our tables.

There would be, indeed, one door of hope. It has been proposed, and it is said the experiment has been tried with success, as a cure of habitual drunkenness, that the drunkard should be shut up in a room saturated with the fumes of alcoholic liquors, that his clothing and bedding should be soaked with whisky, and all his food and drink so thoroughly permeated with it, that, for the space of, say two weeks, the stench of it should be constantly in his nostrils. By this treatment, it is said, that the poor wretch comes very soon to loathe the vile drug so utterly, that he can never again be persuaded to take a drop of it. Something of this sort might be hoped for from this constant din of politics which would occur in our more intelligent families. Where husband and wife were both voters and partisans, especially if they happened to be on opposite sides, the discussion would go on unceasingly, morning, noon, and night; there would be no rest, and if the debate were to be enlivened by choice passages from such political papers as we have described, there would soon come, we believe, such a feeling of nauseation with politics, that the subject would be tabooed for ever.

Thus much we have thought it needful to say of the social aspect of woman-suffrage among the more educated and intelligent classes. Let us now glance at it in its influence upon the social relations of the lower and more ignorant classes.

That these would vote intelligently, or from any conviction of right or wrong in connection with their vote, no one can believe who has any knowledge of these classes.

The great body of domestic servants, especially those of Irish and German origin, and of the Catholic faith, will follow the dictation of their priests unquestioningly, and we say it with no disposition to find fault with the priests, the entire vote of this class would be thrown at their bidding, and almost wholly in one direction. But bad as this would be,—and we regard votes given at the dictation and under the influence of others as among

WOMEN AT THE POLLS.

the sorest evils of free suffrage,—there are other evils to be dreaded, in a social point of view, worse than this. The feeling of antagonism which exists between the more ignorant of the Irish Catholics and their Protestant employers is much stronger on the side of the Irish than we generally imagine. Occasionally a lightning-flash, like that of the great riot of 1863 in New York City, shows it in all its intensity, for a brief period; we see then that those who have been confidential servants, long trusted and regarded as humble but true friends, are ready, under the influence of excitement, to plunder and destroy our own property or that of our friends, if we or they belong to the class against whom their anger is roused. In the political strife, it will often happen that these servants will be enlisted on the opposite side from their employers; and when the contest is a warm and exciting one, what warrant have we for believing that Biddy, in her enthusiasm for the cause, which her priest has told her is the right one, may not resort to some measures to nullify her employer's vote, which would not bear a legal scrutiny? Or, believing that the end would justify the means, that she might not participate in some riot or foul play, which would endanger the life or property of her employers?

A very large proportion of those women and girls who are employed in manufactories, especially in our great cities, are of foreign birth, and would be subject to the same influences as the servant girls.   There would be some danger of influence being exerted in the case of these in another direction, as objectionable as that of the priests, viz.: the threats of employers to dismiss them, in the case of their voting in opposition to the employer's views.   Intimidation of this sort has been largely practiced in the South, in regard to another dependent class, the negroes; and human nature is so much alike everywhere, that it might naturally be expected in the case of factory girls.

The whole class of unskilled and partially skilled female laborers will be, if woman-suffrage prevails, in the market with their votes.   Too poor to afford to spare the time for voting, except for pay, they will, almost without exception, be ready to accept the best offer.   They are, with but slight exceptions, too ignorant to have any intelligent ideas on political questions, and hence will have no conscientious scruples against voting for the side which pays best.

There is still another class who will be found at the polls "early and often," and to whom the election will be a gala-day, since then, of all days in the year, they will be the equals of the best women of the community.   Whoever else fails to be at the polls, when woman-suffrage is permitted, the prostitute will not, and her vote will be given as the keeper of the den of vice in which she dwells may direct. Corrupt men, desirous of office, will secure the votes of these poor wretches for themselves, by a bonus to their keepers, and, when it can be done, will cause them to repeat their votes in one precinct after another, till they have registered votes enough to attain their purpose.

Will it be pleasant for modest, refined, Christian women, to go to the polls in the company of these daughters of shame? Will the loud laugh, the boisterous behavior, and the drunken leer of these poor creatures (who are, after all, to be pitied almost as much as they are to be blamed), cause them to feel any more proud of their sex, or more certain of the great advantages to be gained from woman-suffrage? Would it not be a nobler and better object to attain, to rescue these poor souls from the bondage of sin, to emancipate them from the service and oppression of the devil, than to succeed in bestowing on woman a gift of such doubtful value as suffrage—a Pandora's box, whose evils would prove innumerable?

CHAPTER XVIII.

In discussing the objections to woman-suffrage from the intellectual point of view, it is necessary to recur, for a moment, to the first principles of government. In all governments of the people, and for the people, the intelligence of the voters, who are, in the ultimate resort, the ruling power, is the all-important consideration. If they are lacking in this, whatever the wealth or enterprise of the nation, whatever its advantages of position, soil, or commerce, it is destined to speedy decay. If its voters are ignorant, and accustomed to vote at the dictation of others, or for pay, the government soon becomes the prey of corrupt aspirants for power and heartless demagogues, who will use it for their own base purposes, and having secured their own wealth and power by its means, will aid in its overthrow. It is owing to the ignorance and venality of the masses of voters, that no Celtic nation, neither the French, Spanish, Italian, Portuguese, or Irish, have ever been able to maintain a republican government; and to the same cause is it due, that Mexico and the Central and South American republics have been, ever since their independence, in a state of anarchy.

Bad men have always been able to rally round them, for an insurrection, a sufficient force of voters whose influence in their favor has been gained, either by plunder already seized and distributed, or by promises of money to be gained by revolt; and hence these countries have been kept in a constant state of revolution. In Chili, which has been the most stable of the South American republics, there has been far more widely diffused education, and though too many of the voters are venal, they are generally capable of understanding the political questions at issue. In the Argentine Republic the enlightened President, Don Diego F. Sarmiento, has become so fully convinced of the absolute necessity of intelligence to the preservation of the national existence and the promotion of the nation's prosperity, that he is making the greatest possible efforts for the education of his entire people.

Just at this point is our nation in its greatest peril. We have three classes of voters who are every year endangering our national existence by their ignorance, venality, and the facility with which they may be influenced and led by evil and designing men. These three classes are: the low, brutish, often depraved, and always ignorant class of voters at the North, mostly, though not entirely, of foreign birth or parentage, the shoulder-hitters, plug-uglies, dead rabbits, repeaters, and bummers, and, with them, a still larger class of sim-

12

ilar origin, who, though ordinarily peaceable and quiet, yet always vote according to the orders of their fugleman, who is generally a pot-house politician, though, sometimes, an aspiring demagogue, like Fernando Wood or Captain Rynders. A second class is the "poor white trash" of the South, intensely ignorant, brutish, and prejudiced, who will vote every time according to the instructions of their file leaders, and by whose votes, outweighing those of more intelligent and patriotic citizens, the South was lately plunged in civil war. Great efforts are now making to educate and elevate this class, and they may be successful with the children, but there is hardly much hope for the parents. A third class are the more ignorant and stupid of the negroes, who are at present very much under the control of others, and incapable of intelligent and thoughtful action on political subjects. Their earnest zeal to acquire knowledge amid the obstacles which two hundred years of slavery have engendered, gives us good reason to hope that, in a few years, they will not be the lowest class in point of intelligence. We have shown already, that, while a portion of the educated and intelligent class of women would probably vote, if woman-suffrage were granted, by far the larger part of the votes would come from domestic servants, factory girls, unskilled or partially skilled female laborers, and the depraved and vicious classes, all of whom, with but few exceptions, would either vote under the influence and at the dictation of others, or for the party or politician which would pay them best. This addition of so vast a body of unintelligent and purchasable voters—many of them, it is to be feared, from the facility with which they could disguise themselves, voting several times at each election —to our already excessive number of this class, would be certain to swamp the nation in speedy ruin. No government on earth could exist a score of years with such masses of easily influenced and venal voters. And the evil is likely to be still further aggravated by the speedy influx of immense numbers of Chinese, both men and women (the latter having the worst possible reputation for depravity), who would, in the event of the passage of an amendment to the State constitutions permitting woman-suffrage, become voters at the end of five years after their arrival, and would inevitably cast their votes for pay, and so, almost necessarily, for the most corrupt politicians to be found.

If we are to have universal suffrage, let us by all means have, first, universal education, compulsory, if need be, to fit our prospective voters for their duties. Universal suffrage, where each voter fully understood the issues to be voted upon, and acted conscientiously, might not be attended with many serious evils; but universal suffrage, where three-fourths of the voters could be purchased or influenced by men devoid of principle, would be the ruin of our country.

The objections to woman-suffrage from the *moral* point of view are numerous and weighty.

There is among the acquaintances of almost every upright and true man, some woman (perhaps more than one), upon whom he looks as upon a vision of the lost Eden. Her purity and innocence, her exemplary fulfillment of all the sacred duties of wife and mother, her genuine piety and modesty, fill his soul with respect and admiration. Such pure and excellent women in these days of fashionable education, frivolous accomplishments, and extravagance in dress and display, are unhappily less numerous than they once were; but enough are yet left to make this world a desirable dwelling-place. Who would be willing to see such a woman descend into the arena of party political strife, and enter upon its intrigues, its heated partisanships, its perilous depths of wickedness? It would be like drawing an angel from heaven, to plunge him in the world of woe!

Yet this is what would happen often if women entered upon a political career. We have all seen an ingenuous youth, the soul of honor, resolute in his integrity and virtuous purposes, plunge into politics as his life employment. How long was it ere he had learned to palter with words in a double sense, to make promises which he could not fulfill, to first endure, then sanction, then advocate those devious courses for the sake of party, which, under the specious plea of accomplishing ultimate good by the success of party measures, make politics inconsistent with honesty, and the very name of politician odious to all true men ? If such a wreck of character and integrity in man has made us sad, how much more would it distress us to see a pure, good, and true woman fall into the same snare ? Woman, when she falls away from integrity and truth, has further to fall than man, and by a law of moral gravitation, she falls faster and sinks deeper.

The affectional and emotional nature is so much stronger in her than in man that, in whatever she becomes interested, her whole soul is engaged. Let her once become occupied with politics, and the craft, the policy, the subterfuges, the ignominious party tricks, in which male politicians have engaged, would not satisfy her for a moment. Downward, and still downward she would plunge, till she would astonish and confound her male associates by her daring and reckless audacity in the contrivance of party schemes.

In most of the monarchical countries of Europe, though women have not voted, some of them have, at one time or another, mingled largely in political matters, and never without going more deeply into the mire ; proposing and audaciously carrying through measures of greater iniquity and injustice, and prompting others to grosser sins, than any man would have dared. Yet some of these women in their youth were virtuous and pure-minded, and were dragged down from their lofty position more by the corrupting influences of a political life, than by the temptations of a profligate one.

We need not name the succession of mistresses of the fourteenth and fifteenth Louis of France, who hastened the downfall of the kingdom, and made the horrors of the French Revolution possible; the favorites of the worthless Charles the Second of England, and his equally worthless successor; the coarse, vicious women, whom the first, second, and fourth Georges made their confidants and advisers; nor such restless politicians as Christina of Sweden, Catharine II. of Russia, Christina of Spain, and the Countess of Lansfeldt in Bavaria. Such corruption seems an inevitable result of an active participation in politics; and what a blight would it cast upon families now reared in purity and innocence? How could a mother, whose whole heart was absorbed in political strife, teach her children those lessons of integrity, modesty, and truthfulness, which would come most appropriately from her lips, were they untainted by political corruption?

In its effects upon the morals of the more dependent classes, woman-suffrage seems still more objectionable. Power without knowledge is always an evil, and the consciousness on the part of the ignorant and prejudiced servant-girl, that she possessed a privilege which made her in some sort the peer of her mistress, would so stimulate her pride, self-sufficiency, and impertinence, that a class already almost intolerable from these qualities would become entirely so, and a social revolution would ensue. The intrigues for the votes of these dependent classes would tend greatly to their demoralization, for where all regard to truth, honor, and right is banished from their action on political questions, and the party ascendency is achieved by the most unscrupulous means, the whole moral sense is weakened, and virtue in all its relations becomes only a name.

As to the abandoned class, their very presence at the polls will be an outrage on the public morals. It has always been, and very properly, too, a rule with our civil authorities, if they were unable to suppress houses of prostitution, at least to keep their inmates from practicing their vocation, or tempting others, on our public streets; and though they have not wholly succeeded in this, yet they have mainly compelled them to be quiet, and, by frequent arrests, have greatly diminished the practices which made the great thoroughfares unsafe for honest women at night. But, with the proposed woman-suffrage, these daughters of shame would be paraded through the principal streets in the day-time in squads, and their influence for mischief would be immense. What a lesson of evil would be taught our children on an election day! These poor wretches, bedizened in gaudy finery, with bold, brazen faces, many of them half or wholly drunk, and uttering, with loud laughter, horrible oaths and ribald and obscene jests, what impression must an intelligent child receive in regard to a class of women of whom he or she has hitherto known nothing! If the virtuous mother seeks to ward off the evil effects of such a sight from the mind of the child, by saying that these are wicked, bad women, who ought not to be allowed to walk the streets in this way, how will she be appalled by the answer: "But, mother, they are going to vote. If they were so very bad, would they have the same right to vote that you and other ladies have?" If she attempts to explain that moral character has nothing to do with political privileges, will she not be met again with the inquiry: "But, mother, what makes the government so bad, that they have to let such bad women vote and help make the laws?" The mother will be in a dilemma—either she must recognize these abandoned women as her associates in political privilege, and thus break down the ideas of moral purity and virtue which she has attempted to establish in the minds of her children, or she must condemn the government of her country for adopting the very measure which she and her friends have clamored for. The association with these depraved and vicious women at the polls, will, in itself, be a great source of

THE SENATE CHAMBER AS IT MAY BE.

demoralization to men as well as women. It is bad enough to have a drunken, profane rowdy near you in the line of voters, for an hour or more, while you are waiting your turn to deposit your vote ; but, as most of these fellows have, at one time or another, been in State prison, you can, if too much annoyed, generally get him challenged off; but to be obliged for an hour to stand in line with a drunken and noisy prostitute, compelled to listen to her foul ravings, and to know that she has the same legal right to vote with yourself, and that her vote can neutralize that of the best and purest man in the land, is intolerable, and must disgust every thoughtful, sensible citizen with universal suffrage. On the young voter, it must have one of two effects ; either it will disgust him with the government, or it will lead him astray to follow these abandoned creatures. But there is another phase of the question which has its moral bearings also. The privilege of woman-suffrage implies also the right to hold office and to seek official position. The thirst for office is at once the most engrossing and the most groveling of human passions. Daniel D. Tompkins, once Governor of New York, and Vice-President of the United States, said, late in life, and he spoke from experience : " Let a man once entertain the idea that he may win the presidency of the United States, and there is nothing he will not sacrifice for the purpose of attaining it. His property, his dearest friends, his own family, the shortening of his life, and his soul's eternal salvation, would all go freely, if by their loss he could obtain the place he strove for." And for much lower places, how many have sacrificed all these. With her more ardent and impulsive nature, can we doubt that woman would be, at least, as zealous in seeking office as man.

Let us inquire briefly into the way in which nominations for official positions, such as members of the State Assembly or Senate, members of Congress, State officers, &c., are secured. In a late speech, Miss Anna Dickinson avowed her belief that within ten years she should be a member of Congress. For the sake of illustration, we will suppose that woman-suffrage having been granted in Pennsylvania, a warm personal and political friend of Miss Dickinson, a lady of Philadelphia (Miss D.'s home), is desirous that her friend should receive the nomination for Congress. What must she do to bring about such a result?

She must first secure the primaries. Our fair friends may not exactly understand what this means. We will explain. All these nominations for legislative, State, or Congressional positions, are made by party conventions, composed of delegates chosen at meetings of the voters of that party, or a portion of them, in each voting precinct. These meetings for the choice of delegates to the conventions are called *primaries*.

In the cities the number of voters to a precinct usually ranges from four to eight hundred. Of course, it is not to be expected that any very large proportion of these will come out to the primary meetings for the nomination of delegates.

In truth, only the political managers of the precinct, and the bullies, rowdies, pot-house politicians, and roughs of the party—those who can influence the votes of the more ignorant and vicious classes—are usually present, and the candidates for Congress, or their friends, begin the struggle there, for delegates to the nominating convention who will vote for them. Too often these primaries are places where open bids are made by the candidates for support. The questions are put plumply: "Ef I vote for ye in the convintion, will ye git my brother a place in the Custom-House?" "Will ye git me appointed weigher or gauger?" and so on. The candidate or his friends who make the most liberal bids and promises, or who pay the most money, get the delegates from that primary, and the same thing is repeated throughout the district. Often very heavy sums are paid to secure the nomination.

Attempts have been made repeatedly to improve these primaries. Good and high-minded citizens have sometimes gone to them in considerable numbers, to attempt to control them, and secure the nomination of good men who would not bribe the delegates, either with money or promises; but it has all been in vain; the rowdy class do, and will, control them, and nearly as much in one party as the other.

It is not reasonable to suppose that they would be any better if woman-suffrage was inaugurated. Indeed, there is every reason to suppose that they would be worse, since the number of voters of the ignorant and vicious classes would be so greatly increased. Our fair friend, therefore, if a wife and mother, leaving her husband at home to care for the children, sallies out, of a dark night, to visit one or two of these primaries. It is her first visit to them, and it will be likely to be her last one. Entering, she finds herself surrounded by a fierce, ruffianly crew, men and women, who look with suspicion on her neat and becoming dress, and are prejudiced against her at the outset from this cause. Confusion worse confounded reigns in the room, and the air is redolent with the perfumes of vile whisky, cheap tobacco, and garlic.

It is some time before she can comprehend at all what is the cause of the hubbub; but she finally ascertains that the primary is not yet organized, but that the keeper of a dance-house is discussing his own claims to be a delegate, with the leader of a gang of workhouse women, both agreeing, however, that they will only vote for the candidate who will promise to get for them some appointment by which they can plunder the government. The keeper of a grog-shop urges

THE WIFE AND MOTHER AT A PRIMARY,

THE FATHER STAYS AT HOME, ATTENDING TO THE CHILDREN.

his claims, but wants a chance to get in what whisky he needs for his business without paying the revenue tax on it.

The meeting is at last organized, by the choice of a noted brothel-keeper as chairman, and the cashier of a drinking-saloon as clerk. The nomination of delegates being in order, our fair friend, who is not quite at home in the mode of procedure, begins to canvass among the would-be delegates in behalf of Miss Dickinson, unaware that she should have previously secured her candidate for delegate from among the motley crew, and having made him pledge himself to vote for Miss Dickinson, and her only, have put him forward in the fight. Miss Dickinson's name is received with shouts of derisive laughter or abusive epithets; and when one of the proposed delegates somewhat hesitatingly inquires, " But what'll she do for us ; will she come down with the spondulicks ?" he is at once checked by some of the reprobate class, with, " Hold your tongue. She's smart enough, may be ; but she ain't one of our sort." Disheartened, discouraged, and frightened, Miss Dickinson's friend slips out of the room as soon as possible, and with quick steps, and panting for breath, reaches her own home. Two or three days later she finds that some sharp, unprincipled politician, it matters not of which sex, is nominated, and that Miss Dickinson is not even mentioned in the convention.

This is no overdrawn picture. In the rural districts the corruption and villainy are not so open, and perhaps not so prevalent; but in the cities, the primaries, which must be placated if a nomination is to be obtained, are nests of unclean birds, festering pit-holes of all iniquity. Is it possible to touch pitch and not be defiled?

But, we may be told, in the West, this system of primaries is not in vogue. There, the candidate nominates himself, or is nominated by his friends, and then "takes the stump," or visits each town or voting precinct, often in company with the opposing candidate, and publicly discusses with his opponent the political issues of the election. These stump-speeches are usually made in the open air, when the weather is such as will admit of it, and generally the speaker who has the strongest lungs, and the most taking way with the masses, wins the victory.

Let us suppose, for a moment, that woman-suffrage being granted, a woman of decided intellectual ability, and, if you please, accustomed to public speaking in halls or lecture-rooms, were to be the nominee of one party for governor, and a man of like ability the candidate of the other, and that they "stump the State" together. A woman could have no more unfavorable opportunity of displaying her eloquence than a large open air meeting. To enable her audience to hear, her voice must be pitched on so high a key that her

THE CANVASS FOR GOVERNOR IN A WESTERN STATE. THE MALE AND FEMALE CANDIDATES STUMP THE STATE TOGETHER.

finest passages will come out with a shriek, and the whole effect will be unpleasant. In these days of weak throats, too, it would be difficult to find a woman who could stand the strain of a cam-paign. Then, in a discussion of that sort, sup-posing the two parties to possess equal abilities, the man would have the advantage, from the greater excitability of the woman. The result could hardly fail to be against her. The high-pitched treble voice always wearies a crowd very soon, and the bold position which the female can-didate would be obliged to take would deprive her of the respect due, under other circumstances, to her womanhood; while the moral effect of such an exhibition could not but be injurious to all who witnessed it.

But suppose it possible that a woman of high character could run the gauntlet of the primaries and the nominating conventions, and finally obtain an election. The perils to her moral nature are but just begun. If she is elected to the State Legislature she will be plied with a thousand temptations to act corruptly in regard to railroad chárters and provisions, State aid to them, city appropriations, and a host of other bills in which she will be told there is money; bribes, direct and indirect, will be offered her daily, to do or to refrain from doing something, or to vote or not to vote for somebody. Attempts have been made by exposures, denunciations, committees of inquiry, and in all other ways, to break up the corruption and venality of our legislatures; yet each one seems worse than its predecessor. That members of Congress, both Senators and Representatives, are too often corrupt, and amass great wealth through their adroitness, is, unfortunately, too well known to admit of doubt. Could we hope that women, who are admitted to be the most skillful of lobbyists, would be able to resist these manifold temptations?

For the rest, we should hardly expect women to be very successful as legislators, either in the State legislatures or in Congress. Their proneness to discuss all questions (*i. e.* the class who would be most likely to achieve an election), their impulsiveness, their tendency to be influenced to wrong action by appeals to their sympathies, and the impatience with which they would be listened to, would all be against them. A sensible woman would hardly seek a place in any of our legislative bodies.

The skill and tact which women have on many occasions manifested in diplomacy, when they have been secretly intrusted with diplomatic duties, has led some to suppose that they would be eminently successful as embassadors. We can not coincide in that opinion. Were diplomacy now what the Italian diplomatist represented it, the art of skillful deception, we could imagine that a smart, intriguing woman might achieve some distinction in it, though at the expense of her own character for truthfulness and integrity ; but diplomacy new requires the highest gifts of coolness, imperturbability, thorough statesmanship, profound political knowledge, patriotism, sound judgment, and quick perception; qualities all of which few women can be supposed to possess, and these few would, without exception, be averse to occupying such a position. The skillful and statesmanlike management of our ministers in England and France during the late war, saved us, more than once, from threatened war with those powers at a time when such a misfortune would have well nigh proved fatal to our national existence. Does any one believe that we could have safely replaced Mr. Adams, Mr. Dayton, or Mr. Bigelow, by any female diplomatist in our country ? No! We shall hope to be spared the sight of that day when a woman, however gifted, shall be our embassador at the court of the Tuileries, or at that of St. James.

CHAPTER XIX.

HAVING thus fully stated the objections which seem to us conclusive against the admission of woman-suffrage, we will next proceed to reply to such of the arguments advanced in favor of it by its advocates, as have not been already met in our previous examination of the subject.

We begin with Mr. J. Stuart Mill's position, which, in his work, is the basis of all his arguments in favor of woman-suffrage : the substantial equality of woman with man, in all respects. Mr. Mill, indeed, admits that, in physical power, woman is generally the inferior of man, and that his claim of authority, and her condition of subjection, are both based on his possession of a superior amount of brute force. In all other respects, he contends, that, under the greatest disadvantages, woman has proved herself the equal of man, and that, therefore, she should have the right of suffrage to protect herself from the oppression of his brute force.

That a logician so astute, a thinker usually so calm and dispassionate as Mr. Mill, should have been led astray by such evident fallacies as are contained in this proposition, is only a confirmation of the ancient proverb, "Great men are not always wise." Mr. Mill, as a professed deist, ignores the scriptural account of the creation of woman, and thus fails to discern the original design and purpose of her Creator, in placing her in a subject relation to man, that she might be the complement of his nature, and that the two together might form the unit of a perfected humanity. To him, too, the comment of the apostle Paul, on this design of God in the creation, is of no significance, "For the man is not of the woman, but the woman of the man. Neither was the man created for the woman; but the woman for the man" (1 Cor., xi. 8, 9). And yet, in these words, he would have found the key to the mystery which so stumbles him. Taking the history of the past, and the status of woman in the present, he finds that she has been, in all the historic ages, in a subject condition; that in savage, and sometimes even in civilized nations, this condition has been the result of the exercise of brute force ; in other and more enlightened nations, it has been maintained mostly by the exertion of a stern and dominant will. Never, according to his own testimony, has there been, to any appreciable extent, an exception to this subject condition of women. From his own stand-point, taking no cognizance of the divine revelation, would it not have been more philosophical for him to have inquired why, if there was no just cause for it, this condition of subjection had always existed? No class of reasoners are so ready, as those with whom Mr. Mill is affiliated, to deduce a general law from ages of unbroken custom. Why can not he see that there must have been some reason, other than the mere brutal instincts of man, why women should have, throughout all time, remained in this subject condition, and why they should, in all ages, have acquiesced in it? Again, while he admits the physical inferiority of woman,* is he not led to inquire, whether this very condition of body, in which grace takes the place of strength, beauty that of dignity, and the whole frame indicates how diverse is its purpose, object, and aim from that of man, does not of itself teach that, as in the physical so in the mental and moral structure, woman and man have their distinct and differing spheres of action, and that, occupying these, there can be no more question of equality, superiority, or inferiority, than between any two objects of entirely differing, and yet complementary natures? The rind of an orange differs in form, color, and consistency, from the pulp; yet one is as necessary as the other to the making up of the complete orange; and, while the pulp is inferior in position to the rind, we can not say of either, that it is or is not equal to the other. The one is the complement of the other.

It would seem that a man of Mr. Mill's astute-

* See Appendix B.

ness ought to have seen this; yet, had he recognized it, he would at once have comprehended that, when he relinquished the idea of woman's equality with man, and substituted for it the view of her complementary nature, the argument for suffrage from equality must fall at once to the ground. As the other part of himself, woman can have no claim to a separate representation—a distinct vote from man—for she is represented in his representation—she votes through him. There can be no antagonisms, no conflicting interests between man and woman in this relation, if rightly understood, and hence, no occasion for the woman to protect herself from the aggressions of the man, more than of the man to protect himself from the aggressions of the woman. They have a common interest from their common nature.

That this community of nature and of interest has not been fully recognized in the past, and is not, by all classes, at the present time, is undoubtedly true, and is a misfortune of the sex; yet it would be a very absurd remedy for this want of recognition, to endow the woman with the ballot, when her tyrant (as Mr. Mill would call the man) possessed the same right, and when her possession of it, leaving her still in a hopeless minority, would only afford the opportunity of adding insult to her previous injuries.

There is, moreover, good reason to believe that this community of nature and interests, between the two sexes, is coming to be better understood, and that in the not distant future it will be regarded by all intelligent men and women as the basis of all their relations to each other.

But Mr. Mill, as if aware of the weakness of his previous argument, of the equality of the sexes, proceeds with other arguments in favor of woman-suffrage, some of them a little inconsistent with his doctrine of equality. "Their right to both parliamentary and municipal suffrage" is, he says, "entirely independent of any question which can be raised concerning their faculties. The right to share in the choice of those who are to exercise a public trust, is altogether a distinct thing from that of competing for the trust itself. If no one could vote for a member of Parliament who was not fit to be a candidate, the government would be a narrow oligarchy indeed. To have a voice in choosing those by whom one is to be governed, is a means of self-protection due to every one, though he were to remain forever excluded from the function of governing; and that women are considered fit to have such a choice, may be presumed from the fact that the law already gives it to women in the most important of all cases to themselves—for the choice of the man who is to govern a woman to the end of her life is always supposed to be voluntarily made by herself. In the case of election to public trusts, it is the business of constitutional law to surround the right of suffrage with all needful securities and limitations; but whatever securities are sufficient in the case of the male sex, no others need be required in the case of women. Under whatever conditions, and within whatever limits, men are admitted to the suffrage, there is not a shadow of justification for not admitting women under the same. The majority of the women of any class are not likely to differ in political opinion from the majority of the men of the same class, unless the question be one in which the interests of women, as such, are in some way involved; and if they are so, women require the suffrage as their guarantee of just and equal consideration. This ought to be obvious even to those who coincide in no other of the doctrines for which I contend. Even if every woman were a wife, and if every wife ought to be a slave, all the more would these slaves stand in need of legal protection; and we know what legal protection the slaves have where the laws are made by their masters."

Some portions of this argument are more plausible in their application to woman-suffrage in England, where, even under the new Reform law, none but property-holders have a vote, and where the dependent and vicious classes of women would not be allowed the suffrage under any circumstances, than to this country, where all classes (in the event of the permission of woman-suffrage) would be allowed to vote. But there is, never theless, an amount of sophistry in it which is perfectly astonishing. It is doubtless true that in England many vote for members of Parliament, who would not, and under any circumstances could not, be candidates for seats in that body; but here the theory of our government is, that every citizen who votes is, in some sort, eligible to any elective office in the government. There are undoubtedly exceptions to this in actual practice, though none which must be so of necessity; but the doctrine of one qualification for voters, and another, greatly higher and belonging to a different class, for office-holders, would not be tolerated for a moment here.

So, too, his statement that "the majority of the women of any class are not likely to differ in opinion from the majority of the men of the same class," may be partially, though not wholly true, in England, where only the more intelligent men and women, and those holding property, would be allowed to vote; but it is very far from being true here, where many classes of women would vote under influence, or for pay, while the men of a corresponding class would very often have some political principle to guide them. But it is very singular to hear Mr. Mill, who is strongly opposed to any votes being cast under influence, make such a statement, which implies distinctly that the women would usually vote under the influence of the men of their class; and it is still more singular to hear him, after an elaborate argument to prove that woman ought not to be in subjection to man at all, speak of her voluntarily making choice of the man who is to govern her to the end of her life. He is also sadly unfortunate in the choice of his illustration ; for neither in England nor France, if the ablest writers of both countries, and the vast weight of testimony are to be believed, is the woman's choice of a husband, in a majority of instances, a voluntary one. A voluntary choice implies the power of actively making a selection ; at the best, except in the case of the sovereign, the woman has only the power of accepting or refusing the hand offered her, not of selecting such a one as she might have desired ; and how few are the instances in which the wishes of parents or friends, ambitious desires for wealth, equipage, or display, the wish to be the mistress of a home, or the fear of not receiving a more eligible offer, do not exert a controlling influence in the matter ?

Nor can we regard without surprise his assertion, that " women require the suffrage (in matters relating to their interests as women) as their guaranty of just and equal consideration." It can not be possible that Mr. Mill supposes for an instant that any sufficient number of women could or would vote in Great Britain, to give them the control, either in a single borough or in Parliament ; and unless they obtained such a control,

13   T

would they not, as a hopeless minority, be in a worse position, so far as any "guaranty of just and equal consideration" was concerned, than if they were without suffrage?

We have shown, we think, clearly, that under the true idea of society—that which regards the family, and not the individual, as the unit of it—there can be no occasion for women, as women, to vote, since they are already represented; and we may add that, any attempt at voting on their part, while it would place them in a condition of unnatural and needless antagonism to man, would, by releasing him from the responsibility he now feels to legislate for their good, make their situation in every respect worse than it now is.

Another argument which the friends of woman-suffrage have continually urged in behalf of their favorite measure has been, that woman, by her presence at the polls and in our political gatherings, legislatures, &c., would exert a refining and purifying influence upon our politics. It is even stated that Mr. Beecher has more than once brought forward this argument for woman-suffrage. We can hardly credit it; for we have too high an opinion of his knowledge of human nature to believe that he could deliberately utter such an absurdity. The snow falls upon the city pure and white, and for the moment it seems to have invested it with its own purity. But, in a day or two at the farthest, this very snow, smirched and foul from the mud and filth witn which it has mingled, becomes even more offensive to the eye than the foul streets of the city were before it descended, and we give a sigh of relief when it disappears.

So would it be with women after mingling in political life, and marching to the polls once or twice, even had they been previously all as pure as the driven snow. But no one knows better than Mr. Beecher, that with our system of universal suffrage, there would be more bad than good women to take part in the ballot; not, perhaps, that there are more ignorant and depraved than good women in the community (we hope not, certainly), but that very many of the good and pure women would stay at home, while the bad women would all come to the polls under the various influences which would be exerted to bring them out. Does he believe that these classes would make the polls, or the legislators elected by their votes, better, purer, and more refined than now? Would they not very soon be infinitely worse? And would not the country, with this large addition to the corrupt and venal voters, very soon sink to ruin?

No! the reformation of our politics will not, can not come from that direction. We must restrict the number and elevate the character of our voters, before we can hope for any material improvement. If it were possible to apply the intellectual test of ability to read and write, and the moral test of an unblemished character, and to insist, in addition to these, upon a residence of not less than five years by all aliens, after the declaration of their intention to become citizens, before they should be allowed to vote, we might hope for a better government, more honest legislators, and more refinement and elevation in our politics. A favorite mode of expression with the advocates of woman-suffrage in reference to the success of their project, is to speak of it as " the emancipation of women ;" and they often allude to " the coming freedom of women." These phrases have grown out of the recent emancipation of the colored race here, and of the serfs in Russia; but there is a fallacy in their application to women. Emancipated from what slavery, freed from what bondage, we may ask? That very many women are the slaves of fashion, that they are in bondage to their love of display, and ambition to excel others in dress and equipage, is undoubtedly true ; but, so far as we can understand these writers, this is not the sort of slavery from which they expect emancipation. There are other women who are, in some sort, slaves and drudges to their houses—scrubbing, washing, sweeping, dusting, till every thing around them is so painfully clean that they are in distress lest somebody should soil it; but neither is this the bondage from which freedom is sought. We will not think so badly of these women as to suppose that it is the matrimonial bond from which they desire all women to be set free, though there are undoubtedly some cases of oppression and cruelty in married life; and there are, very probably, more bad and tyrannical husbands than depraved and shrewish wives. Yet there are so many happy and united families, in which this bond of union is not in any respect allied to slavery, that we can not believe these fair speakers and writers have any design of establishing a system of universal divorce.

What, then, can be this slavery from which woman is to be emancipated, and how is her emancipation to be accomplished? It must be, to many of the sex, an unconscious bondage, and to a large majority, one from which they have no desire to be freed.

Inquiry among the leaders of the woman-suffrage movement on the subject, brings a variety of answers. Miss Anthony will tell us, perhaps, that it is "man—the horrid creature—from whom woman desires to be set free. He has always been the tyrant and oppressor of women in all ages, and it is high time we were emancipated from his sway." "Not quite so fast, Miss Susan," exclaim some of the other leaders, "you forget that we have husbands, very good fellows, too, who suffer us to do very much as we please, and some of whom render us essential service by their advocacy of our schemes; and then, too, there is that dear, delightful George Francis Train, you would not desire, surely, to be rid of him?"

Well, then, if it is not men, nor husbands, nor household drudgery, nor fashion, nor display, from which you desire to be set free, dear ladies, what is it? The civil disabilities under which you have labored in regard to inheritance, conducting business in your own names, the punishment of crimes against you, are fast passing away, and the influence you can exert upon our legislatures, in a quiet way, will be sufficient to remove whatever traces of wrong may still remain. Evils which can be removed by the exercise of your wills and influence, clearly do not deserve the name of slavery. You do not receive, perhaps, in all employments, the wages you deserve and should have; but this is not slavery, since it is in your own power, as we have shown, greatly to improve your own condition in this respect, without insurrection or revolution, simply by abstaining from undue competition with each other, by association, and by co-operation.

The absence of the privilege of suffrage can not be considered as slavery, for slavery is something positive, not negative; a direct oppression, not an absence of a privilege which you have never enjoyed; and if you call yourselves slaves from the want of this, you have ample company, since in no community of the United States do the voters much exceed one-fifth of the entire population. We might urge, also, that you are already represented more efficiently than you could be by a direct vote; that your position in the organization of human society is such, that you do not need the ballot, and that your admission to the ballot would only increase the aggregate vote, without altering its character, except for the worse— the classes of women who would vote under influence being more numerous, proportionately, than of men; but we have already sufficiently stated and illustrated these positions.

But admitting, for a moment, that this were the only possible sense in which women could be said to be in bondage, the question arises whether the exercise of suffrage would give them the freedom they crave. Women who voted might properly be divided into two classes: a small one, who, having made politics their study, voted independently; and a very large class, mostly dependent in one way or another, who voted under the direction and influence of others.

In regard to this latter class, we might well ask, which would be the greater slave—the woman who did not vote, or the one who voted only under the direction and dictation of others?

As to the former, they would soon find that an active interest in politics was the most engrossing and enslaving of all pursuits; and from woman's natural tendency to devote herself wholly to any subject in which she becomes deeply interested, we might expect to find her devotion to politics make her the most abject of slaves.

We can not but regard this phrase, " the emancipation of women," as an unfortunate one. It expresses a fallacy and not a fact. In no conceivable sense are the great mass of women slaves; and of course they are in no need of emancipation.

We are sometimes told that woman-suffrage is not so new a thing after all; that it was practiced in New Jersey for thirty-three years. The statement is true; and as those thirty-three years were between 1776 and 1807, a period when the doctrines of the Declaration of Independence might be supposed to have exerted the greatest influence on the minds of the Americans, it will be interesting to examine into this practice of woman-suffrage, and learn what were the circumstances under which it was granted and subsequently annulled. There have been so many erroneous statements made on this subject, that we have deemed it advisable to give in full the following very complete history, compiled evidently from the highest authorities, and originally published in the Newark *Daily Advertiser*. We quote it from Mrs. Dall's work, " The College, the Market, and the Court," and when we add that it was compiled by Lucy Stone and Antoinette Blackwell, our readers will agree with us, that it presents the woman's side of the question as fairly as the facts will justify :—

' In 1709, a provincial law confined the privilege of voting to 'male freeholders having one hundred acres of land in their own right, or fifty pounds current money of the province in real and personal estate;' and during the whole of the colonial period these qualifications continued unchanged.

"But on the 2d of July, 1776 (two days before the Declaration of Independence), the Provincial Congress of New Jersey, at Burlington, adopted a Constitution, which remained in force until 1844, of which section 4 is as follows :—

"' Qualifications of Electors for Members of Legislatures. *All inhabitants of this colony*, of full age, who are worth fifty pounds proclamation-money, clear estate in the same, and have resided within the county in which they claim a vote, for twelve months immediately preceding the election, shall be entitled to vote for representatives in Council and Assembly, and also for all other public offices, that shall be elected by the people of the county at large.'

"Section 7 provides that the Council and Assembly, jointly, shall elect *some fit person within the colony* to be governor. This Constitution remained in force until 1844.

"Thus, by a deliberate change of the terms, 'male freeholder,' to 'all inhabitants,' suffrage and ability to hold the highest office in the State were conferred both upon women and negroes.

13*

"In 1790, a committee of the legislature reported a bill regulating elections, in which the words ' *he or she*,' are applied to voters ; thus giving legislative indorsement to the alleged meaning of the Constitution.

"In 1797, the Legislature passed an act to regulate elections, containing the following provisions :—

" ' Sec. 9. Every voter shall openly, and in full view, deliver *his or her ballot*, which shall be a single written ticket, containing the names of the person or persons for whom *he or she votes*, &c.

" ' Sec. 11. All free inhabitants of full age, who are worth fifty pounds proclamation-money, and have resided within the county in which they claim a vote, for twelve months immediately preceding the election, shall be entitled to vote for all public officers which shall be elected by virtue of this act ; and no person shall be entitled to vote in any other township or precinct than that in which he or she doth actually reside at the time of the election.'

"Mr. William A. Whitehead, of Newark, in a paper upon this subject, read by him in 1858, before the New Jersey Historical Society, states that, in this same year (1797), women voted at an election in Elizabethtown for members of the Legislature. 'The candidates between whom the greatest rivalry existed, were John Condit and Wm. Crane, the heads of what were known, a year or two later, as the "Federal Republican," and "Federal Aristocratic" parties—the former the candidate of Newark and the northern portions of the county; the latter, that of Elizabethtown and the adjoining country, for Council. Under the impression that the candidates would poll nearly the same number of votes, the Elizabethtown leaders thought that, by a bold *coup d'état*, they might secure the success of Mr. Crane. At a late hour of the day, and, as I have been informed, just before the close of the poll, a number of females were brought up, and, under the provisions of the existing laws, allowed to vote. But the maneuver was unsuccessful; the majority for Mr. Condit in the county being ninety-three, notwithstanding.'

"The Newark *Sentinel*, about the same time, states that 'no less than seventy-five women voted at the late election in a neighboring borough.' In the Presidential election of 1800, between Adams and Jefferson, 'females voted very generally throughout the State; and such continued to be the case until the passage of the act (1807) excluding them from the polls. At first the law had been so construed as to admit single women only; but, as the practice extended, the construction of the privilege became broader, and was made to include females eighteen years old, married or single, and even *women of color;* at a contested election in Hunterdon County in 1802, the votes of two or three such actually electing a member of the Legislature.'

"That women voted at a very early period, we are informed by the venerable Mr. Cyrus Jones, of East Orange, who was born in 1770, and is now ninety-seven years old. He says that ' old maids, widows, and unmarried women very frequently voted, but married women very seldom;' that 'the right was recognized, and very little said or thought about it in any way.'

"In the spring of 1807, a special election was held in Essex County, to decide upon the location of a court-house and jail; Newark and its vicinity struggling to retain the county buildings, Elizabethtown and its neighborhood striving to remove them to Day's Hill.

"The question excited intense interest, as the value of every man's property was thought to be involved. Not only was every legal voter, man or woman, white or black, brought out, but, on both sides, gross frauds were practiced.*

* Mrs. Dall had the opportunity, in 1867, of conversing with Mr. Parker, a venerable member of the Society of Friends, who was a member of the New Jersey Legislature of 1807, and, we believe, one of the committee who reported the bill repealing this provision of the Constitution. Mr. Parker told her "that the women were not at that time anxious to retain the privilege (of voting); but that if they had been, the Legislature was so irate that the change would have taken place. Lads, both white and colored, and under age, had dressed in women's clothes, to swell the ballot, which was more than double what it should have been; the irritating question being the possible removal of the county buildings.

Mr. Whitehead states, in a communication to the Rev. George B

" The property qualification was generally disregarded; aliens, and boys and girls not of full age, participated, and many of both sexes 'voted early, and voted often.' In Acquackanonk township, thought to contain about three hundred legal voters, over eighteen hundred votes were polled, all but seven in the interest of Newark.

" It does not appear that either *women or negroes* were more especially implicated in these frauds than the white men. But the affair caused great scandal, and they seem to have been made the scape-goats.

" When the Legislature assembled they set aside the election as fraudulent; yet Newark retained the buildings. Then they passed an act (Nov. 15, 1807) restricting the suffrage to white male adult citizens twenty-one years of age, residents in the county for the twelve months preceding, and worth fifty pounds proclamation-money. But they went on, and provided that all such whose names appeared on the last duplicate of State or county taxes should be considered worth fifty pounds; thus virtually abolishing the property qualification.

" In 1820, the same provisions were repeated, and maintained until 1844, when the present State Constitution was substituted.

Bacon of Orange, N. J., quoted in Rev. Dr. Bushnell's " Women's Suffrage—The Reform against Nature," page 111, that " the women voted, not only once, but as often as by the change of dress, or complicity of the inspectors, they might be able to repeat the process."

"Thus it appears, that from 1776 to 1807—a period of thirty-one years—the right of women and negroes to vote was *admitted and exercised;* then from 1807 to 1844—by an arbitrary act of the Legislature, which does not seem to have been ever contested—the constitutional right was *suspended,* and both women and negroes excluded from the polls for thirty-seven years more. The extension of suffrage, in the State Constitution of 1776, to 'all inhabitants' possessing the prescribed qualifications, was doubtless due to the Quaker influence, then strong in West Jersey, and then, as now, in favor of the equal rights of women.

"Since 1844, under the present Constitution, suffrage is conferred upon 'every white male citizen of the United States, of the age of twenty-one years, who shall have been a resident of this State one year, and the county in which he claims a vote, five months next before the election,' excepting paupers, idiots, insane persons, and criminals.

"This Constitution is subject to amendment by a majority of both houses of two successive Legislatures, when such amendment is afterward ratified by the people at a special election.

"Lucy Stone,
"A. B. Blackwell."

It is worthy of notice, that this voting was under a freehold or property qualification, one which would, of course, exclude the dependent and vicious classes almost entirely; yet the result was so deplorable in the first case in which there was a warmly contested election, that the Legislature felt compelled to prohibit further voting by women, in order to put an end to the scandal. If such was the result under all these restrictions, what might be expected in the almost unlimited freedom of universal suffrage? If such things were done in the green tree, what would be done in the dry?

CHAPTER XX.

Among the arguments for bestowing suffrage upon woman to the same extent to which it is exercised by man, perhaps the one most frequently reiterated by its advocates, is that it would have such an elevating effect upon woman, that it would inspire her with higher hopes, loftier ideas, and greater energy in working out her destiny.

With that singular incapacity for logical reasoning, and that lack of practicality, which are such marked characteristics of many of these female orators, some have insisted that the ballot would at once raise female wages to a fair rate, would increase the social consideration of women, cause politicians to interest themselves in finding offices and places for them, and would prevent any of them from lacking remunerative employment.

One of these orators exclaims : " Shall Sena tors tell me in their places, that I have no need of the ballot, when forty thousand women in the city of New York alone are earning their bread at starving-prices with the needle !"

We might reply, very justly, that there is no necessary, hardly any possible, connection between the premise and conclusion of this plea; that the ballot can neither hinder nor help these forty thousand women (the number, by the way, is greatly exaggerated) in regard to the starving prices at which they are earning their bread by the needle. All this we have shown conclusively elsewhere in this volume. But we prefer to let one of their own sex, a gifted woman, and a believer in the abstract right of woman-suffrage, answer them :— *

" But what will the ballot do for those forty thousand women when they get it ? It will not give them husbands, nor make their thriftless husbands provident, nor their invalid husbands healthy. They can not vote themselves out of their dark, unwholesome sewing - rooms, into counting-rooms and insurance offices, nor have they generally the qualifications which these places require. The ballot will not enable them to do any thing for which their constitution or their education has not fitted them, and I do not know of any law now, which prevents them from doing any thing for which they are fitted, except the holding of government offices. I can think of no other occupation, which the right of suffrage will open to woman, and of public officers the number must be, in proportion to the population, insignificant."

The same writer meets with still greater clear-

* Gail Hamilton (Miss A. M. Dodge), in her " Woman's Wrongs : a Counter-Irritant."

v

ness and force, the other claims which the advocates of woman-suffrage urge with such pertinacity. We quote her views the more readily, because, though she holds to woman-suffrage, as an abstract right of the sex, she is too clear-sighted and sensible to expect from it any of the thousand benefits which some of its advocates predict:—

"Is it said that the impetus given to women by the social elevation consequent on the possession of the ballot will act in every direction, will quicken all her energies, will impel her into a thousand paths which now she never dreams of entering, and will give her an importance in the eyes of men which will effectually secure her from their oppression?

"But how is this work to be wrought? Does the possession of the ballot really mark any practical social elevation for women? Will they stand, either in their own view, or in that of men, any higher? Will they have more social influence, or, if their vote be the duplicate of the male vote, will they have any separate political influence? The vote in the hands of the freedman marks a real change. He was a slave; he is a man, and the ballot is at once the sign and the staff of his freedom. But women are free-born. They have an acknowledged, or, at least, an uncontested right to form and to express opinions on every subject, in every way that man has, save one.

Much real power of expression, much actual influence they possess, which men do not. They have no consciousness of inferiority. Those women who are wise and thoughtful, who understand politics, political and historical, and who comprehend situations, are too high to be degraded by the absence of the ballot. Classing them with idiots does not make them idiots. The classification fixes the status of the classifiers, not of the classified. Their rank and power in society, and their self-respect, will not be touched by suffrage. The influence of any woman's vote is slight, compared with that of her voice. As for the feeble and frivolous women—the women who are given over to trivialities, who know and care nothing for politics, and reckon their ignorance an accomplishment—will the ballot raise them up into dignified human beings? I hope so. It is, indeed, almost the only ground of hope; it is almost the only direction in which there seems to be a prospect of any definite advantage from female suffrage ; but I fear not. If women can live in the deep, strong excitement of the times, if their ears can be filled with the discussion of questions which affect the honor and safety of the country, and yet brain and heart remain untouched, there is reason to fear that the franchise will fail to enfranchise them. All this is no reason for withholding it. I only intimate that such withholding can not be considered the cause of the apathy which prevails, and that the bestowal of the ballot will hardly dispel the apathy. It is only that the ballot has no power to elevate those who are unworthy to hold it. The 'mobs and rowdies' have long held the ballot, but are no less mobs and rowdies. The ballot neither elevates nor depresses. It takes its character from its possessor. . . . What incitement to honor, profit, education, do women miss in missing the ballot? What barrier will it remove; what stimulus present? The brilliant prizes of life are already open to female competition. There are still unequal laws, but not so many, or so severe, as to prevent any woman's becoming whatever she has power to become, in any walk of life except the political. Within her grasp lies all the freedom which she has the nerve to secure. Prejudice itself has softened down into an insipidity which is no obstacle to a really robust soul. There may be petty jealousies to impede and annoy, but these the ballot will not remove; and these, excellence, without the ballot, will remove. Art, literature, science, theology, medicine,—all lie in her manor, but how largely are they left uncultivated! Miss Dickinson has had a career more brilliant than that of most men, but she stands almost alone upon the platform. Miss Hosmer's position is honorable and secure; but her followers are few. Mrs. Stowe has left all men far behind her; but the female story-writers are no better than they were before Uncle Tom came, and spoke, and conquered. What has the ballot to do with such women? It can give them no more money, for they already command the highest market price. It can give them no social standing, for they rank first now. Does the want of it keep any one from adopting their career? I venture to say that there is not at this moment in the whole country a woman who is held back from public speaking, or from any of the finer or higher arts, for lack of voting. If women held, to-morrow, the right of suffrage, there would not be any more female lawyers, preachers, artists, doctors, than there are to-day. There is nothing now to hinder a woman from taking charge of a church, if she and the church wish it. Indeed, women, to-day, hold pastorates, and no one molests them. Probably there is not a village or a city in New England, where a woman would not be listened to respectfully, and given full credit for all her wit and wisdom. Let any woman who is moved to address a public assembly, announce such an intention, and she will have a larger audience than a man of similar ability, and she will have at least an equally appreciative hearing. If she can sustain herself, she will be sustained by the public. Still we have not reached the masses—the women who have no inward, irresistible bent to any thing, who have no ambition for a career, but who must earn their own living—who, while the leaders are conquering all opposition, all circumstances, still remain, thirty-nine thousand and five hundred out of forty thousand, for whose sake the ballot is demanded, and whose fortunes the ballot is expected to create. We have, as yet, found no answer to the question, What will the ballot do for them? 'A thousand employ-ments it will give them,' say its advocates, but they do not specify ten; indeed, I can not find one.

"Is it, in fact, the want of the ballot that keeps them at starving prices, any more than it is the want of the ballot that keeps them back from art and science? I think not. All suffering is pitiable; but I can not spend all my pity upon these forty thousand. I pity myself. I pity the twice forty thousand women in New York who are annoyed, hindered, and injured by the incapacity of foreign servants, that do not know the difference between a castor and a tureen, or between truth and falsehood; but whose lives might grow smooth and peaceful, through the advent of forty thousand intelligent American servants. These forty thousand women are starving over their needles, but if a busy house-mother wants a plain dress made, she must pay ten dollars for the work, bespeak it a month beforehand at that, and submit to whatever abstraction of pieces the dressmaker or her apprentices choose to make. Not to speak of dressmaking, it is no easy matter to secure really good plain sewing; and really good plain sewing, so far as I know, always commands good pay. Why, then, do not these women who are starving over the needle, make fine dresses for twenty dollars, instead of coarse trousers for twenty cents? Why do they not become milliners and mantua-makers, and earn a fortune, and an independent position, instead of remaining slop-makers, earning barely a living, and never rising above a servile and cringing dependence? It is because they have not the requisite skill or money; but of these they can not vote themselves a supply. Here is a girl who wants some other work than sewing. She goes to a counting-room, and is offered, by way of trial, a package of letters to copy. The work is expected to occupy about a week, and she is to be paid twenty-five dollars. She brings back the letters, copied in a clear, round hand, but so carelessly and inaccurately, that her work is worthless. Here is a pretty, bright young woman, engaged with a room full of companions in a similar work, and actually boasting that her employers ' can not do any thing with us. They make rules that we are to be here at such times, and to leave the room only at such times, and do only such and such things; but we will do just as we like;' and I am not surprised by and by to hear that there is trouble brewing, nor do I see how the right of suffrage is to remove the trouble. There are so many things to be taken into the account, that one has need of great caution in forming opinions; but it seems to me that the great and simple cause of the low wages paid to women is the low work they produce. They are equal only to the coarse, common labor; they get only the coarse, common pay; and there are such multitudes of them that their employer has every thing his own way. The moment they rise to a higher grade of work, the crowd thins, and they become masters of the situation. It may not be their fault that they are not skilled artisans, but I suppose trade takes into account only facts, not causes. The laws of supply and demand are just as rigorous as if the brutal and profane head-shopman were a wooden automaton. There are a few employers who modify them by moral laws; but to the great mass work is worth just what it can be got for, and so long as work can be got at starving prices, living prices will not be paid. What can the ballot do here? Nothing but mischief. The relations between employer and employed the law seldom touches but to disturb. 'Hands off' is all we want of government—its own hands, and all others. Freedom, not fostering, is its aim, or fostering only through freedom. Only so far as government continually tends to non-government, continually tends to relegate its power to the individual, to decrease itself and to increase the citizen, is it performing the true function of government. But if women are prevented from establishing themselves in business, through want of means, they need not on that account work at starving prices. I suspect that every one of those forty thousand women could find a comfortable home in New York—a home in which she would have plenty of wholesome food and sufficient shelter, and in which she could earn, besides, two or three dollars a week, if she would accept the home. The work would be more healthful and far less exhaustive than the starvation sewing. Household service is always in demand.

"A woman needs no capital to enter upon it. Even skill is not indispensable. There are thousands of families to which, if an intelligent, virtuous, and ordinarily healthful woman should go and say, ' I have been starving with my needle, and I desire now to try housework. I know very little about it, but I have determined to devote myself to it, and am resolved to become mistress of it,' she would be welcomed. Here, by exercising those virtues and graces which every human being ought to exercise—by being faithful, good-humored, and efficient, she could speedily become an honored and valued member of the family, and secure herself a home that would last as long as the family held together. She could make herself as useful to the family, as the family is to her. Where is the sense in a woman's starving because she has no food in her hands, when a woman is starving by her side because she has

14

no hands for her food? I feel indignant when I hear these multiplied stories of wholesale destitution. I am disposed to say to these women: If you choose to stay at home and perish, rather than go into your neighbor's kitchen and supply your wants, do so; but do not appeal to those for pity from whom you refuse employment. I know there are many who are tied to their own wretched homes; but if those who are unencumbered would resort to the kitchens of the rich, it would relieve the stress of competition; those who remain would command a better price for their labor, and starvation would be permanently stopped.

"I do not say this because housework is woman's sphere, but because it is honest work that calls her, and any honest work in her power is better than starvation, and more dignified than complaint and outcry. If it were picking apples or gathering huckleberries, instead of housework, I should recommend that, just the same. The case of the woman is precisely the case of the man. If a man had palpable, artistic genius, we should constantly desire for him artistic employment; but if he could by no means succeed in securing it, we should certainly advise him to chop wood, however disagreeable wood-chopping be to him, rather than die; and if he choose to shiver and starve at his home, rather than come and cut my wood, for want of which I stand shivering, I should take his starvation with great equanimity. So with women. No one has a right to tell women what they ought to do, to dictate to them their sphere. But when women cry out that they are dying for the want of the ballot, we have a right to say : 'Not so. Unquestionably you are dying, and unquestionably you have not the ballot; but the two do not stand in the relation of effect and cause.'"

We can very readily understand how it should come to pass that there should be at this time so much excitement on the question of woman-suffrage. The late war called into sudden and beneficent activity thousands of heroic, brave women ; tested by its great emergencies, lifted above themselves by its grand excitements, they found themselves capable, while the stress lasted, of wonderful deeds, as surprising to themselves as to any one else. Well-educated women, hitherto distrustful of their own powers, undertook, and with success, the management of great enterprises of mingled philanthropy and business; they kept, with perfect accuracy, complicated and difficult sets of books of account, packed and shipped goods, sometimes to the amount of millions of dollars, superintended hospitals, arranging all the details with the most perfect system and order, improvised hospital comforts and luxuries from the most unpromising materials, visited camps and battle-fields, remaining sometimes under fire when the most stout-hearted men retreated. They roused the occasionally flagging contributions of the country, by eloquent appeals, and sometimes by oral addresses of such deep pathos, that large audiences would be affected to tears, and what was more to the purpose, to the most bounteous giving; and in all ways developed powers of the possession of which they had previously no consciousness. It is greatly to the honor of these noble women, that at the close of the war, after three or four years of the most intense and wearing excitement which human nature was capable of enduring, they should have gone back to their homes, as quietly and with as little seeming consciousness of the great work they had accomplished, as if their years of toil had been but a pleasant pastime. And yet they were greatly changed. The pale face, the occasional expression of intense weariness, a weariness which the grave alone could hide, the abstracted gaze, as if the soul was looking back on all it had seen and suffered, these alone would have sufficed to show that there was a change from their girlish gayety, or their womanly self-possession.

But the change was far deeper than this. The development of higher gifts, and a more profound and thoughtful nature than they had previously been conscious of, made the frivolities and superficiality of their old life intolerable. Henceforward, except where the vital powers had been so much overtasked that they could not rally, their lives must be passed in unresting activ-

ity. To them the poet's words were deeply significant—

> Life is real, life is earnest,
> And the grave is not its goal;
> Dust thou art, to dust returnest,
> Was not spoken of the soul.

To some these opportunities for activity came
in the shape of philanthropic enterprises: the care
of hospitals, the ministering to the sick and sorrowing, the instruction and elevation of the ignorant and degraded, the rescue of the imperiled
or fallen, or the care of the orphaned, the homeless, or the tempted. Into all these institutions
they infused a new life and power, and showed
that they were in their true vocation.

Some (a comparatively small number) in whom
the consciousness of power dominated over the
claims of the ordinary philanthropies, believed
themselves called to a wider sphere of action; to
the inauguration of reforms in society, in political
life, in the very organization of government.
Aware of what they had been able to accomplish
amid the white-heat of a great civil war, and not
having hitherto reached the limit of their intellectual abilities, they went forward fearlessly, but
found themselves, presently, hampered by unexpected obstacles, and learned, to their cost, that
there were bounds which they could not pass. It
was natural that the efforts of this class should be
early directed to the acquisition of suffrage for

women; and that they should cherish undue expectations from it. Had they not demonstrated that they possessed equal executive abilities, equal business capacities with men? and looking upon their own grand achievements with a kind of proud humility, they said: "What we have done, our sisters could have accomplished under similar circumstances;" if, then, they were capable of doing men's work, even in its higher, perhaps its highest, callings, why should they not enjoy all men's privileges? Why, indeed?

But they have yet to learn, and some of them are slower in acquiring this lesson than any other, that there is a higher sphere of action for woman than the enjoyment of man's prerogatives or the usurpation of his duties and labors. He who, in his blessed word, has taught us the true relations of the sexes, and has made us to understand that woman's nature is the complement of man's, and that both are necessary to make up the unit of a perfect humanity, has also demonstrated to us in the type of this perfect humanity, the God-man, Christ Jesus, that the subject-condition in this life is the one of the highest honor, and that in the future it will receive the greatest glory. "For even the Son of Man came not to be ministered unto, but to minister, and to give his life a ransom for many." If, then, the Divine Redeemer, the only perfect representative of the complete human nature, has thus glorified the subject-condition by himself assuming it, and only laying it aside with his mortal life (since one of his last acts before his crucifixion was to engage in the office of washing his disciples' feet), how confidently may those who, in the like spirit, have submitted to the subject-condition here, look forward to that glorious future, when they shall be as the angels which excel in strength, still, indeed, the ministers of God's will, but ministers crowned with glory and honor. This subject-condition did not, in the case of Jesus Christ, and does not in theirs, imply any thing necessarily humiliating or degrading; it is rather in itself one of honor and responsibility.

The work to which these brave, heroic spirits are called, is not, indeed, one of political revolution; it is something higher and better. The army of the Union to which they with others ministered was a great one, and the care of its sick and wounded tasked their highest powers; but they are now called, if they will but heed the call, to a greater ministry, to ameliorate more wide-spread suffering, to do a grander work. Be it theirs, by associated and organized effort, to promote the practical education of the humbler classes of their own sex, to elevate them from the slough of poverty and despondency, in which so many of them are sunk, not by the gifts of an indiscriminate charity, but by kindly sympathy, encouragement, and counsel; protecting them from oppression and wrong, aiding even their feeblest efforts to struggle up to a higher position; assisting in the attempts of both husbands and wives to escape from the bondage of intemperance and its concomitant evils; facilitating the acquisition of trades and other forms of skilled labor by the young; encouraging and helping the organization of associations to prevent overcrowding and undue competition in the lower grades of work where they produce the greatest suffering; explaining and enforcing the benefits of co-operative labor and supplies; and, where it is necessary, invoking earnestly the legal protection of the interests, temporal and moral, of women.

Here is a vast and most beneficent work—a work which will give ample employment to the intellects and activities of thousands of our most accomplished women, and which will confer, if rightly managed, untold benefits upon the women of our country. Were the ballot the agency for good which its most enthusiastic advocates describe it, one week of such work as we have here indicated would accomplish more for the advantage of American women, than could be gained from the ballot in all the ages of the future.

It would be a ministry, a service, it is true; and those who engaged in it would be, in the best sense, the servants of the Most High; but, in thus following the example of Him, who went about doing good, they would find their work and ser vice compatible with the greatest joy and the highest honor.*

* Mr. J. Stuart Mill, in some of the most eloquent passages of the closing chapter of his book on "The Subjection of Women," thus bemoans the condition of these women, qualified for a life of active usefulness, but who are, as he thinks, denied any suitable outlets for their activity: "There is nothing, after disease, indigence, and guilt, so fatal to the pleasurable enjoyment of life as the want of a worthy outlet for the active faculties. Women who have the cares of a family, have this outlet, and it generally suffices for them; but what of the greatly increasing number of women, who have had no opportunity of exercising the avocation which they are mocked by telling them is their proper one? What of the women whose children have been lost to them by death or distance, or have grown up, married, and formed homes of their own? There are abundant examples of men who, after a life engrossed by business, retire with a competency to the enjoyment, as they hope, of rest, but to whom, as they are unable to acquire new interests and excitements that can replace the old, the change to a life of inactivity brings *ennui,* melancholy, and premature death. Yet no one thinks of the parallel case of so many worthy and devoted women, who, having paid what they are told is their debt to society—having brought up a family blamelessly to manhood and womanhood—having kept a house as long as they had a house needing to be kept—are deserted by the sole occupation for which they have fitted themselves; and remain with undiminished activity but with no employment for it, unless, perhaps, a daughter or daughter-in-law is willing to abdicate, in their favor, the discharge of the same functions in her younger household. Surely a hard lot for the old age of those who have worthily discharged, as long as it was given to them to discharge, what the world accounts their only social duty. Of such women, and of those others to whom this duty has not been committed at all—many of whom pine through life with the consciousness of thwarted vocations, and activities which are not suffered to expand—the only resources, speaking generally, are religion and charity. But their religion, though it may be one of feeling and of ceremonial observance, can not be a religion of action, unless in the form of charity. For charity many of them are by nature admirably fitted; but to practice it usefully, or even without doing mischief, requires the education, the manifold preparation, the knowledge, and the thinking powers, of a skillful administrator. There are few of the administrative functions of government for which a person would not be fit, who is fit

We honor the efforts of those who seek to rescue from the paths of the destroyer those who
have become the slaves of lust; theirs is an
arduous but a blessed work; yet, how much
more blessed is the work of those who rescue
from temptation those who have not yet fallen!
She who has not sinned has great advantages over

to bestow charity usefully. In this, as in other cases (pre-eminently in
that of the education of children), the duties permitted to women can not
be performed properly without their being trained for duties which, to
the great loss of society, are not permitted to them. . . .

"If there is any thing vitally important to the happiness of human
beings, it is that they should relish their habitual pursuit. This requisite
of enjoyable life is very imperfectly granted, or altogether denied, to a
large part of mankind; and by its absence many a life is a failure, which
is provided, in appearance, with every requisite of success. But if circumstances, which society is not yet skillful enough to overcome, render such
failures often for the present inevitable, society need not itself inflict
them. The injudiciousness of parents, a youth's own inexperience, or
the absence of external opportunities for the congenial vocation, and their
presence for an uncongenial, condemn numbers of men to pass their
lives in doing one thing reluctantly and ill, when there are other things
which they could have done well and happily. But on women this sentence is imposed by actual law, and by customs equivalent to law.
What, in unenlightened societies, color, race, religion, or in the case of a
conquered country, nationality, are to some men, sex is to all women;
a peremptory exclusion from almost all honorable occupations, but either
such as can not be fulfilled by others, or such as those others do not
think worthy of their acceptance. Sufferings arising from causes of
this nature usually meet with so little sympathy, that few persons are
aware of the great amount of unhappiness even now produced by the
feeling of a wasted life. The case will be even more frequent, as increased cultivation creates a greater and greater disproportion between
the ideas and faculties of women and the scope which society allows to
their activity." We have, we think, demonstrated in the passage which
precedes this note, that for the classes whose lack of enjoyable employment Mr. Mill so eloquently deplores, there is something better than the
ballot, and better than that indiscriminate dispensation of charity which
he seems to regard as their only other resource.

her erring, but repentant sister. How much of sin and bitter repentance may be prevented by such labors as we have indicated; how many homes now desolated by vice may be made happy; and how many wives and mothers, in imminent danger of falling, may be held up and made to stand firmly! How many abodes of wretchedness and filth may, by kindly counsel and instruction, be made comfortable and cheerful homes! An organization somewhat akin to this, though more distinctly religious, has been established in Germany by the philanthropist, Wichern, and some associates, male and female, of kindred spirit, under the name of "The Inner Mission," and it has accomplished a vast amount of good. Let us have our "Inner Mission" here, and let those noble women who showed such executive and administrative ability during the late war, be its founders and managers.

There are other fields of effort yet open to this newly-awakened activity of woman; fields in which she may exhaust the aspirations of her nature, without ever reaching their bounds. Are her tastes and sympathies interested in the promotion of high art? Is "a thing of beauty a joy forever" to her? How wide is the scope for the exercise of her powers of invention, creation, and combination? In painting, in sculpture, in those arts of design which are of humbler name, she may aid in enlightening and beautifying the world,

and if her highly cultivated taste excel her powers of execution, how easily may she, as the friend
and patron of artists, give them that appreciative
encouragement which is often more cheering to
their sensitive natures than the most lavish ex·
penditure without intelligent interest.

There are other realms of art, too, in which
woman reigns of right. In music, she can, if
endowed with a fine and flexible voice, thoroughly
trained, move the heart and thrill the soul, as no
man ever did or can. And this is not, as some
have supposed, because the soprano voice is so
much more effective than the tenor, but because
the woman puts more soul into her singing, and
forgetting her own consciousness, is borne heaven-
ward by the exalted strains, while the man almost
inevitably thrusts his own personality into his
music.

And what is true of music, is also, in a less
degree, perhaps, true of poetry. The elements
of the true poetic nature are oftener found in
woman than man; and the sole reason why women have not oftener been successful in attaining
the loftier heights of poetry, has been that they
have been too much afraid to abandon themselves
to its best inspirations; they have mingled too
often their own personality with the great thoughts
which sought utterance. The genuine poets of
the future will, many of them, be women. In
still another department of art, now degraded by

the utter want of good taste, and in which the worst possible contrivances of women, alike devoid of intellectual and moral capacity for their work, have been eagerly copied, the artistic designing and planning of woman's dress, there is a wide scope for the genius of highly cultured and gifted women.

What an admirable means of instruction in the principles of beauty in form, lines, design, and color, might dress be made. How complete its adaptation to the figure, complexion, and bearing of the wearer. And how might economy, both in style and cost of material, be made compatible with elegance and excellence. We should be delivered from those hideous designs, whose only object seems to be to transform the most transcendent beauty into a thorough fright; and in the reign of exquisite taste which would ensue, the eye would no longer be pained, nor the heart sickened, by the grotesque deformities which are now palmed upon society as the latest fashions.

There would be a positive gain to our systems of education, both the public and the charitable, if they were to a much greater extent than they now are, under the control and supervision of thoroughly trained, sensible women. The deaconesses and Protestant sisterhoods in Europe, trained to educational and charitable labors, and the Sisters of the Sacred Heart and of Mercy in the Catholic Church, accomplish great good in their several spheres, in bringing the children of the middle and poorer classes under instruction. Organized and persistent effort is greatly needed in this country, especially in our great cities, to bring the vast numbers of vagrant and truant children into schools. It is estimated that, in New York and Brooklyn alone, one hundred and fifty thousand children, between the ages of five and sixteen years, never enter a school; and from these hordes of young vagrants, the criminal classes are constantly recruited. By systematized and judicious effort, much can be done to educate and train up these children aright; and women must do it, if it is to be done successfully.

Another wide field of activity for these women who desire to be useful, is to be found in the management of charitable and benevolent institutions. The reformatories, homes for the friendless, orphan and half-orphan asylums, homes for the aged and infirm, schools for feeble-minded and imbecile children, nurseries, *crèches*, children's and foundling hospitals, asylums for consumptives and incurables, industrial schools for girls, working-women's homes, houses of correction, homes for fallen women, and all the wide range of reformatory, corrective, and charitable institutions, will generally succeed better under the management of able and judicious women, than under the charge of men; and though the experiment has not yet been tried on a large scale, we incline to the belief that they would prove skillful in the management of deaf-mute and blind asylums. Every thing depends, of course, upon the selection of women for these posts, since a pragmatic, wrong-headed, or otherwise incompetent woman, could, even to a greater extent than a man of the same character, do almost irreparable injury to the institution.

But for women possessing the high abilities and the ardent piety, which are the necessary qualifications for the work, there is no sphere where there is so great an opportunity of usefulness as is to be found in connection with the Christian Church. She who lays her intellectual gifts, her graces, her superior culture, and her ability, to plan and work for Christ and his Church, upon the altar, brings a noble sacrifice. Foreign missions call loudly on our women of culture and talent, for recruits to the heroic band who have been for years struggling with the darkness of heathen minds, the powerful influence of caste, the degrading doctrines of Brahminism and Mohammedanism, in relation to the future life of woman, and the general condition of depression and wretchedness of the sex on the Asiatic and African continents.

Formerly, women who went out to the East, as the wives of missionaries, were looked upon as a sort of necessary evil; little or nothing was expected from them in the way of missionary labor, and some of the missionary boards preferred that the missonary should be a celibate. More than once was the question argued in the meetings of these boards, whether the wives were not, on the whole, a hinderance, rather than a help, to the success of their husbands.

The remarkable efficiency of many of these women in a few years overcame these prejudices, and now, not only is it considered desirable that every male missionary should have a wife, who will be a help-meet for him in his labors, and who will take an active part in teaching, and exerting her influence for the elevation of her sex from the ignorance and degradation which now surround them, but very considerable numbers of single women are sent out as teachers of the heathen women, on a wider scale than had previously been attempted, and preparations are making to establish Christian women, educated as physicians, in Mohammedan, Hindoo, and Chinese countries, because they can reach their own sex in the higher classes through their professions, where men could obtain no access to them. In these various classes of duties, there is a field for as many women as will devote themselves to the work.

But the home-field is not less importunate in its demands for more laborers than the foreign. On the frontier, the wives of home-missionaries, and female missionary teachers, will find ample scope for work which will accomplish more for the mental and moral improvement of these States of the future, than almost any other agency.

In our great cities and towns, and even to a considerable extent in the more scattered farming districts, the necessity for mission schools, for friendly Christian visitation from house to house, for Sunday-school instruction among the ignorant, poor, and vagrant classes, for those ministrations to temporal necessities which are so often the means of calling the minds of these poor people to the consideration of religious truth, and the thousand other methods of reaching the lower classes for their good, are already employing the thoughts, the hearts, and the hands of many Christian women; but the number might and should be greatly increased. This is a work which money alone can not do; money is needed, undoubtedly, and our Christian, philanthropic men, may be relied upon with considerable certainty, to furnish that—they have never yet been found wanting, when properly approached for such causes—but what is absolutely indispensable is, that personal effort and influence which women of tact and high religious enthusiasm can best exert.

There is still another department of this field in which educated and refined Christian women can do a work whose influences shall be felt through all coming time. There are, in all our large cities, many thousands of young men who have come thither to fill places as clerks, errand boys, and

apprentices to the various mechanical and manufacturing occupations. They have left country
homes often where they were under good influences, and have come to the great city, where they
are homeless and friendless. The cheerless board-
ing-house, with its hall bedrooms and untidy table,
does not invite their stay in it a moment longer
than can be helped; and they go forth into the
streets to satisfy their craving for society and entertainment, two wants which are uppermost in their
minds. Satan takes good care that neither of these
shall be lacking on his side. The friendless, lonely
young man, unguarded by any strong religious
principle, is not long at a loss for either companionship or pleasure in a great city. On every
hand, the theater, the concert-saloon, the beer-gar-
den, the billiard-room, glowing with light and
beauty, stand conspicuously before him, and
places of even baser character are not hard to
find. To keep these young men from such resorts
there must be other resorts, also glowing with
brightness and beauty, where wholesome—not dull
—entertainment and pleasant society may attract
and keep the yet unhardened from the dangerous
influences surrounding them.

The "Young Men's Christian Associations" are
doing a good work in this direction, but they need
help—such help as Christian employers can give
by taking a careful interest in the intellectual and
spiritual welfare of all those in their employ, and

seeing to it, personally, that they have suitable companionship and proper sources of entertainment; and, above all, they need help from noble Christian women. No attraction to good is so powerful to young men of this class, as the influence and notice of pure, gentle, and intelligent women. Their influence is, beyond comparison, greater than that of all others with these youths, who have left tender and pure-minded mothers and sisters in their far-away homes.* If attracted away from the haunts of vice, and strengthened in all good purposes and virtuous undertakings, they will become, in a few years, proprietors and employers, where they are now clerks and apprentices. Then, how vast will be the power which they will exert for good in the community—a power due almost wholly to the influence of these Christian women, who, at the cost, doubtless, of a considerable sacrifice of their feelings and natural reserve, have won them from the haunts of vanity and sin, to become, under their guidance, honorable, high-minded Christian men.

Several of the Christian churches in Europe, and three or four denominations in this country, have been in the habit for some years of setting apart, by some simple form of consecration, after suitable instruction and training, such

---

* We are gratified to learn that, in New York City, a considerable number of excellent and philanthropic women have banded themselves together for this and other humane purposes, under the appropriate title of "Sisters of the Stranger."

women as felt that they were called to the work, as deaconesses, or, as they are called in some of the churches, "Protestant Sisters."

The work of the deaconesses is, in general, visiting and nursing the sick, ministering to the poor, gathering the poor and vagrant children into parochial schools, and, in some instances, teaching them; encouraging and aiding those who have not attended church to do so, assisting the clergymen under whose general direction they work, in such of his pastoral duties as may come within their range, and less frequently, though to a considerable extent, nursing in and superintending hospitals and asylums, acting as matrons and managers in Magdalen asylums, penitentiaries, and prisons for women.

The Deaconesses' Institute at Kaiserswerth, on the Rhine, long under the care of its founder, Pastor Fliedner, and now conducted by his widow and daughters, is the best known of all these, in part from the fact that Florence Nightingale received her special training there. It has sent out several hundred deaconesses, who are mostly at work in Europe, Asia, Africa, and America. They enter upon their work for five years, but take no vow, and are at liberty to marry if they choose. Most of them continue in their work beyond the five years, and if they remain in it till disabled by illness, infirmity, or old age, they have a home at Kaiserswerth to which they are welcomed, and where they spend the evening of their days. This institute is under the care of the Lutheran Church. A somewhat similar institution, at Strasburg, under the care of the Protestant Reformed Church of France, has also accomplished a great amount of good. Smaller establishments exist in the Dordogne, under the care of Pastor Bost; in Paris, also under the direction of the Protestant Reformed Church; at Basle, in connection, we believe, with the Basle Missionary Society, and in some other towns of Central Europe. In England, the organization of sisterhoods has been a High Church, and to some extent a ritualistic development; and though they have accomplished some good, it has caused a prejudice against them that they copied too closely the objectionable features of the Catholic order of Sisters of Charity. That order, despite its life vows, its peculiar costume, its lack of a broad and generous culture, its fanaticism, and its zeal in propagating under all circumstances and at all times the Romish faith, has accomplished a vast amount of good, and has given Romanism a more powerful hold on the hearts of the masses, than all its other agencies. In this country, the Lutherans, the Moravians, the Mennonites, the Tunkers, and, in a few instances, the Congregational churches, have had and still have their deaconesses; not always trained like those of the European institutions, but always selected from those who manifested a vocation for the work. Analogous to these, in some particulars, are the women preachers and elders among the Friends. Some churches, and at least one diocese of the Protestant Episcopal Church, have favored the establishment of sisterhoods, trained to this philanthropic and Christian work, from some of which (notably the Sisterhood of the Holy Communion in New York, and a similar organization in Baltimore, under the direct patronage of Bishop Whittingham) were sent some of the most accomplished nurses and lady superintendents of hospitals who served in those capacities during the war.

We have been thus particular in our review of the work which still demands the exertion of the marvelous energies, the great abilities, and the remarkable administrative powers of the women who were the glory and pride of our country during the recent war, for the purpose of showing to them that their time and intellect need not be frittered away on such insignificant objects as woman-suffrage, but that they can find "ample scope and verge enough" for the exercise of all their powers, in the great duties which we have spread before them. There are those among them, we feel certain, who will rise,—there are some, indeed, who have already risen "to the height of this great argument," and we can not but commend their example to those of their sisters who seek but to know their duty, and are willing, so soon as it is known, to do it with their might.

CHAPTER XXI.

WERE we to estimate the importance of the movement for woman-suffrage, by the force of the arguments of the women who have undertaken its advocacy in this country, we should deem the labor we have bestowed on the subject as well nigh lost, for there can be no serious discussion, when one of the parties puts forth only words without argument. There can be no doubt that Mrs. Stanton, Miss Anthony, and the other eight or ten ladies who have made themselves conspicuous in this movement, possess considerable talent; they ought to be familiar with the whole subject of woman-suffrage, for some of them have been declaiming in its favor for twenty years and more; if there are any strong arguments for it, they certainly should have them at their fingers' ends; but, after a careful reading of their addresses and speeches, and a frequent perusal of the *Revolution*—their organ—we have failed to find any thing which could be, by courtesy, called an argument, in favor of what they claim to be the greatest reform of the century. There is declamation in plenty; exaggerated and inaccurate statistics of the number of working-women who are starving for want of the ballot; of the number of the impoverished and vicious classes; careless misrepresentations of the arguments against woman suffrage; the most laughable *non sequiturs*, from assumed, but false premises; sharp, and sometimes witty flings against opponents, and a great amount of froth and fury, utterly irrelevant to the subject; but of real argument, not a word.

Of course there is nothing to answer in such ebullitions; and, were it not that a few writers elsewhere, among them Mr. Mill and Mrs. Dall, have brought forward all the arguments which can be adduced in its favor, we should have deemed it the wiser course to let the public judge of the cause by their weak defense of it, satisfied that they could make no considerable progress with thoughtful minds.

Many of Mr. Mill's arguments do not apply to the condition of affairs here, being written for the people of England, where the property-qualification is an essential feature of the suffrage; others we have met, we believe, satisfactorily. Mrs. Dall indulges too much in mere declamation, but she adduces more arguments than any of her sisters, and these we have endeavored to answer fully.

The effect of this frothy declamation, and assertion without proof, upon the community, has been just what might have been expected; a large proportion of the sensible, practical women, who, at a first superficial survey of the subject, thought that it might be well for women to enjoy the abstract right of suffrage, though they would have been opposed to any frequent exercise of it, have become completely disgusted with the want of reason and argument which these self-appointed advocates have manifested, and are now clear and decided opponents of woman-suffrage, under any and all circumstances. Let us give a few instances, which will serve to show the existing feeling on the subject.

About a year ago, a working-women's association was organized in New York City, Miss Anthony being active in it from the first. Its main object was, such systemization of woman's work, as should lead to their receiving better wages, and should prevent undue and unfair competition. Miss Anthony insisted that these objects could be attained only by the acquisition of the suffrage. The working-women, who had come into the organization in considerable numbers, listened at first with respectful silence, and some hope, but soon perceiving that there was nothing but declamation and froth in these harangues, and finding that the only measures which were practical and feasible, were steadily ignored by Miss Anthony, and that there was no way of shaking off this " Old Man of the Sea," they began to drop off by ten or a dozen at a time, till finally Miss Anthony was left with but two or three adherents. The working-women, meantime, organized anew, and made it one of their organic conditions that neither woman-suffrage nor its advocates should have any place henceforth in their association.

There were at first a considerable number of sincere friends of the movement for the elevation of woman, and her more thorough culture—persons of both sexes, who honestly thought that some benefit might inure to woman from the possession of suffrage. They had no political ends to serve, and no personal ambitions to gratify. A year or two of declamation from the leaders has satisfied most of these, either that the ballot would be productive of more evil than good to woman, or, that of all the agencies for her advancement, it was the least significant and the least important. Among these we may name Mr. Greeley, Geo. W. Curtis, Miss A. Dodge (Gail Hamilton), Miss C. E. Beecher, and one, at least, if not more, of her sisters, and, we believe, also, Mr. W. L. Garrison.

Chicago, as in duty bound, was early, forward in this movement, a Sorosis being formed, in which this was the prominent idea, and a newspaper in defense of woman-suffrage in particular, and woman's rights in general, started, under the editorial charge of one of the most gifted, brilliant, and eloquent women of the city—one who had already achieved a high reputation by her labors in behalf of the soldiers during the war.

Chicago is a fast city, and these enterprises presently attained maturity—and decay. The

Sorosis failed first, and singularly enough, on a question of the individual rights of one of its members. The interest in the paper speedily began to wane, and not all the ability of its editor could increase or even maintain its circulation. We are not informed whether it still exists, but at the latest advices, it was evidently destined to speedy dissolution. Meantime, the true friends of woman have been gradually arriving at the conclusion that her highest interests and her best opportunity for improving her condition lie in quite another direction, and that her advancement can be best promoted by a more thorough and more practical education, especially in artistic, horticultural, and other industrial pursuits, by trades-unions, co-operative societies, and association. Miss Beecher has led the way among her own sex in the systematic development of plans for this purpose, and " Gail Hamilton " has demonstrated, with more than her accustomed force, that the evils under which women suffer are very largely due to their own ignorance, indifference, or recklessness.

So rapidly is this sound and healthy reaction affecting the masses of intelligent women, that were the vote to be taken among them solely to-day, the preponderance against woman-suffrage would be, at least, ten to one.

" But," say some of the advocates of woman-suffrage, " if there are *any* women who want to vote, the door ought to be opened so that *all can* who choose."

Why, O sapient orator! should they be? Let us put the proposition in another shape. If there are any minors (no matter of what age) who want to vote, the doors ought to be opened, so that all can who choose. Does that proposition seem absurd? It is not more so than the other. Still another form might be given to it with equal justice. If a woman wants any thing (no matter whether it is reasonable or unreasonable), she ought to have it. We are hardly prepared to accept either proposition as our rule of action, because that we believe that neither party (the women or the minors) are always the best judges of what is for their good. Let us be convinced that they are, and we will cheerfully aid in according them all that they have set their hearts upon.

We entered upon the preparation of this work with the avowal of our high regard for the sex, and our desire to promote their real interests in all possible ways. If we have opposed woman-suffrage with zeal, if we have sought to dissuade women from entering on certain pursuits and callings, it has been, not from any unkindly motive or any desire that they should be restrained from occupying any sphere or fulfilling any duty to which God has called; them but because we were convinced that the suffrage, and the pursuits to which we objected, would prove an injury and a blight upon their character and reputation. We would have all women what some whom it has been our happiness to know, are : modest, virtuous, pure, and loving, of amiable disposition, clear intellect, and sound judgment; in short, God's last, best earthly gift to man, his help-meet, friend, and counselor.

It is a source of great gratification to us, to know that the views we have advocated in this volume are fast gaining ground in our own country ; that here, sooner than anywhere else on earth, woman is likely to be enfranchised from every bondage which prevents her from occupying the sphere which the Creator designed she should occupy; while yet she maintains with honor and dignity, that subject-condition to which she was assigned in Eden.

There is progress, not always, perhaps, in exactly the right direction, though often the deviation is but slight, but still progress in all respects in the condition and rights of women, and progress is infinitely preferable to stagnation.

Looking back as some of us can, to a period forty years ago, we shall see how great are the changes which have transpired in woman's condition in that time.

The young woman of those days, at eighteen, was a very good cook; she could wash and iron skillfully, could sew, knit, and spin. Except on state occasions, her dress was a plain, neat calico ;

or, in winter, of woolen stuff; her cheeks had the glow of health, for she knew nothing of disease; her life was simple and pure, and she looked forward with a confidence which time seldom failed to justify, to the day when she should be a happy bride and reign a queen in her own household. This was the bright side. But useful and happy as she was, her education was but scanty; she could read and write, she knew a little of the elements of arithmetic, geography, and possibly a trifle of grammar and history. Politics did not much disturb her, though she had a vague idea, that for the preservation of the country, all men ought to vote as her father did, and wondered that any were so perverse as not to do so. If she possessed a natural taste for music, she attended the singing-school, was duly escorted therefrom by a rustic swain, and in process of time joined the village choir, and perhaps performed with remarkable skill her part of one of those wonderful fugues, in which the whole choir seemed engaged in playing the game of tag. As to instrumental music, she knew nothing more of it than could be extracted from the accordeon, though, perchance, she might be able to accompany her lover with her voice, as he played some simple tune on the fiddle or flute. To own a piano, and especially to be able to play a tune upon it, was only the privilege of the families of the very rich; and even with them

was regarded as an almost sinful waste of time.
It was very doubtful if she had ever learned to
dance; if she had, it was only some simple qua-
drilles, or the old-fashioned contra-dance. The
polka and waltz, to say nothing of the Schottische,
the Lancers, or the German, would have shocked
her sense of propriety. Of all the sciences and
belles-lettres, which go to make up a modern,
fashionable education, she was utterly ignorant,
and if she had ever heard of, or read any novels,
they were either, " The Children of the Abbey,"
" The Scottish Chiefs," " Thaddeus of Warsaw,"
" The Mysteries of Udolpho," " Dunallan,"
" Thinks I to Myself; or, Coelebs in Search of a
Wife;" or, by a bare possibility, " Redwood," or
some volume of " Waverley," then just issued.
She could not have entertained a young gallant
for five minutes with small talk about the last
novel, and as to magazines, they were not; but if
the young gentleman would stay to tea, he could
have choice wheat, or rye bread, which her own
hands had made, and cake which would surpass any
thing to be found at the confectioner's; rich, golden
butter, which was wholly the product of her skill;
and though the table was old and dark, it was
covered with a snow-white cloth, which, very possibly, she herself had spun. Visiting her a few
years later, you would find her with her beauty a
little faded, it may be, and the face perhaps less
joyous and *spirituelle;* her cares as wife and

mother had rendered her somewhat more of the earth, earthy; yet all were performed with a conscientiousness and fidelity, a neatness and attention to detail, which left nothing uncared for. She had no time now for books or intellectual improvement, but must go on as she had begun, as a model wife and housekeeper in all things appertaining to the comfort of her family.

If, in this simple, healthful life of the young maiden of forty years ago, we find little which is not now changed for the worse, except it may be a higher and better intellectual culture (though even this is a little in doubt), the progress in a better life of the household has been far greater. The health of the women of the higher classes at the present day, is much less sound and stable than that of the matrons of forty or even thirty years ago; but though this is a serious drawback to the happiness and comfort of the family life, the higher education, the wider range of thought, the more complete intellectual companionship, in a great measure, compensate for the other ills, and if we can but substitute a more rational education for the absurd fashionable one, which every reasonable person must so heartily deprecate, the ratio of progress will be such as to give us new cause of congratulation. There are cheering signs of the near approach of this beneficent reform. The great error of the past forty years in the education of women, has been that we have sought to bring about mental development while ignoring entirely the claims of both the body and the moral nature. Such one-sided culture could not fail to be harmful, and the more successful it has been, the more injury has it done. The mind, debilitated by the cramming process, has sought relief in the stimulating influence of the most vapid and trashy sensational novels, and an equally trashy magazine literature, and has at last reached that condition in which memory is weakened, consecutive serious thought has become impossible, and the whole intellectual powers are too often occupied with the most frivolous topics. The body, neglected in all except its outward adornings, gives speedy tokens of its premature decay in weakness, ill-health, and inability to bear even slight exposures to the vicissitudes of weather, which the young maiden of forty years ago would have regarded as only enhancing her enjoyment. The physical frame should have been developed in harmony with the mind by vigorous and health-giving enterprise, and by the performance of domestic duties, and then both body and mind would have been capable of higher and better attainments. But the moral nature has been as much neglected as the body in the fashionable education of the day. The principles of truthfulness, spotless honor, and strict, unflinching integrity, have not been practically enforced. Petty deception, injustice, class distinc-

15*

tions, and falsehood in little matters, have been passed over as things of no moment, even when they have not been actually encouraged, so long as they inured to the teacher's benefit. The moral culture in our boys' schools and colleges has been bad enough, and we are feeling its evil effects throughout the whole structure of society; but that of our fashionable female seminaries is greatly worse, inculcating a lower sense of honor, giving predominance to false standards of right and wrong, prompting to no high aims, searing the conscience, and hardening the heart.

But we are not without hope that the worst point has been reached even in the schools. More attention is certainly given to physical education than formerly, and though its outcroppings, in the protracted and exciting dances kept up till near morning, in the almost equally exciting skating parties, where the health is often greatly periled, and in the questionable velocipede riding, are not exactly in the right direction, even these in moderation may be better than an entire absence of exercise, or the moping walk in long procession through the public streets, which was at one time the semi-weekly penance called exercise, in many of the fashionable schools.

What is really wanted, and is beginning to be practiced by our best teachers, is not so much any system of female gymnastics, Indian clubs, swinging of dumb-bells, pulling at weights, and all the

KITCHEN EDUCATION.

varied motions which have been invented to call the different muscles into activity. Though these are very good in their way, as some form of exercise which shall occupy and interest the mind while it keeps the body in motion—climbing mountains, cultivating botany in the field, rowing, the study of geology and mineralogy *in situ*, and, as an agreeable alternative to these, the exercise of the sublime art of bread-making, the skillful washing, clear-starching, and ironing of some of the many dainty garments which constitute their wardrobe. The vigorous wielding of the broom is also not a bad exercise, especially on a hard and heavy carpet. It calls into active motion the muscles of the chest and shoulders, and is fully equal for this purpose to the rings or the Indian clubs of the gymnasium. It is a pity that spinning on the great wheel could not be revived. The motions were not too violent, and while they were not incompatible with steady and consecutive thought, they contributed greatly to an erect and graceful carriage of the head and shoulders.

The moral culture will, we hope, come in time. The example of the best of the training-schools and the colleges and high schools for both sexes, will not be without its influence; but while so many of these fashionable schools are controlled by those who are actuated by no lofty principle, who seek patronage on other grounds than those of the moral excellence of their instruction, and who are accustomed in their intercourse with wealthy patrons to

> Bend the supple hinges of the knee,
> That thrift may follow fawning,

we can hardly expect that they should all become remarkable for their inculcation of the loftier virtues. It is something gained that sensible, practical, intelligent women, themselves long connected with the education of girls, see these evils, and are taking measures to obviate them as far as possible. We look with great interest for the results of the noble plan proposed by Miss Catharine E. Beecher, in her paper read before the National Educational Convention at Trenton, in August, 1869, which we have printed in full in the appendix to this work.* It marks an era in the education of woman in this country. We hail this thorough canvass of woman's position, rights, and duties, which is now in progress, for another reason, while we feel certain that the more thoroughly the subject is discussed, the more clearly will the impracticability of female suffrage be demonstrated, and there will yet come out of the discussion much of positive good for woman. The disabilities under which woman has labored, the imperfection of female education, the lack of sufficient employment, the great over-crowding in the lower grades of work, and the unjust difference

* See APPENDIX A.

between the compensation given to women for certain kinds of work, and that paid to men for doing the same things, the want of a vocation so strongly felt by a class of earnest, educated, but hitherto unemployed women; all these, and other kindred grievances of the sex, have not hitherto received their full share of consideration. But the present agitation, notwithstanding the efforts of some injudicious partisans on both sides, will now effect a thorough ventilation of the whole subject, and as there is no desire on the part of any intelligent, right-minded man to do injustice to woman, we may feel confident that all the real wrongs will be righted as soon as they can be fairly reached. Most of them, indeed, are already in progress of amelioration. The promptness with which both the larger trades-unions and the recent Labor Congress, which closed its session in August, 1869, have recognized and admitted to their organizations the real representatives of the working-women's trade associations; and the readiness with which most of the employers have acceded to the requests of the associations for increase of women's compensation, give strong ground for hope that henceforward we shall have less complaint of the inferior wages of women. The over-crowding of applicants for work which unskilled or but partially skilled women can perform, and the consequent reduction of their wages to the point of starvation, is a matter requiring time and patience to remedy. The best panaceas for it are those which we have urged so strongly, and which others are now urging—better industrial education, the diversion of a large proportion of these working-women to domestic employment, the avoidance of country competition and under-bidding, and, as soon as it can be accomplished, trade associations and co-operation.

The earnest and really noble women, who, conscious of their ability to be something other than the gay, frivolous butterflies of society, are seeking for a worthy vocation, will find in the suggestions we have made to them in the previous chapter—suggestions which their best friends will reiterate—a better way of utilizing their remark-able gifts, than in agitation for the ballot for women, a boon which, like the fabled apples of Sodom, would turn to ashes and bitterness the moment they seized it.

For them, if they have, as they have manifested in the past, the true heroic spirit, there is a grand and noble future. To be the world's bene-factors, to illumine its dark places, to give hope and joy to the downcast, peace and comfort to the erring, health to the sick; to lift up those who have fallen, and bid them, as the Divine Master had done before, to go and sin no more, to rescue the orphaned and vagrant child from a life of wretchedness and sin, to raise the victims of appe-tite from their degradation, and make homes now desolated by intemperance, happy and peaceful, and to diffuse over our own and other lands the blessed influences of lives full of all pure and generous deeds—these are objects worth living for, worth dying for. The women of America who shall organize and develop this glorious mission for good, will deserve and will receive from a grateful country such honors as no crowned queen, no proud empress, can ever hope to attain. On them, too, will fall Heaven's highest benediction : " Inasmuch as ye have done it unto one of the least of these my brethren, ye have done it unto me."

Thus, then, we take leave of our readers. We have sought, with all plainness of speech, but with the deepest regard and reverence for women, to show them from Scripture, from history, and from reason, what were the best remedies for the evils and wrongs from which they suffered ; what the advancement and progress to which they should attain. Desiring to see them, in the future as in the past, women and not men, beings of gentleness and grace, our companions, our sympathizing friends, and not either our slaves or our tyrants, we have endeavored to indicate to them in what directions their condition might be benefited, their lives made happier and more useful, and their own comfort and joy enhanced.

Knowing the evils that were to be apprehended from their participation in political life, and the weighty reasons which forbade their entering upon it,—reasons lying at the very foundation of all society and government, and inherent in their very nature, as well as those which were specially pertinent to our American conditions of suffrage, to the good order of society, and to their own modesty and delicacy—we have endeavored to set these before them as plainly and clearly as possible, and to answer the arguments of those who have advocated woman-suffrage.

How far we have succeeded, remains to be seen; but if our humble effort shall have stimulated any of the sex to more earnest endeavor after a higher and more useful life; if it shall have aided to relieve any woman from the unjust burdens borne so patiently, and have turned any from the vain pursuit of the *ignis fatuus* of the ballot, we shall feel that those months of toil have not been wholly in vain.

APPENDIX A.

[Miss Beecher's essay, read before the National Educational Convention at Trenton, N. J., in August, 1869, and subsequently published in *Appleton's Journal*, is, in the main, so pertinent to the topics discussed in this work, and presents so strongly the need of a better, practical, and industrial education for women, as something of far greater advantage to them than the possession of the suffrage, that we felt we could not better aid in carrying out the philanthropic purposes of its author than by giving it the advantage of the extensive circulation of our work.— L. P. B.]

SOMETHING FOR WOMEN BETTER THAN THE BALLOT.

BY CATHARINE E. BEECHER.

Now that negro suffrage is accomplished, the next political struggle that will agitate this country, as well as Europe, will be that of *labor* and *capital*, and, connected with it, the question of *woman-suffrage*.

That there is something essentially wrong in the present condition of women, is every year growing more and more apparent, while the public mind is more and more perplexed with diverse methods proposed for the remedy. In one of our leading secular papers, we read this statement of the case from the pen of a working-woman :—

" There are so few departments of labor open to women, that, in those departments, the supply of female labor is frightfully in advance of the demand. The business world offers the lowest wages to eager applicants, certain that they will be ravenously clutched. And, indeed, to see the mob of women that block and choke these few and narrow gates open to them—the struggle—the press—the agony—the trembling eagerness—you might suppose they were entering the temple of fame or wealth, or, at least, had some cosy little cottage ahead, in which competence awaited the winner. Nothing of the sort. These are blind alleys, one and all. The mere getting in, and keeping in, are the meager objects of this terrible struggle. A woman who has not *genius*, or is not a *rare exception*, has no opening—no promotion— no career. She turns hopelessly on a pivot; at every turn the sand gives way, and she sinks lower. At every turn light and air are more difficult, and she turns and digs her own grave. Do you say these are figures of speech? Here then, are figures of *fact*. There are *now thirty thousand* women in New York, whose labor averages from *twelve to fifteen hours a day*, and yet whose income seldom exceeds *thirty-three cents a day*. Operators on sewing-machines, and a few others, enjoy comparative opulence, gaining five to eight dollars a week, though from this are to be paid three or four dollars for a bed in a wretched room with several other occupants, often without a window or any provision for pure air, and with only the poor food found where such rooms abound. Thousands of ladies, of good family and education, as teachers receive from two to six hundred dollars a year. Few women get beyond that, and a large proportion of them are mothers with children. Over these poorly-paid laborers broods the sense of hopeless toil. There is no bright future. The woman who is fevered, hurried, and aching, who works from daylight to midnight, loathing her mean room, her meaner dress, her joyless life, will, in ten years, neither better herself nor her children. The American working-woman has no share in the American privilege given to the poorest *male* laborer — a growing income, a bank account, and every office of the Republic, if he have brain and courage to win them."

This describes the condition and feelings of not all, but of a large class of women in our larger cities, who must earn their own livelihood. But, in the medium classes, as it respects wealth, the unmarried or widowed women feel that they are an incumbrance to fathers and brothers, who often unwillingly support them from pride or duty. For such, also, there is "no opening—no promotion—no career;" and they must remain dependent chiefly on the labor of others till marriage is offered, which, to vast numbers, is a positive impossibility.

This has lately been proved, from the census,

by a leading New York paper. In that it is shown that, in all our large cities, the male inhabitants, under fifteen and over the usual marriageable age, are greatly in excess of the females, and, consequently, the women at the marriageable age are greatly in excess of the marriageable men. Thus, in New York City, according to the statements of the New York *Times*, there are eleven thousand more females than males, of all ages, while there are one hundred and thirty-two thousand more women of marriageable age than men of that age. This is probably a large estimate, but the disproportion is at all events enormous.

And, in the rural districts of New York State, we find a similar state of things; for the excess of females, of all ages, is twenty-one thousand, while the excess of marriageable women, if at the same ratio as in New York City, is two hundred and sixty-three thousand. Thus, it appears that, in the single State of New York, there are over three hundred thousand women to whom marriage is impossible. The same state of things will be seen in all our older States.

The most mournful feature in this case is the fact that most of these women have never been trained for any kind of business by which they can earn an independent livelihood. The Working-woman's Protective Union, of New York City, reports that, of thirteen thousand applicants, not one-half were qualified to do any kind of useful work in a proper manner. The societies that are formed to furnish work for poor women report that their greatest impediment is that so few can sew decently, or do any other work properly.

The heads of dress-making establishments report that very few women can be found who can be trusted to complete a dress, and that those who are competent find abundant work and good wages. The demand for really superior mantua-makers is almost universal in country places, and even in many of our cities.

In former days sewing was taught in all schools for girls, but now it is banished from our common schools, and the mothers at home are too neglectful, or too ignorant, or too pressed with labor, to supply the deficiency.

It was reported in the New York *Tribune*, not long since, that there are at least twenty thousand professed prostitutes in New York City alone, while Boston, in proportion to its number of inhabitants, shows a larger number, and all our cities give similar reports. This, also, is an estimate probably much in excess of the reality; but the truth is bad enough and mournful enough. Multitudes of these unfortunates have only two alternatives—on the one hand, poor lodgings, shabby dress, poor food, and ceaseless daily toil from ten to fifteen hours; on the other hand, the tempter offers a pleasant home, a servant to do the work, fine dress, the theater and ball, and kind attentions, with no labor or care. Where is the strength of virtue in those who despise and avoid these out-casts, that might not fall in such perilous assaults?

It is this dreadful state of temptation which accounts for the fact that crime increases faster among women than among men. Thus, in Massachusetts, during the last ten years, among the men of that State, crime *decreased* at the rate of eight thousand five hundred and seven less than during the ten preceding years, while, among women, crime *increased* at the rate of three hundred and sixty-eight during the same period; that is, over eight thousand *less* men, and over three hundred *more* women, were guilty of crime than in the previous ten years.

But, turning from these to the daughters of the most wealthy class, those who have generous and elevated aspirations also feel that for them, too, there is " no opening—no promotion—no career," except that of marriage, and for this they are trained to feel that it is disgraceful to seek. They have nothing to do but wait to be sought. Trained to believe marriage their highest boon, they are disgraced for seeking it, and must affect indifference. Meantime, to do any thing to earn their own independence is what father and brothers would deem a disgrace to themselves and their family. For women of high position to work for their livelihood, in most cases custom decrees as disgraceful. And then, if cast down by poverty, they have been trained to nothing that would earn a support, or, if by chance they had some resource, all avenues for its employment are thronged with needy applicants. Ordinarily, and with few exceptions, there are only two employments for such women that do not involve loss of social position, viz., school-teaching and boarding. But every opening for a school-teacher has scores, and sometimes hundreds, of applicants, while often the protracted toils in unventilated and crowded school-rooms destroy health. To keep boarders demands capital to start, and an experience and training in household management and economy rarely taught to the daughters of wealth. In this country housework is regarded as dishonorable, and rich men make no attempts to train their daughters to any other business that would be a resort in poverty.

Few can realize the perils which threaten our country from the present condition of women. The grand instrumentality, not only for perpetuating our race, but for its training to eternal blessedness, is the family state, and in this woman is the chief minister. As the general rule, man is the laborer out of the home, to provide for its support, while woman is the daily minister to train its inmates. But there are now many fatal influences that combine to unfit her for these sacred duties. Not the least of these is the decay of female health, engendering irritable nerves in both mother and offspring, and thus greatly increasing the difficulties of physical and still more of moral training.

The factory girls, and many also in shops and stores, must stand eight and ten hours a day, often in a poisonous atmosphere, causing decay of constitution, and forbidding healthful offspring. The sewing-machine lessens the wages of needlewomen, while employers testify that those who use it for steady work become hopelessly diseased, and can not rear healthy children. In the more wealthy circles, the murderous fashions of dress make terrible havoc with the health of young girls, while impure air, unhealthful food and condiments, lack of exercise, and over-stimulation of brain and nerves, are completing the ruin of health and family hopes.

The state of domestic service is another element that is undermining the family state. Disgraced by the stigma of our late slavery, and by the influx into our kitchens of ignorant and uncleanly foreigners, American women forsake home circles for the unhealthful shops and mills.

Then the thriftless young housekeepers from boarding-school life have no ability either to teach or to control their incompetent assistants, while ceaseless "worries" multiply in parlor, nursery, and kitchen. The husband is discouraged by the waste and extravagance, and wearied with endless complaints, and home becomes any thing but the harbor of comfort and peace.

Add to all this, the now common practice which destroys maternal health and unborn offspring—the loose teachings of free love—the baleful influence of spiritualism, so called—the fascinations of the *demi-monde* for the rich, and of lower haunts for the rest, with the poverty of thousands of women who but for desperate temptations would be pure, and the extent of the malign influences undermining the family state—that chief hope of our race—is appalling.

Woman, in the Protestant world, is educated only *for marriage*, hoping to have some one to work for her support, and, when this is not gained, little else is provided.

The Roman Catholic Church, while it honored the institution of marriage as a sacrament, and upheld its sanctity, yet taught that woman had a still higher ministry; and for this, large endowments, comfortable positions, and honorable distinction, were provided. The women who devoted their time and wealth and labors to orphans, to the sick, and to the poor, were honored above married women as *saints*, who not only laid up treasures in heaven for themselves, but also a stock of *merits* to supply the deficiencies of others. The idea of self-sacrifice and self-denial in that church was so honored as to run into mischievous extremes, so that rich establishments of celibates

16

of both sexes multiplied all over Christendom till they became burdens and pests.

This drove the Protestant world to the other extreme, so that no provision at all has been made for the single woman. She must marry, or have no profession that leads to independence, honor, and wealth. To fit young men for their professions, thousands and millions are every year provided, securing by endowments the highest class of teachers, in addition to every advantage of libraries, apparatus, and buildings. But woman's profession has no such provisions made for its elevated duties.

How much there is included in woman's distinctive and appropriate duties, and how much science and practical training are demanded properly to prepare for them, few realize. The selection, preparation, and care of food and drinks for a family are, in Europe, made an art and science, to which the most literary and cultivated devote attention. The selection, fitting, and making of clothing are other branches for which science and training are demanded. The care of young infants, and the nursing of the mothers demand science and practical training as much as any profession of the other sex. The management and governing of young children require as much training and skill as the duties of the statesman or warrior. The nursing and care of the sick, if performed by conscientious, scientific, and well trained nurses, would save thousands of the victims of ignorance and neglect.

And then there are out-door professions connected with a home which are as suitable for women as for men. The business of raising fruits and flowers is especially suited to woman, as also the management of the dairy; and for these the other sex are regularly instructed in endowed agricultural schools, while women can not share these advantages. The arts that ornament a home, such as drawing, painting, sculpture, and landscape gardening, are peculiarly appropriate for women as professions by which to secure an independence. Yet but a few have the opportunities which are abundantly given to the other sex.

These are all employments suited to woman, and such as would not take her from the peaceful retreat of a home of her own, which by these professions she might earn. Were there employments for women honored as matters of science, as are the professions of men; were institutions provided to train women in both the science and practice of domestic economy, domestic chemistry, and domestic hygiene, as men are trained in agricultural chemistry, political economy, and the healing art; were there endowments providing a home and salary for women to train their own sex in its distinctive duties, such as the professors of colleges gain—immediately a liberal profession would be created for women, far more suitable and attractive than the professions of men. Let this be done, and every young girl would pursue her education with an inspiring practical end, would gain a profession suited to her tastes, and an establishment for herself equal to her brother's, while she would learn to love and honor woman's profession.

It would soon become the custom, as it now is in some European countries, for every woman to be trained to some business that would secure to her honorable independence.

The grand difficulty, which those who are seeking the ballot would remedy, is, the want of honorable and remunerative employment for unmarried or widowed women. It is not clear how the ballot would secure this; while a long time must elapse before public opinion would arrive at this result.

But the attempt to establish institutions, well endowed to support women instructors, and carrying out as liberal a course as men have provided for themselves, would have an immediate influence, while it would escape the prejudice and the difficulties incident to giving woman the ballot.

Few will deny that the various departments of domestic economy demand science, training, and skill, as much as any of men's professions. But the world has yet to see the *first* invested endowment to secure to woman's profession what has been so bountifully given to men. Never yet has a case been known of a highly-educated woman supported by an endowment to train her sex for any one department of woman's profession. Such favors being withheld, the distinctive profession of woman is undervalued and despised. To be a teacher of young children would be shunned by the daughter of wealth as lowering her social position. To become a nurse of the sick for a livelihood, or a nurse of young children, would be regarded as a degradation; while to become a domestic assistant in the family state would be regarded as the depth of humiliation to any in a high social position.

In the Roman Catholic Church, the woman of high position, culture, and benevolence, is honored above all others, if she remains single, and devotes her time and wealth to orphans, to nurse the sick, to reclaim the vicious, and to provide for the destitute. She becomes a lady abbess, or the head of some sisterhood, where high position, influence, and honor, are her reward.

And the priesthood of that church employ all their personal and official influence to lead women of benevolence and piety to devote time, property, and prayers, to the salvation of their fellow-creatures from diseases of body, ignorance, and sin.

But Protestant women, as yet, have been influenced to endow institutions for *men*, rather than for their own sex. The writer obtained from the treasurers of only six institutions for men the following statement of benefactions from women :

Miss Plummer, to Cambridge University, to endow one professorship, gave $25,000; Mary Townsend, for the same, $25,000 ; Sarah Jackson, for the same, $10,000; other ladies, in sums over $1,000, to the same, over $30,000.   To Andover Professional School of Theology ladies have given over $65,000; and, of this, $30,000 by one lady. In Illinois, Mrs. Garretson has given to one professional school, $300,000.   In Albany, Mrs. Dudley has given, for a scientific institution for men, $105,000.   To Beloit College, Wisconsin, property has been given by one lady, valued at $30,000.

Thus, half a million has been given by women to these six colleges and professional schools, and all in the present century.   The reports of similar institutions for men all over the nation, would show similar liberal benefactions of women to endow institutions for the other sex, while for their own no such records appear.   Where is there a single endowment from a woman to secure a salary to a woman teaching her own proper profession ?

But a time is coming when women will honorably perpetuate their name and memory by bestowing endowments for their own sex, as they have so often done for men.

The first indication of this advance is the organization of an association of prominent ladies and gentlemen of the city of New York, for the purpose of establishing institutions in which highly-educated women shall be supported by endowments to train their own sex for the practical duties of the family state, and also, to some business that will secure to them an independent home and income.

The plan aimed at is large and comprehensive, but will commence on a small scale, and be enlarged as means and experience shall warrant. When completed, it will include these departments:—

1. *The Literary Department*, which will embrace a course of study and training for the main purpose of developing the mental faculties. Much that goes under the head of acquiring knowledge will be omitted until it is decided what profession the character and tastes of a young girl indicate as most suitable. When this is decided, the studies and practical training will be regulated with reference to it, and the pupil will select that department of general knowledge most connected with her special profession.

The public mind is fast approaching this method in the education of young men who do not aim at what have heretofore been called the liberal professions, and who enter institutions where the course of study is adapted to the profession to be pursued. At the same time, our colleges are gradually modifying mediæval methods to those which bear more directly on practical life.

2. *The Domestic Department*, in which the pupils of the literary department will be received and examined as to their practical acquaintance with the varied duties of the family state, aiming to supply every deficiency in past training, so as to fit them to be economical, industrious, and expert housekeepers. The principal of this department will have a family of about twelve, consisting of her assistant principal and ten pupils, who will be carried through a regular course of domestic labor and instruction, and then vacate their place to another class of pupils. In another family, consisting of stationary residents, another assistant principal will superintend the training of servants to be conscientious and faithful cooks, chambermaids, and table-waiters, and, when trained, will provide suitable places for them.

3. *The Health Department*, in which the pupils of the literary department will be trained to preserve their own health, and also to superintend the health of a family. In this department the attempt will be made to train scientific nurses of the sick, monthly nurses of mothers and infants, and nurses for young children. With scientific training will be combined moral instruction and influences to induce the sympathetic, conscientious, and benevolent traits, so important in these offices.

4. *The Normal Department*, in which women will be trained to the distinctive duties of a school-teacher.

5. *The Department of the Fine Arts*, in which all those branches employed in the adornment of a home will receive attention; drawing, painting, sculpture, and landscape gardening, which are peculiarly fitted to be professions for women, will be included in this department.

6. *The Industrial Department*, the chief aim being to train women to out-door avocations suited to their sex, by which they can earn an honorable independence. The raising of fruits and flowers, the cultivation of silk and cotton, the raising and manufacture of straw, the superintendence of dairies and dairy-farms, are all suitable modes of earning an independence, and can all be carried on by women without any personal toils unsuited to their sex. And agricultural schools to train women to the science and practice of these professions are the just due to women as much as to men. And here it is well to notice that our national government has given to every State in the Union a portion of the national lands to endow agricultural colleges, and they have been taken, and in most cases have been wasted, by speculators, and in no instance have American women received any share. But the States in the late rebellion have not taken their portion, and, when they receive it, the Southern women, it is hoped, will claim their proportion, and thus establish institutions to train women to earn their own independence. If only a majority of women, in such a

case as this, and also in the case of detrimental and unjust laws, would unite and petition for redress, they would gain all they ask, and by a more direct and suitable method than by obtaining the law-making power, and then enforcing such acts of justice.

The wisdom of the former course is indicated by the results of a recent meeting of New York ladies. Among the resolutions adopted at this meeting was one claiming that women should be trained for their appropriate professions as men are, and that institutions for this purpose should be as liberally endowed as are the colleges and professional schools for men. This resolution was adopted unanimously, and was as unanimously approved by the leading papers of the city, both secular and religious.

It is an unfortunate feature of some who, with the best of motives, are laboring to relieve the burdens of their sex, that they assume that the fault rests with men, as if they were in antagonism with woman's interests and rights. But in all Christian countries men are trained to a tender care of wives, mothers, and sisters, and a chivalrous impulse to protect and provide for helpless womanhood is often stronger in men than in most women who have had no such training.

The grand difficulty is that the teachings of our Heavenly Father, as to the care of the feebler members of his great family, have been imperfectly realized by women as much as by men, and therefore they have never understood their rights, nor claimed the advantages which are now seen to be their just due. It is certain that all just and benevolent men feel the wrongs and disabilities of womanhood as much as most women do, and have been as much perplexed in seeking the most effective remedy.

The ladies' meeting in New York, and the universal approval by the public prints of the resolutions adopted, prove that the most benevolent and intelligent minds of both sexes deem it only an act of justice to establish institutions for training women to their appropriate professions, which shall be as liberally endowed as those for the other sex ; and that these endowments shall support well-educated women as liberally as the professors of our colleges.

In pursuance of this indication, the American Woman's Educational Association proposes to commence seeking endowments to establish such an institution in close vicinity to New York. Each of the various religious denominations is represented in their board of managers, and the constitution forbids a majority of any one denomination as managers. It is hoped that the ladies of New York (of all parties and sects) will set an example of harmonious action in establishing one model institution, which, no doubt, would be reproduced all over our land. Should this be done, it is believed that all the wrongs of woman would be redressed, and that the ballot for woman, and its risks and responsibilities, would be no longer sought. The family state would thus rise to its high and honored position, and woman, as its chief minister, would feel that no earthly honors or offices could compare in value with her own.

Then every woman would look forward to a cheerful home of her own, where she could train the children of her Heavenly Father for their eternal home. If not married, or if not blessed with children, she could gather the lost lambs of her Lord and Saviour, and lead them to the green pastures and still waters of eternal life.

APPENDIX B

It will be noticed by the reader that we have, in this discussion, said nothing concerning the views held on the subject of marriage by some of the advocates of woman-suffrage; nor on the effect which would be inevitably produced on the permanence and inviolability of the marriage tie, by granting this privilege to women.

Having laid down, in the beginning, the Scriptural view of the relations of the two sexes, a view which we conceive to be vitally important to the discussion of the whole question, we were disposed to leave the subject of marriage untouched, regarding these declarations of Scripture sufficient to satisfy our readers of our position.

But the avowals of Mr. Mill, in his recent volume, the published declarations of some of the leaders of the woman-suffrage movement in this country, and the low ground on which all of them base the relation, have caused us to reconsider our determination, and to say a few words on this important subject.

Marriage we hold to be an ordinance of God, in which one man, in the presence of witnesses, and before his Creator, whom, by that act, he calls also to witness his vows, takes one woman to be his wife, promising to love, cherish, protect, and honor her, to be true to her, and to her only, so long as they both shall live ; the wife, on her part, pledging herself equally to be true to her husband, to honor, love, and obey him, so long as they both shall live. This is no mere partnership of two equals, to be dissolved with or without cause, at the will of either or both parties. Aside from death, it can, according to the explicit declaration of the Divine founder of the relation, be dissolved only for one cause—the violation of their marriage vows by one or the other party. A separation, but without the privilege on either side of marriage to another, might be justified on the ground of cruelty, intemperance, desertion, or complete incompatibility of temper. This position, we believe to be maintained by the Scriptures, and by the Christian Church in all ages.

Mr. Mill, on the contrary, takes the ground that marriage is a mere partnership, professedly for life, but capable of being dissolved at any time, at the will of the parties ; though he dissuades them from such dissolution, except for good and sufficient cause. The corollary which he draws from this position is, that being equal partners, there is no rightful headship in one more than in the other ; that, from the accident of his seniority, or his greater mental culture, the man may be the head ; or, the circumstances being changed, the wife may

be ; or, they may share their headship together.
To the objection that this would lead to collisions
and separation, he replies, that this would never
occur except where the connexion altogether had
been a mistake, and then it would be a blessing
to both parties to be relieved from it.

Some of the leaders in the woman-suffrage
movement, Mrs. Ernestine L. Rose for one, we
believe, take even stronger ground than this.
They avow that marriage has not even the sanc-
tions that belong to an ordinary partnership; that
" every woman has a right to choose who shall be
the father of her child;" " that true marriage, like
true religion, dwells in the sanctuary of the soul,
beyond the cognizance or sanction of State or
Church;" and scoff generally at the idea of any
permanence or sanctity in the marriage tie.

We do not believe that Mrs. Stanton, Miss
Anthony, Mrs. Davis, or several of the other
prominent women of the suffrage movement, are
prepared to sanction all these extravagant and
disorganizing sentiments ; though we have never
been able to learn that any of them have publicly
repudiated them; but there is a looseness of view
on this important subject, inherent in the movement itself.

Miss Dodge (Gail Hamilton), in one of the
most eloquent passages in her " Woman's
Wrongs," treads on very dangerous ground on
this subject; and, though she would probably

scout the idea of being the advocate of divorce and the opponent of legal marriage, her language bears on its face that interpretation. Hear her :—

"Wherever man pays reverence to woman, —wherever any man feels the influence of any woman, purifying, chastening, abashing, strengthening him against temptation, shielding him from evil, ministering to his self-respect, medicining his weariness, peopling his solitude, winning him from sordid prizes, enlivening his monotonous days with mirth, or fancy, or wit, flashing heaven upon his earth, and mellowing it for all spiritual fertility,— there is the element of marriage. Wherever woman pays reverence to man—wherever any woman rejoices in the strength of any man, feels it to be God's agent, upholding her weakness, confirming her purpose, and crowning her power,—wherever he reveals himself to her, just, upright, inflexible, yet tolerant, merciful, benignant, not unruffled, perhaps, but not overcome by the world's turbulence, and responding to all her gentleness, his feet on the earth, his head among the stars, helping her to hold her soul steadfast in right, to stand firm against the encroachments of frivolity, vanity, impatience, fatigue, and discouragement, helping to preserve her good nature, to develop her energy, to consolidate her thought, to utilize her benevolence, to exalt and illumine her life,—there is the essence of marriage. Its love is founded on respect, and increases self-respect at the very moment of merging self in another. Its love is mutual—equally giving and receiving at every instant of its action. There is neither dependence nor independence, but interdependence. Years can not weaken its bonds; distance can not sunder them. It is a love which vanquishes the grave, and transfigures death itself into life."

Now this is a very beautiful, and, barring a little of the rhapsody, a very true description of that union of hearts which constitutes a perfect marriage. Such unions there are, thank God, and they constitute the bright spots on earth's darkness; but, if Miss Dodge supposes that no marriage can be other than an adulterous one, which does not contain all these elements, she sadly mistakes God's ordinance and the spirit and tenor of both the gospel and history. How many cases are there, where the affection, reverence, and confidence of the two parties, at marriage, fall far short of this, and yet, subsequently, develop into a near approach to it? Are these no true marriages? Again, how many instances do we all know, where the parties, through all their lives long, coming far below this very exalted standard, yet lead peaceful and well-ordered lives, and enjoy such harmony and satisfaction in each other's society as is possible in temperaments not ardent, and in intellects not of the highest grade. Must we strike out these from the list of true marriages? Yet further, there are those who have infirmities of temper, which lead to not infrequent collisions, but yet entertain a strong affection for each other, and, in the intervals of these ebullitions, are loving and tender. Are these adulterous mismatches? It would be a blessed world, indeed, if all the married came up to Miss Dodge's noble ideal, and perhaps at the millennium they may; but meantime, it is a naughty world, and we fear that, for every one of these instances of perfect connubial bliss, there are to be found not less than fifty, and perhaps a hundred, which make no near approach to it. Yet, believing as we do in the upward progress of the race and its capacity for improvement, we should be slow to declare all marriages except these few, violations of the true idea of marriage, until we had ascertained whether it was not possible for those who now occupy a low plane to come up higher.

But Miss Dodge goes on to say : " The current of human progress is undoubtedly—perhaps has always been—setting in this direction. Its motion is slow, sometimes apparently backward, but never permanently checked. Every legal enactment that tends to equalize the sexes, to give husband and wife the same position before the law, smooths the way for the desired end. Every elevated friendship between a man and a woman prefigures it. All the subjugations of the marriage rite and of common law are against it. Every thing which coerces that whose only value lies in its freedom is an obstruction. So long as the law commands subordination, it forbids the grace of a spontaneous deference. Man never will be truly monarch, till woman of her own will places the crown on his brow; and that she will never do till her will is free. Each being in a false relation to the other, there will be constant antagonism where there ought to be unbroken harmony. They will hinder and irritate where they ought to help and soothe. Man may have mastery by strength of thew and sinew; but he masters only thew and sinew. The fine spirit escapes him. The subtile soul, bruised, outraged, deformed, but defiant, mocks him from afar.

"So long as the tendencies of growth, however feeble and awry, are to fill out the empty shell of marriage with true spiritual richness, we may hold our peace. But when our preachers and teachers come to us and set down this empty shell square in the path of progress, and say, ' This is all—all that has been, all that shall be, all that God intended ever should be,' the stones may cry out upon them. It is the very priests thrusting God from his most holy temple. It is the ministers of that Gospel which emancipates woman from centuries of servility, remanding her to her burdens. Christ made no distinction, but opened the door wide to woman as to man. These restrict her to a single form of service, while oppressing her with a thousand forms of servitude. They subordinate her best uses to her lowest functions. They degrade her into a hewer of wood and a drawer of water, and add blasphemy to falsehood with a 'Thus saith the Lord.'"

Miss Dodge is too sensible and clear-headed a woman, we are persuaded, to advocate the abolition of the marriage rite and of all laws intended to regulate marriage; and yet to many her words in this extract will seem to have this signification, and this alone. She has been imprudent in her use of language on this subject before, and has incurred odium which we do not believe she fully deserves thereby.

But the fundamental difficulty with Miss Dodge is that, though recognizing, she fails to comprehend the reality of woman's complementary nature, and harps on the equality of the sexes, when she really knows, if she would but consider, that there is no perfect equality between them.

That many rush into marriage with no thought of its real character, and no knowledge of their adaptation to those to whom they are wedded, in temper, tastes, affection, or intellectual capacities, is too true; and very often they find, too late, that they are grievously mismated; but the remedy for this great evil is not, as these advocates of the equality of the sexes assert, in the abrogation of all marriage rites, and the leaving both sexes perfectly free to choose, by some occult law of affinity, how they will be mated. The perfect union which Miss Dodge so glowingly describes will not come in this way. Opinions will be as discordant, hasty and ill-considered matches will be as common, and quarrels as frequent, if women propose for husbands, as they are now, when men propose and women accept or reject. It is all very well to talk of woman's being free, and of her own will placing the nuptial crown on man's brow; but woman, in all the past, has been disposed to robe the man of her choice in ideal perfections, and very often, when she believed him a demigod, he has turned out to be only a creature of clay, and very poor clay at that. Will she be any wiser, or judge character any better in the future than in the past? We hope so, but we doubt. Let us now listen to another woman, the peer of Miss Dodge in learning and in intellectual grasp, and her superior in her mastery of the higher problems of political economy and ethics, as she gives her views on this question of the equality of the sexes.

The gifted author of "Woman's Rights and Duties" thus discourses on the subject :* "The power of the strong over the weak is so immovably fixed in the nature of things, that any attempt to improve the condition of women, if not founded on the assumption that men must hold the chief rule in society, will carry the seeds of failure in

* Vol. i. p. 208, *et seq.*

its bosom. Every fanciful attempt to place the two sexes on a perfect equality, has ended without the slightest benefit to women. When we view the wide regions of uncivilized life, the first thing that strikes us is the corruption to both sides, which results from this natural deficiency on the part of the female sex. We can not but contrast the spirit of tyranny it generates in the one party and the servility in the other, with the humanizing influence of those bonds of relationship or friendship, which are cemented by a mutual sense of equality. The same individual who is a devoted and generous friend, has sometimes proved a brutal oppressor to his wife; nor is it surprising: for in the rude mind, services received as duties generate contempt—as free kindness, they generate love and fidelity. But we may be assured there is no natural law without some beneficial uses. Man was designed for civilization, and though, in uncivilized life, the weakness of woman is found to be almost invariably productive of misery, the effect, when reason begins to prevail over barbarism, may perhaps appear very different. There can be no civilization without order, and the progress of order could scarcely be secured without some provision that should lead mankind, promptly and universally, to a division of labor and duties into the public and private.

" The utmost confusion and embarrassment would arise, if it were quite uncertain which of the two heads of a family should attend to the details of the household, and which pursue the profession or duties that were to provide for their common support. On what principles should education be conducted ? It can not be said that rearing the young would naturally confine the female to the domestic duties ; we see that in savage life it does not do so. She is compelled to labor much harder in proportion to her strength than the other sex ; she is exempted from nothing that her strength can perform. In civilized life it can not be supposed that man would labor for her if she was just as strong and able, as bold and as daring as himself; all the feminine virtues would cease to exist, or be even imagined, and the whole race be so much the harder and coarser. The confusion would be so great from the uncertainty which of the two parties should abandon their professional duties, to attend to the details of domestic life, that, I think, such an awkward condition of society would compel the institution of castes, that a certain portion of the community might be brought up to particular sorts of employment alone. Let any one but follow out in imagination the details of a condition in which all the professions and employments of civil life were given indifferently to men or women, as their physical strength might permit. The picture could scarcely be drawn out with seriousness, but the embarrassments would not be the less real because the notion is ludicrous. All inconvenience is avoided by a slight inferiority of strength and abilities in one of the sexes. This gradually develops a particular turn of character, a new class of affections and sentiments that humanize and embellish the species more than any others. These lead at once, without art or hesitation, to a division of duties needed alike in all situations, and produce that order without which there can be no social progression.

" In the treatise of ' The Hand,' by Sir Charles Bell, we learn that the left hand and foot are naturally a little weaker than the right; the effect of this is, to make us more prompt and dexterous than we should otherwise be. If there were no difference at all between the right and left limbs, the slight degree of hesitation which hand to use, or which foot to put forward, would create an awkwardness that would operate more or less every moment of our lives, and the provision to prevent it, seems analogous to the difference nature has made between the strength of the sexes.

" Nature, then, having placed the stronger mind where she gave the stronger body, and accompanied it with a more enterprising, ambitious spirit, the custom that consigns to the male sex the chief command in society, and all the offices which require the greatest strength and ability, has a better foundation than force, or the prejudices that result from it. The hard, laborious, stern, and coarse duties of the warrior, lawyer, legislator, or physician, require all tender emotions to be frequently repressed. The firmest texture of nerve is required to stand the severity of mental labor, and the greatest abilities are wanted where the duties of society are most difficult. It would be as little in agreement with the nature of things to see the exclusive possession of these taken from the abler sex, to be divided with the weaker, as it is in the savage condition, to behold severe bodily toil inflicted on the feeble frame of the woman, and the softness of feeling which nature has provided her with for the tenderest of her offices, that of nurturing the young, outraged by contempt, menaces, and blows.

" It is, therefore, an impartial decree which consigns all the offices that require the greatest ability to men. For, is it less the interest of woman than of man, that property, life, and liberty should be secured—that aggression should be quickly and easily repressed—that contentment and order should prevail instead of tumult? —that industry should be well paid—provisions cheap and plentiful—that trade should cover their tables and their persons with the comforts, conveniences, and luxuries which habit has rendered necessary, or an innocent sensibility pleasurable? Is it less momentous to them that religious opinions should be free from persecution—that a

17   A A

wise foreign policy should maintain these blessings in peace, and preserve us from the tribula-
tion of foreign dominion? In objects of less
selfish interest, are women less anxious than
men, or more so, to see the practice of slavery
expelled from the face of the earth? or our colonial government redeemed, in every remaining
instance, from the stain that has too often attended
it, of being numbered with the most oppressive
of European? In the dangerous and difficult
sciences of medicine and surgery, is it less important to women than to men that the life which
hangs by a thread should be trusted to those
whose nerves and ability insure the greatest
skill? Or in law, that the decision of rights, the
vindication of innocence, should be in the hands
of those who can most patiently endure the driest
studies and most boldly follow human nature
through all its various forms and all its foul
pursuits? Ills enough, Heaven knows, ensue from
the weaknesses and incapacity of men, but to confer the offices, which demand all the skill and energy
that can be had, on those who are weaker still,
would be injurious alike to both. The commanding
and influential stations in society belong, therefore,
naturally and properly to the male sex; this, of
necessity, entails the chief rule in private life also.
But it is here that the rights of women come in,
and that the danger of unjust encroachment upon
them commences. Every thing that tends to

lessen the comparative purity and refinement of women is most pointedly adverse to their real interests ; these are the qualities that enable them to be the guardians and sustainers of national morals; and their rights must be founded on their natural attributes and their moral dignity. To these respect and consideration can not be denied, and every step mankind advances in civilization gives strength to those sentiments. Women have neither the physical strength nor the mental power to compete with men in the departments which depend on those qualifications ; and however little we were to suppose their inferiority, in the long run they would always be defeated and discredited in their competition for employment with the abler sex. Were so unnatural a state of society to arise, as that they should become the competitors instead of the assistants of man, they would lose their hold on his protection and tenderness, without being able to shield themselves from his harshness. The business of life would be far worse conducted, when the division of labor so clearly pointed out by nature was done away ; and the just influence which women ought to have would be destroyed by breaking down the barrier of opinion which consigns them to the duties of a domestic and private station, and preserves them from the contamination of gross and contentious scenes.

" But the same arguments that establish the right

of the male sex, to the sole possession of public authority, must leave the *chief* control of domestic life in their hands also. All the most laborious, the greater and more lucrative social offices, being filled by them, it follows that, generally speaking, it is they who produce the wealth and property of society, and the property they create they have assuredly the best right to control; within the rules of virtue and law, they may spend it as they will. The children whom the husband supports, the wife who accepts him, engaging to follow his fortunes, must be content to live as he pleases, or as his business requires. This is the law of nature and reason. If his tastes or his profession be unpleasant to her, she must see to it beforehand; for ever after their interests must be one. In every important decision that is taken, one counsel must prevail; if it can not be mutual, it must be assigned as a legal right to the owner of the property and the abler sex. Hence he is the head of the family; he must be responsible to law and opinion for the decorum of his house, and must have the power of restraining what he holds to be discreditable or wrong. Happy if he could be made equally responsible, even to his own conscience, for unjustly encroaching on rights which should never be taken from a woman, except for positive vice or incapacity! Her right to all the self-government that can be left to her, without deranging *his* purposes or *his* enjoyment, is as real as his own; and his purposes and enjoyments are not to be measured by mere pride or fancy, but by reason and justice; even then he remains judge in his own cause. As the right of man to the chief power, public and domestic, has been deduced from his greater ability, so the aptitude of the female mind and character for the details of domestic life, and the improvement of society, in manners and morals, establish her rights, also, to a share of control; otherwise, her utility must be greatly impaired, and her enjoyment cruelly and needlessly sacrificed."

APPENDIX C.

Just as the last sheets of this work were passing through the press, two volumes of essays were published in England, treating on many of the same topics which are here considered, though necessarily from the English point of view. One of these, "Woman's Work and Woman's Culture," is a large octavo volume, and, besides the introductory essay by the editor, Mrs. Josephine E. Butler, has very able papers by Frances Power Cobbe, Jessie Boucherett, Rev. G. Butler, Principal of the Liverpool College, Sophia Jex-Blake, James Stuart, Charles H. Pearson, Herbert N. Mozley, Esq., Julia Wedgwood, Elizabeth C. Wolstenholme, and John Boyd-Kinnear. The various aspects of what is so generally called "The Woman Question," so far as English women and English society are concerned, are treated with remarkable ability and moderation, and the work is one which ought to be widely read. The other volume, "Ourselves," is a series of spicy, lively essays, by Mrs. E. Lynn Linton, exceedingly readable, and portraying the good and evil that is in woman as only one of themselves could do it. It will, we doubt not, do good.

The essay, in the first volume named, on the "Social Position of Women," by John Boyd-Kinnear, is so remarkable for its forcible presentation of facts, and corroborates so fully the positions we have already taken in this work, that we feel that our readers will enjoy a few passages of it, but we must beg leave to say, in advance of our presentation of them, so striking is at times the resemblance of the thoughts, that we had no knowledge of Mr. Kinnear's views, or of his essay, when our chapters on these topics were written, and, of course, he could have no possible knowledge of ours.—L. P. B.

. . . . "The most prevalent understanding at present, undoubtedly is, that women should do as little as possible of any active, any outside work. Let them become wives and mothers, it is said—these are their natural functions; and let them leave the business of the world to men. We concede grudgingly, and under a sort of protest, that they may do a little charity, visit some select ed poor, decorate churches, and teach under the clergymen in Sunday-schools. All beyond that is thought exceptional, if not odd.

"And yet it ought to startle us into doubt of the soundness of our notions, when we find, ever and anon, how infinitely obliged we are to women when they dare to be even more than odd. The country was more grateful than it has been to any man since the Duke of Wellington, when Miss

Nightingale took the extraordinary step of going out to Scutari, and bringing order and decency into the chaos of neglect that had grown up around medical men and staff-officers. On a more limited scale, there is many a parish that owes the deepest thankfulness to some good woman who has quietly organized its schools, or broken down the cruel routine of its workhouse. If it is well when these things are done, can we deprecate their being done more often; and still insist that women are out of their sphere when employed in other duties than 'suckling fools and chronicling small-beer?' It is probably the case that modern social changes have indirectly operated to lower the public idea as to the duties of women, just as they have ousted women from some of the employments that were formerly appropriated to them. In the feudal times, woman, factitiously elevated by the notions of chivalry, and so often called on to play the part of men when left as chatelaine of the castle in their husband's absence, or head of the family of the yeoman, who had to follow his lord to the field, could hardly at any time sink back into the mere household ornament or drudge. In every rank women had their prescribed duties, and these were so large, that unmarried girls were often attached to a lady's little court, that from her they might learn, and, under her, practice the proper accomplishments of a gentlewoman. But girls had another resource. The convent opened its gates to rich and poor.   In these communities, whoever could not marry, and whoever did not choose to marry, was sure of an honored and secure asylum.   There they were at least not idle. Beside the regular offices of religion, there was the management of property, the acts of charity, the learning and the teaching of the literature of the time.   If we think copying manuscripts, illuminating borders, or working tapestry, not very profound studies, or interesting amusements, yet surely they were far less vapid than the chief avocations of modern young ladies.   But, above all, they were at least an alternative to matrimony. While such refuges existed, no girl could be forced into a reluctant marriage, either by compulsion of parents, or because, on the death of parents, there would be no home for her to live in.   I am far indeed from desiring the restoration of the conventual system, with its vows of perpetual celibacy and servitude; but it is right to remember that, with many evils, it brought at least some compensations.   To be unmarried was then to be the spouse of Christ, the revered 'mother,' the member of a sisterhood surrounded with all the honor and sanctity of the Church; nowadays, it is to live and die in the dreary lodgings, and under the half-contemptuous title of an old maid.

"Thus it has come to pass that women have, by change to times of settled peace, and by the reformation of religion, lost something of dignity,

17*

of usefulness, and of resources. And, thus it has been brought about that, having scarce any choice but marriage, marriage has come to be considered as the sole function to which it is right or decent they should look. This notion is heightened among, at least, the upper classes, by the ideas which the law of primogeniture fosters. It is thought a father's duty to provide largely for the eldest son; consequently, the daughter's portion must be pinched. Many are left enough to live on, but not enough to enable them still to move in the society in which they have been brought up. Their choice lies, then, only between marrying money, or abandoning all their connections, habits, and amusements. Foreseeing such a time, a wealthy marriage becomes a matter to which they, and their mothers for them, eagerly look forward. The more luxury increases, the more urgent seems the necessity for their securing a luxurious provision. Unluckily, at the same time, and from the same causes, there grows up an increased disinclination among young men to enter into marriage. Then, the efforts of the young ladies become more desperate, and being more apparent, of course, still less and less successful. So matters go on from bad to worse. It is esteemed a discredit to pass the second season, after they come out, without securing an engagement. Rich young men become so valuable a prize, that selection is renounced, and even barefaced vice is no disqualification to their being well received in wealthy drawing-rooms. The young men feel and improve all the privileges of their position ; they are careless of hiding what is no longer reprobated, and they begin unreservedly to speak of, and to be seen talking to, the notorious harlots of the day. Young ladies, seeing that the harlots are run after and themselves neglected, begin (God knows it may often be with innocent ignorance) to ape the style, and in some degree, the manners, of the attractive harlot. It is now the harlots that set the fashion in dress ; that prescribe the fashionable drives in the park; and that still, because in some things modest women can not vie with them, form the attraction that daily carries young men more and more away from the society of modest women. But still the fatal emulation is kept up. Whoever wants to judge of its character, has only to frequent the fashionable London drive at the fashionable hour, and there he will see the richest and most shameful woman-market in the world. Men stand by the rails, criticizing with perfect impartiality and equal freedom, while women drive slowly past, some for hire, some for sale—in marriage ; these last with their careful mothers at their side, to reckon the value of the biddings, and prevent the lots from going off below the reserved price.*

* Horrible as is the picture which Mr. Boyd-Kinnear has here drawn of the mercenary spirit of British mothers of the upper classes, and of

" Such is the pitch to which we have arrived by telling women that marriage is their sole duty.

the readiness of young ladies of high rank to imitate the manners, the dress, and the shameless conduct of the *demi-monde*, in the hope of thereby winning husbands, there is the most abundant evidence that it is not exaggerated. Mrs. Linton, in her volume of essays—" Ourselves "—thus testifies to the prevalent tendencies of these "girls of the period," as a writer in the *Saturday Review* had previously done :—

"These characters are no mere fictions of the Saturday journalist's brain. They exist, and they make their existence a loud and staring fact. In the Park, the streets, the drawing-room, you see their painted cheeks, their dyed red hair, and liberal expanse of bust and back, and you hear their spicy talk, well seasoned with slang, and always hovering about that doubtful line of topics at which bold men laugh and modest women blush. We may wince as much as we like, and flounce and flutter, and deny, but the fact remains the same. Here, in the very heart of what is called good society—here, as the companions of our daughters, the wives of our brothers, the playfellows of our sons, and the friends of our husbands, is a sect of women, young and mature alike, who have taken the *hetairæ* of the day for their models, and who paint, and dress, and talk, and make up their lives as near after the patterns set by their prototypes as is possible to them. How can we deny it, when we see the archpriestess of the sect living in that wealthy temple of hers, in Bond Street, whence every now and then some deluded votary, more indignant than wise, turns round against her cyprian-abbess, and denounces and exposes? The guilt, and the shame of such things, do not lie with those who speak of them, but with those who do them ; not with the writers of those slashing articles in our weekly censor, but with the models who stand in the way to be slashed. For my own part, I only hope there will be no holding of the hand yet awhile, and that so long as these sins exist among us, there will be found faithful friends to use the knife and the actual cautery, and so to cut out and to burn unsparingly, while one corrupted fiber remains."

Elsewhere, Mrs. Linton says : "I, who am a matron myself, with pleasant, brown-haired girls, as yet innocent of aqua amarilla and Madame Rachel, I solemnly swear that I would rather see my daughters dead now in their youth and beauty, than in the way to become girls of the period, and frisky matrons to follow."

The fashionable women of America have sins and follies enough to answer for, sins of frivolity and display, of indolence, and ignorance of what is good and true ; but—we say it in no pharisaic spirit—we are

Its terrible evils are chiefly visible among the upper classes; but who can tell what mischief is done throughout every rank of society by examples so conspicuously set? When the best sanction of social morality, the reprobation of vice by women, is cast aside in the highest circles, who can tell how widely the encouragement may act? It is happily limited as yet in our country by two checks, the purity of the throne, and the strength of religious feeling in the middle classes. And we may hope and believe that these influences will ultimately prevail, so far at least as to shame into respect for external decency those who now flaunt their defiance of morality and modesty in the public eye. But not the less is it apparent that men and women.degrade each other when social opinion inculcates that life's chief aim is luxurious enjoyment, and that to secure a good establishment is the one purpose for which a girl should be brought up. . . . . .

"In this is summed up the fatal error of the day in the position assigned to women. We disregard, even if we do not deny, the fact that they have souls as well as bodies,—souls not only to be saved, but to be cultivated, instructed, made fit to do what work God has assigned such souls

devoutly thankful that, as yet, they are under no temptations to imitate and emulate the painted and bedizened daughters of shame, or enter the lists with them in winning rich and fashionable rakes for husbands. Far distant be that day when we shall be called to write such bitter things of our countrywomen.

to do on earth, as well as to grow meet for the nobler duties that may await them in Heaven. Herein arises no question whether they are intellectually equal with the souls of men or not. Enough that they *are* intellectual; the conclusion follows that the intellect ought to be employed. And concede only this simple, this indisputable proposition, and it will guide us through all our difficulties. Grant that we have to think of the minds of women as their chief part; and how different must be the education we give them, as well as how different the work we must expect from them : the one dependent on the other; the education to make them capable of the work, the work as the outcome of the education.

" The wider usefulness which ought to be intrusted to women is craved for by themselves. It is easy for us to speak of the frivolity of their pursuits and cares, when we force them, by all the moral power we can bring to bear, to be nothing more than frivolous. But against this constraint, their own higher and better nature constantly rebels. Some, of course, there are among them, as among men, who are not capable of more than triviality. But it is incontestable that the majority of women would most eagerly welcome a truer education than they are now permitted to have The cry among the poor is hardly more strong for leave to work, than it is among the rich for leave to be useful. Against every difficulty and tacit opposition, many girls of the higher classes eagerly fling themselves into such branches of parish, church, school, or other local work, as are at all allowed to them. The more active minds form sisterhoods, in which the nursing of the sick and the tending of the poor are the principal occupations. There is no doubt that much of the encouragement which has lately been given to ritualism, may be traced back to its recognition of the longing of women to devote themselves to what they are able to think, and to what, in some sort, are really active and important services. Those who know how readily recruits are found among women for all sorts of lay mission work, will bear witness to their longing to labor in fields that are not naturally inviting to the frivolous. Again, the recent establishment of lectures for women, on subjects often abstruse, and given by men whose position is guarantee that they will not deal with the subjects in a too popular method, has elicited proof that, in every part of the kingdom, women are anxious to avail themselves of every opportunity of cultivating their minds, and of developing faculties which have not even the attraction of any immediate application. . . . .

"It does not fall within the scope of this paper to enter into the details of an educational system that would remedy the defects so prevalent at present. It is enough here to point out the principles which ought to regulate such a system. The principle is the same for women as for men. That is a true education which teaches how the faculties which its Maker has implanted in the soul can be made most serviceable to our fellow-creatures. For in serving others consists self-elevation. Whatever is divine in ourselves, is most fully developed by the endeavor to make it beneficial to our neighbor. Herein is scope, and motive, and reward for the most patient effort of self-culture. Nor is it to be overlooked that, in the wonderful scheme of God's earthly government, the doing of good to others is the direct means by which what is called success in life is achieved for ourselves. Unthinkingly, often, the man of the world who by honest effort struggles to raise himself, raises hundreds around him. All science, all commerce, all industry, by which human fame or fortune is made, spread blessings around. Not less do they lead to fame and fortune, if pursued for the sake of the blessings they confer. Women's education and work make no exception to this happy rule. If a woman were to try to do the very best for herself in a worldly sense, she could take no surer course than by fitting herself to confer the largest benefits on those around her. For her, then, I ask the best, when I ask that she should be trained so as to be best able to do good. Beyond elementary education this process must vary in the case of every individual, according to her individual temperament and her position in life. Only let the highest faculties be in each case most regarded—the capacities for literature, for art, for industry, for government, for organizing, for instructing, for sick-nursing, with the thousand subdivisions and modifications of each, present a wide enough field, within which every girl can find some innate taste to gratify, some special aptitude to cultivate. Let her count that her duty which she can best exercise. Let fathers and mothers count it their most solemn duty to help and guide their children to render themselves thus worthy workers in their Father's vineyard, that so, when the day is done, they may receive every one the reward of their work.

" Does any one object that in thus developing the higher nature of women, in teaching and admitting them to the performance of important duties, there is danger that any of the peculiar charms of their sex should be lost? Surely, neither in men nor in women is it to be found that a sense of life's deeper realities and responsibilities, and an interest in things outside themselves, are hostile to the qualities that make the delight of companionship. The struggle, indeed, which women just now have to make in order to escape from the trammels of a false position, do sometimes lead them to take up an attitude which we should not perhaps like to see them all assume. I do not admire, any more than their critics, the type of the 'strong minded' woman, as it is occasionally presented to us. I am not arguing in favor of woman-militant, or defending any errors of taste into which some may occasionally fall. But, on the other hand, we all have the happiness of knowing a far greater number of examples of women, intelligent and cultivated, active in every good work, interested in all that is worthy of interest, who by such development of their faculties have added additional grace and luster to their natural attractions. Even men who only look for agreeable companions, acknowledge that they are to be found rather among the educated than the uneducated. What further answer is needed to the apprehensions which only silly men venture to express, that learning and employment would make women bores, and destroy the pleasures of society?

"And the world has room and need for all the higher work of which women are capable. In cities, in villages, in prisons and in workhouses, in art-galleries and in letters, in all branches of industry, and in every field of benevolence, the world will be grateful to the women who can do it service. In many things the world gropes and stumbles, because it has not enough of women's hands to guide it. In many other things in which men and women may labor together, there is a cry for more labor. In some things even men's work is less perfect than it would be if they had women's work to compare with their own. For women, I again say, I do not call the same as men, but different—their complement, the necessary element to the completeness of human nature. Even in our highest public duties, we should be incalculably helped by admitting the directness, the simplicity, the instinctive honesty of a woman's unperverted mind. Often their counsel would be less cowardly than men's, simply because they would more regard what is ultimately right, and less what is probably and immediately profitable. And in thus counseling us, women would save us from many disasters into which our own selfish and short-sighted policy is daily leading us, because we choose to forget that what is not right can not be profitable ultimately, whatever the promise of safety or wealth it may hold out for the moment. . . . . .

" But in matters affecting our home administration, surely no candid mind can dispute the fact that women's opinions would be a most valuable corrective of our own. I leave out of sight all the questions which practically affect women, either as regards their property or their persons; for every day we concede to them, as individuals, rights of self-government which the surviving barbarism of our laws still denies to them as a section of the community. But looking to matters in which, as members of the community, women have an interest as great as men have, it is obvious that we should reap incalculable advantage from their considering along with us the national questions of education of the young, of the management of the poor, of the treatment of criminals, and of the guidance of emigration. Whoever thinks that on these topics women would be less careful, cautious, and judicious counselors than men are, simply betrays that he takes for his type of womanhood 'the girl of the period,' as he has helped to make her, and knows nothing of the number of women who have thought out and matured the working of all these most difficult problems of social humanity. But, in narrower spheres than those that belong to the domain of politics, we equally want the recognized help of women. Whatever the nation resolves on, each locality must administer; and, in the administration, there is need for all the experience and all the wisdom that both sexes can contribute. These very questions—education, poor relief, prisons, hospitals, and emigration, are local questions. In every one of these there are departments which scarcely any but women are competent to deal with. Why do we not—I will not say, merely, admit—but why do we not urge women to help us with the classification and redemption of female paupers, and pauper children, and prisoners? How can we, with our rough reasoning and generalization even attempt to deal with what a cultivated woman's intuition can alone discriminate and appreciate? Once again, for fear of being, perhaps willfully, misunderstood, I repeat that I do not

assert that every woman would be of value in
such work; I certainly could still less say so of
every man. But I do say, that there are thousands of women in every district who are competent to help in such work—to help in a way in
which no male help would avail.

"For the sake, then, of the country and of its
dearest interests, we ought to invite women to
bear part with us in the great Christian duty of
doing good to our neighbor; for the sake of women
themselves, we ought so to train them that they
may understand that duty and do it. Think of a
woman's empty life, as too often now public opinion makes it—her training in a few showy gifts,
almost avowedly to help her in husband-hunting—
her seclusion from all that interests the best men,
her incapacity to rule even her own household
and her own children, because, alas! she has never
been taught how to do either; think of her life,
but half useful if she does marry, and an utter
blank if she does not—and then say how great the
loss, the pity, and the shame, of an up-bringing
that has such results. Women and men alike the
losers; but if the pity be for the women, the
shame is for the men; for it is by the indifference
and misjudgment of men that women are so
brought up. It is because fathers do not think of
their daughters' future, because they too often
regard them as only so much goods to be got rid
of in the market, and therefore only to be dressed

and adapted for the market, that the daughters are so unfit for any higher function. When we cry out about women's frivolity, or vanity, or luxury, we impeach the education which has cultivated these feelings, and has not been directed to develop any of the higher and nobler faculties with which women are so endowed.

" I appeal then to men, because by their strength they are the masters ; I appeal to women, because even now their domestic influence is so great ; I appeal to all that mass of thought which forms the public opinion by which we are governed, to give to the women of the present and of coming generations a fair chance ! Let us think of them and deal with them as fellow-workers with us, it may be in different departments, but, at least, in the one great duty of doing good on earth. Let us teach them and train them so that they can work with us in that duty. Shall we, in doing so, make them unmaidenly, unwifely, unmotherly ? No : rather, more perfect in all womanly gifts and graces, of which those will first enjoy the happiness who are nearest to them in their homes. We can not unsex women by cultivating more highly the qualities that are the especial glory of their sex. We shall not make them masterful by teaching them how best they can serve. The purity, the charity, the tenderness that is in them, we now corrupt and crush by misdirection, and by forbidding them any object save that which a possible husband and children may supply. Allowed only to expand—allowed to be bestowed on a wider circle of sympathies—allowed to seek out a sphere beyond the range of self-interest, these qualities will be enhanced in strength, and will become to us the richer blessings. Women and men will be drawn the closer in the bonds of mutual service, and love, and comfort, when we seek women's aid, and train them to give their aid no longer only in our idleness and amusements, but in the daily round of duties which makes the noblest portion of our lives."

THE END.